THE CATHOLIC UNIVERSITY OF AMERICA
CANON LAW STUDIES
Number 111

Suspension of Clerics

AN HISTORICAL SYNOPSIS AND COMMENTARY

A DISSERTATION

Submitted to the Faculty of Canon Law of the Catholic University of America in partial Fulfillment of the Requirements for the Degree of

DOCTOR OF CANON LAW

BY THE

REV. ELIGIUS G. RAINER, C.SS.R., J.C.L.,
Priest of the Baltimore Province

THE CATHOLIC UNIVERSITY OF AMERICA
WASHINGTON, D. C.
1937

Imprimatur:

ANDREW B. KUHN, C.SS.R.,
Superior Provincialis.

BROOKLYNII, DIE 19 APRILIS, 1937

Nihil Obstat:

VALENTINUS T. SCHAAF, O.F.M., J.C.D.,
Censor Deputatus.

WASHINGTONII, D.C., DIE 11 MAII, 1937

Imprimatur:

✠MICHAEL J. CURLEY,
Archiepiscopus Baltimorensis.

BALTIMORIAE, MD., DIE 11 MAII, 1937.

MURRAY & HEISTER
WASHINGTON, D. C.

PRINTED BY
THE CARROLLTOWN NEWS
CARROLLTOWN PA.

To Mary

Christ's Virgin Mother

This Work

is

Affectionately and Gratefully

Inscribed

FOREWORD

Of all the penalties which the Church has instituted for the disciplining of her refractory clerics, suspension is the one most employed. It is one of her spiritual penalties, and is called such, not by reason of its origin, that is, not by reason of the spiritual jurisdiction which renders ecclesiastical superiors competent to inflict it, but by reason of the effects consequent upon its infliction. It is true, these effects are not of a purely spiritual character, as are grace and the accompanying virtues. They are, however, mixed. In other words, external acts proper to orders or offices or benefices which either by their nature or instrumentality produce grace, constitute the essential elements of these effects. Should there at times be involved questions of revenues or other temporalities, these are to be considered as something secondary and indirect. The primary effects always touch mixed goods which have been restricted in some manner by the suspension.

The present dissertation does not essay to enter into the various crimes for which a suspension is inflicted. Its end is merely to state general principles and not to set down specific applications, except perhaps as means to clarify a principle already enunciated. Furthermore, its intent is not to offer an exhaustive presentation regarding the infliction, the manner of judicial and extrajudicial procedure, the means of legal redress, the violation and remission of suspension. The chapters treating of these matters and certain incidental and minutely discussed considerations interspersed throughout the dissertation were undertaken not only to elucidate better the nature of suspension, but also to bring together in one monograph a connected study of various phases of suspension which may serve as a norm in cases involving this penalty.

The first part is an historical study, in which the existence and development of the nature of suspension throughout ecclesiastical history are briefly indicated. It has seemed necessary to divide this historical development into four periods, because progress in the growth of this clerical penalty of suspension manifested somewhat of a change at four different times. Thus, in the early centuries, when nothing definite can be ascertained as to the real nature of this penalty, a division is made to bring out the fact that the idea of forbidding the exercise of certain offices was not foreign to the minds of the early legislators. Then, the successive divisions concern themselves with accurateness in terminology, definiteness as to the nature of suspension through its effects, and finally, the institution of new penalties, whether total or partial, including the abrogation and derogation of already existing suspensions. By way of introduction to the historical development of suspension, a few words are given in reference to public law, which stress the fact that, since the Church is a perfect society, she rightfully enjoys the power to coerce her delinquent clerics. It is shown that this right to suspend her clerics is a power which she received from her divine Founder, Jesus Christ, when He established her as a perfect juridical entity.

The second part of this dissertation deals with suspension in relation to the principles contained in the new law of the Code. From the presentation of the various chapters, it will be seen how necessary a correct idea of this punishment is for all the clergy, for the superior, for the inferior, for the confessor and for the penitent. It is necessary for all the clergy, that they may realize the import and seriousness of the penalty as seen from its effects. It is necessary for the superior, that he may know, when, for what cause and in what manner he can inflict a suspension, and also what norms he must follow to remit its effects. It is necessary for the inferior, that he may realize, when a suspension has been justly and validly visited upon him, that he is bound to acknowledge its justice and submit to its effects under pain of an irregularity *ex delicto*, but that the possibility of legal redress is not denied him. It is necessary for the confessor and penitent, that they may know what rights, duties and obligations the Code assigns relative to the absolution and remission of suspension.

A word should be added regarding the choice of the form *vindictive penalty* rather than *vindicátive penalty*. It is true, the Latin text of the Code makes use of the term *poena vindicativa*. However, the corresponding English word *vindicátive*, according to the best dictionaries, has not the same signification which the Latin term wishes to convey Both Webster's and Funk & Wagnalls' Dictionaries define the word *vindicátive* as "that contributes to vindication". But, with regard to the word *vindictive*, these dictionaries give as its first meaning, "having a revengeful spirit" and as its second meaning, "punitive". The latter meaning is precisely the one which the Latin *poena vindicativa* wishes to convey. It is with this secondary meaning in view that the word *vindictive* has been chosen to express the full significance of the Latin terminology *poena vindicativa.*

The writer takes this occasion to express his gratitude to the Very Reverend Andrew B. Kuhn, the Provincial of the Baltimore Province, for the opportunity afforded for advanced study. He also acknowledges his indebtedness to all the members of the Faculty of the School of Canon Law of the Catholic University of America, for invaluable suggestions and guidance.

TABLE OF CONTENTS

BIBLIOGRAPHY

Sources

Acta Apostolicae Sedis, Commentarium Officiale, Romae, 1909—

Acta et Decreta Concilii Plenarii Baltimorensis Tertii, A.D. MDCCCLXXXIV, Baltimorae, John Murphy, 1886.

Acta Sanctae Sedis, 41 vols., Romae, 1865-1908.

Codex Iuris Canonici Pii X Pontificis Maximi iussu digestus Benedicti Papae XV auctoritate promulgatus, Romae: Typis Polyglottis Vaticanis, 1917.

Codicis Iuris Canonici Fontes, cura Emi. Petri Card. Gasparri editi, 7 vols., Romae [later Civitate Vaticana]: Typis Polyglottis Vaticanis, 1923-1934. (Vol. VII ed. cura et studio Emi Justiniani Card. Seredi.)

Collectanea S. Congregationis de Propaganda Fide, 2 vols., Romae: Typographia Polyglotta S.C. de Propaganda Fide, 1907.

Corpus Iuris Canonici, editio Lipsiensis Secunda post Aemilii Richteri curas . . . instruxit Aemilius Friedberg, 2 vols., Lipsiae, 1922.

Corpus Iuris Civilis, vol. I, *Institutiones*—recognovit P. Krueger; vol. II *Codex Justinianus*—recognovit et retractavit P. Krueger; vol. III, *Novellae Constitutiones*—R. Schoell; opus Schoelli morte interceptum absolvit G. Kroll Berolini, 1928-1929.

Fulton, J., *Index Canonum,* New York, 1892.

Hardouin, Jean, *Acta Conciliorum et Epistolae Decretales ac Constitutiones Summorum Pontificium,* 12 vols., Parisiis, 1714-1725.

Hefele, C., *Conciliengeschichte,* 9 vols., Freiburg im Breisgau, 1875.

Mansi, J. D., *Sacrorum Conciliorum Nova et Amplissima Collectio,* 53 vols., Arnheim, 1901-1927.

Migne, P. J., *Patrologiae Cursus Completus, Series Latina,* 221 vols., Parisiis, 1847-1870.

Pontificale Romanum, 3 vols., Ratisbone, 1908.

Reference Works

Aertnys, Jos.—Damen, C.A., *Theologia Moralis Secundum Doctrinam S. Alphonsi De Ligorio Doctoris Ecclesiae,* II. ed., 2 vols., Taurinorum Augustae, 1928.

Alterius, Marius, *Disputationes de Censuris Ecclesiasticis,* 2 vols., Romae, 1616.

Andreae Ioannes, *In Quinque Decretalium Libros Novella Commentaria,* 4 vols., Venetiis, 1581.

Ayrinhac, H. A., *Penal Legislation in the New Code of Canon Law,* New York, 1920.

[Bachofen], Charles Augustine, *A Commentary on the New Code of Canon Law,* 8 vols., St. Louis: B. Herder, 1920.

Ballerini, A.,—Palmieri, D., *Opus Theologicum Morale,* 7 vols., Prati, 1893.

Barbosa, A., *Collectanea Doctorum tam Veterum quam Recentiorum in Ius Pontificium Universum,* 4 vols., Lugduni, 1716.

Bargillat, M., *Praelectiones Iuris Canonici,* 36.-37. ed., 2 vols., Parisiis, 1915-1923.

Benedictus XIV, *De Synodo Dioecesana,* 2 vols., Romae, 1806.

Biederlack-Führich, *De Religiosis,* Oeniponte, 1919.

Blat, A., *Commentarium Textus Codicis Iuris Canonici,* 5 vols., Romae, 1921-1927.

Bouix, D., *Tractatus de Iudiciis Ecclesiasticis,* 3. ed., 2 vols., Parisiis, 1884.

Cappello, F., *Tractatus Canonico-Moralis de Censuris juxta Codicem Iuris Canonici,* Taurinorum Augustae, 1933.

......, *Tractatus Canonico-Moralis de Sacramentis;* vol. I, *De Sacramentis in Genere, de Baptismo, Confirmatione, Eucharistia,* 2 ed., Taurinorum Augustae, 1928; vol. II, pars I, *De Poenitentia,* Taurinorium Augustae, 1926; vol. III, *De Matrimonio,* 2. ed., Romae, 1927.

Cavigioli, J., *De Censuris Latae Sententiae,* Taurini, 1919.

Catholic Encyclopedia, The, 15 vols., New York, 1912.

Cerato, P., *Censurae Vigentes Ipso Facto A Codice Iuris Canonici Excerptae,* editio secunda recognita, Patavii, 1921.

Chelodi, J., *Ius de Personis,* 2. ed., Tridenti, 1921.

......, *Ius Poenale et Ordo Procedendi in Iudiciis Criminalibus juxta Codicem Iuris Canonici,* Tridenti, 1925.

Claeys-Bouuaert-Simenon, *Manuale Iuris Canonici,* 2. ed., Bandae et Leodii, 1926.

Collison, P., "Non Omnis Censura Ab Homine Est Reservata", *Dissertatio Ad Gradum Doctoris In Facultate Iuris Canonici Consequendum Scripta Apud Pontificium Institutum Angelicum,* Romae, 1935.

Conte, Matthaeus, a Coronata, *Institutiones Iuris Canonici,* 4 vols., Taurini; Marietti, 1928-1935.

Cocchi, G., *Commentarium in Codicem Iuris Canonici,* 8 vols., Taurini, 1925-1927.

Craisson, D., *Elementa Iuris Canonici,* 2 vols., Parisiis, 1873.

D'Annibale, J., *Summula Theologiae Moralis,* 2 vols., Romae, 1908.

De Meester, A., *Iuris Canonici et Iuris Canonico-Civilis Compendium,* 3 vols., Brugis, 1921-1928.

De Smet, A., *Tractatus Theologico-Canonicus de Sponsalibus et de Matrimonio,* Brugis, 1927.

Droste-Messmer, S., *Canonical Procedure In Disciplinary And Criminal Cases of Clerics,* New York, 1887.

Eichmann, E., *Das Strafrecht des Codex Iuris Canonici,* Paderbon, 1920.

Fanfani, L., *De Iure Religiosorum, ad Normam Codicis Iuris Canonici,* Taurini-Romae, 1925.

Fagnanus, P., *Commentarium in V Libros Decretalium,* 4 vols., Venetiis, 1696.

Ferraris, L., *Bibliotheca Prompta Canonica, Iuridica, Moralis, Theologica,* 9 vols., Parisiis, 1861-1863.

Gasparri, P., *Tractatus Canonicus de Matrimonio,* ed nova ad mentem Codicis Iuris Canonici, Typis Polyglottis Vaticanis, 2 vols., 1932.

......, *Tractatus Canonicus de Sacra Ordinatione,* 2 vols., Parisiis, 1893-1894.

Gonzalez-Tellez, E., *Commentaria Perpetua Decretalium,* 4 vols., Lugduni, 1715.

Haring, J., *Grundzüge des Katholischen Kirchenrechts,* 2 vols., Graz, 1924.

Hermann, J., *Institutiones Theologiae Dogmaticae,* 2 vols., Lugduni, 1926.

Hinschius, R., *Kirchenrecht,* 6 vols., Berlin, 1895.

Hickey, J., *Irregularities and Simple Impediments,* The Catholic University of America, Canon Law Studies, n. 7, Washington: The Catholic University of America, 1920.

Hollweck, J., *Die Kirchlichen Strafgesetze,* Mainz, 1899.

Hostiensis, H., *Commentaria in V Libris Decretalium,* 3 vols., Venetiis, 1581.

Hyland, F., *Excommunication,* The Catholic University of America, Canon Law Studies, n. 49, Washington: The Catholic University of America, 1928.

Kober, F., *Die Suspension der Kirchendiener,* Tübingen, 1862.

......, *Der Kirchenbann,* Tübingen, 1863.

Konings, A., *Theologia Moralis,* 2 vols., New York, 1876.

Leech, L., *A Comparative Study of the Constitution "Apostolicae Sedis" and the "Codex Iuris Canonici",* The Catholic University of America, Canon Law Studies, n. 15, Washington: The Catholic University of America, 1922.

Lega, M., *De Delictis et Poenis,* Romae, 1910.

Lyszczarczyk, V., *Compendium Privilegiorum Regularium Praesertim Ordinis Fratrum Minorum,* Leopoli, 1906.

Maroto, P., *Institutiones Iuris Canonici ad Norman Novi Codicis,* 2 vols., Madrid, 1919.

Marc, C., Gestermann, F.,—Raus, J., *Institutiones Morales Alphonsianae,* 19. ed. 2 vols., Lugduni, Lutetiae Parisiorum, 1933.

Melo, A., *De Exemptione Regularium,* The Catholic University of America, Canon Law Studies, n. 12, Washington: The Catholic University of America, 1921.

Michiels, G., *De Delictis et Poenis,* Lublin-Polonia, 1934.

......, *Normae Generales Iuris Canonici,* 2 vols., Lublin-Polonia, 1929.

Murphy, E., *Suspension Ex Informata Conscientia,* The Catholic University of America, Canon Law Studies, n. 76, Washington: The Catholic University of America, 1932.

Noval, J., *Commentarium Codicis Iuris Canonici,* lib. IV, *De Processibus,* 2 vols., Romae, 1920.

Oietti, B., *Synopsis Rerum Moralium et Iuris Pontificium,* 4, vols., Romae 1911.

Ottaviani, A., *Institutiones Iuris Publici Ecclesiastici*, 2 vols., Typis Polyglottis Vaticanis, 1935.

Pejska, J., *Ius Canonicum Religiosorum*, Friburgi Brisgoviae, 1927.

Petrovits, J., *The New Church Law on Matrimony*, The Catholic University of America, Canon Law Studies, n. 6, Washington: The Catholic University of America, 1919.

Pistocchi, M., *De Re Beneficiali Iuxta Canones*, Taurini, 1928.

......, *I canoni penali del Codice ecclesiatico esposti e commentati*, Torino-Roma, 1925.

Reiffenstuel, A., *Ius Canonicum Universum*, 4 vols., Venetiis, 1710.

Richter, E., *Kirchenrecht*, 2 vols., Leipzig, 1882-1886.

Roberti, F., *De Delictis et Poenis*, Romae.

......, *De Processibus*, 2 vols., Romae, 1926.

Roelker, E., *Principles of Privilege According to the Code of Canon Law*, The Catholic University of America, Canon Law Studies, n. 35, Washington: The Catholic University of America, 1926.

Salucci, R., *Il Diritto Penale secondo il Codice di Diritto Canonico*, Subiaco, 1926.

Saegmueller, J., *Lehrbuch des Katholischen Kirchenrechts*, Freiburg, 1909.

Schaefer, T., *De Religiosis*, Münster, 1927.

Schmalzgrueber, F., *Ius Ecclesiasticum Universum*, 12, vols., Romae, 1845.

Smith, S. B., *Elements of Ecclesiastical Law*, 3 vols., New York, 1888.

St. Alphonsus *Theologia Moralis*, editio nova cum antiquis editionibus diligenter collata in singulis auctorum allegationibus recognita notisque criticis et commentariis illustrata cura et studio P. Leonardi Gaude, 4 vols., Romae: Typis Polyglottis Vaticanis, 1912.

Strykius, S., *Opera Omnia*, 14 vols., Frankfurt, 1743.

Suarez, F., *Opera Omnia*, 26 vols., Lugduni, 1608.

Thomassinus, L., *Vetus et Nova Ecclesiae Disciplinae*, 10 vols., Moguntiaci, 1787.

Thesaurus, S.A., *De Poenis Ecclesiasticis*, Romae, 1760.

Vermeersch, A.-Creusen, J., *Epitome Iuris Canonici*, 3 vols., Romae, 1928.

Wernz, F.,-Vidal, P., *Ius Canonicum ad Codicis normam exactum*, vol. II: *De Personis*, 2 ed., Romae: Universitas Gregorgiana, 1928; vol. V: *Ius Matrimoniale*, 2 ed., 1928; vol. VI: *De Processibus*, 1927.

Wernz, F., *Ius Decretalium*, 6 vols., Romae, 1906-1912.

Woywod, S., *A Practical Commentary on the Code of Canon Law*, 2 vols., New York, 1925.

Periodicals

Apollinaris, Romae, 1928—

Archiv für katholisches Kirchenrecht, Mainz, 1857—

Commentarium pro Religiosis et Missionariis, Romae, 1920—

Ephemerides Theologicae Lovanienses, Lovanii, 1924—

Il Monitore Ecclesiastico, Romae, 1879—
Ius Pontificium, Romae, 1921—
Nouvelle Revue Theologique, Parisiis, 1869—
Periodica de Re Morali Canonica, Liturgica, Romae, 1905—

CHAPTER I.

AN HISTORICAL SYNOPSIS OF THE DEVELOPMENT OF SUSPENSION

The Right of the Church to Suspend Clerics

The Church's right to suspend clerics is consequent upon her status as a perfect autonomous society. She has, it is true, supreme legislative and judiciary power. But her mission to lead souls to eternal Beatitude would be wholly ineffective, unless there existed at the same time the right to coerce the contumacious[1] by the infliction of both spiritual and temporal penalties[2]. It is important that in every well constituted society there should be present the faculty to exclude the unworthy, to remove from office corrupt magistrates or at least, to suspend temporarily the exercise of their powers.[3]

To the Church is entrusted the supernatural life of the faithful. To her it belongs to distribute that life, to strengthen it where it is weak, to revive it where it has fallen into decline. How is the Church to meet this obligation unless she be perfect and sovereign, unless she employ perfect legislative, judiciary and coactive power? How can she compel the recalcitrant unless she have at her command all the necessary means to attain her end, which her status as a perfect society, established by Christ demands?[4] One of these means is the power to punish her delinquent subjects, even though they be her officials.

Administratively, the Church is ruled by officials who receive their status by reason of their incorporation into the ecclesiastical hierarchy. Each official is given a determined part of the flock of

[1] Canon 2214; Ottaviani, *Institutiones Iuris Publici Ecclesiastici,* I, 324.

[2] Ottaviani, *Institutiones Iuris Publici Ecclesiastici,* I, 323.

[3] Wernz, *Ius Decretalium,* VI, n. 147.

[4] Hermann, *Institutiones Theologiae Dogmaticae,* I, 286. Ottaviani, *Institutiones Iuris Publici Ecclesiastici,* I, 57.

Christ and is bound in conscience to concern himself about the spiritual and temporal welfare of his charge. When a cleric is given an office, he assumes his responsibility with the express or implied promise to carry out his duties conscientiously and to have at heart the weal and woe of the whole community.[5] The success and permanence of the society depends strongly on the faithful exercise of the office entrusted.[6]

Since, therefore, her spiritual and temporal progress as a society would be impaired and the attainment of her end would be rendered difficult by the scandalous lives of her officials, the Church is certainly within the scope of her power to institute a penalty that would touch her officials exclusively. This penalty is the one known today as suspension. In effect, this penalty whether medicinal or vindictive forbids a cleric to exercise the rights of his office, his orders or any benefice he might possess.[7]

This coercive power which the Church is fully justified in exercising to suspend her clerics, has come to her by an implicit grant from her divine Founder, Jesus Christ.[8] His own words to the Apostles bear this out. "Whatsoever you shall bind upon earth," He told them, "shall be bound also in heaven and whatsoever you shall loose upon earth shall be loosed also in heaven".[9] These words refer not only to the power of forgiving sins but also to every kind of spiritual jurisdiction, including penal sanctions.[10] Ottaviani asserts that this right of binding and loosing which Christ conferred on the Apostles is limitless and includes equally the right to coerce. From the general character of the expression, "Whatsoever you shall bind . . . whatsoever you shall loose," not only those who wish to keep the law are meant, but also those who are unwilling and recalcitrant.[11]

[5] Kober, *Die Suspension,* p. 2.
[6] Kober, *Die Suspension,* p. 1.
[7] Canons 2278, § 1; 2298, n. 2.
[8] Wernz, *Ius Decretalium,* VI, n. 147
[9] Matt. XVIII, 18.
[10] Boudinhon, "Excommunication," *Catholic Encyclopedia,* V, 678.
[11] *Institutiones Iuris Publici Ecclesiastici,* I, 325.

From the First to the Sixth Century

In considering the many penalties which the Church employed in her infancy, this penalty of suspension, now so definitely established can not with any degree of certainty be distinguished. The terminology used in the early Church is extremely general. The word "excommunication" included all penalties and inferred the meaning that "the one penalized had been placed outside of the communion to which his grade in the Church entitled him, either wholly or in part."[12] Furthermore, it was not uncommon for the legislator to employ the word *censure* to include also, with various distinctions, every kind of ecclesiastical punishment, namely, public penalties, deposition, suspension, excommunication or interdict.[13]

During the first three centuries, suspension, excommunication and interdict were not accurately distinguished. There was no clearly defined technical expression to designate the penalty of suspension as such. There was a total lack of any uniform precision in terminology both with regard to the legislation of general and particular councils and also with regard to the works of the early Fathers.

However, even though a specific terminology is wanting in these first centuries, nevertheless, it seems that the idea was not altogether foreign to the minds of the ecclesiastical legislators.

The Apostolic Canons are witnesses to this fact.[14] First of all, they speak of two different penalties, one graver than the other. Possibly the milder penalty is suspension because, if this proved ineffective the graver penalty of deposition followed. Canon five of the Greek text used the words ἀφοριζέσθω and Καθαιρείσθω which Fulton[15] translates as suspension and deposition respectively.

[12] Gans, "Censure," *Catholic Encyclopedia*, III, 528.

[13] Wernz, *Ius Decretalium*, VI, n. 144; Richter, *Kirchenrecht*, p. 774.

[14] The origin of the Apostolic Canons is disputed. Authors claim the Greek text to be the very legislation of the Apostles themselves promulgated by Clement. Some, like Beveridge and Hefele, believe them to belong to the end of the second or beginning of the third century. Others maintain that they could not have been composed before the council of Antioch (341). Cfr. Shahan, "Canons," *Catholic Encyclopedia*, III, 279.

[15] *Index Canonum*, p. 83.

Furthermore the words μηκέτί λεἰτόύϱγέἰν taken from canon fifteen of the Greek text of the Apostolic Canons also point to suspension. This same text in Mansi which is canon fourteen intimates that the delinquent can not be in the public service of the Church.[16]

In the early councils, too, the idea of suspension is somewhat manifest. There appear expressions like *abstentio*[17] and *abstineri.*[18] Likewise one very frequently meets a phrase such as *sacerdotali functione deinceps abstineant.*[19] All seem to point to suspension.

The council of Ancyra in the year 314 makes a statement which brings out clearly the distinction between suspension and deposition. The priests who had been guilty of idolatry are permitted the enjoyment of the honor of their office, but "they may neither sacrifice nor preach nor fulfill any priestly office."[20] The meaning seems to be that the priests retained their office, but certain functions peculiar to that office were denied them. According to Strykius,[21] deposition deprives one of everything, office and rights, whilst suspension only restricts the exercise of certain rights; consequently, there can be as many suspensions as there exist rights to be curtailed. Then again, as regards suspension the cleric does not lose his office nor his clerical status. This comparison of Strykius brings out quite clearly the similarity between the penalty spoken of by the council of Ancyra and the modern penalty of suspension.

Kober[22] is of the opinion that the idea of suspension can be found in canon eight of the first council of Nice, (325).[23] There

16 "Ne porro in ministerio publico sit Ecclesiae."—Canon XIV—Mansi, I, 31. Fulton, *Index Canonum*, p. 85.

17 Pontificale Romanum, tit. *Ordo Suspensionis* . . . III, 198.

18 Migne, *Patrologia Lat.*, IV, 347.

19 I Council of Rome (252)—Mansi, I, 866.

20 "Priests who sacrificed [during the persecution] but afterwards repenting, resumed the combat not only in appearance but in reality shall continue to enjoy the honor of their office, but they may neither sacrifice nor preach nor fulfill any priestly office."—Hefele, *History of the Councils*, I, 201. Canon I—Mansi, I, 514.

21 *Opera Omnia*, IV, Disp. IV. (De Suspensione in Genere), c. I, n. 46-48.

22 *Die Suspension*, p. 22.

23 "Concerning those who call themselves Cathari, if they come over to the

seems to be implied in this canon a form of suspension from the episcopal office. However, it is difficult to see how a cleric could be subject to such a penal effect when no previous personal crime existed. The suspension referred to, can not, therefore, be classed as the suspension as it exists today which is only used to punish the personal crimes of clerics, but rather it may be considered as an impediment. Moreover granted that culpability had previously existed, the prescription of the canon still remained in force and not only in this case but also in the case of those who had received orders while they, in good faith, adhered to the sect of the Cathari. Consequently, the suspension spoken of by Kober, it seems, can not be strictly called the penalty of suspension. Nevertheless, this fact goes to prove that the idea of suspension was not foreign to the minds of the early legislators.

Then as regards the fathers, some authors attest that the most ancient record of the use of suspension dates back to St. Cyprian who lived about the third century.[24] In his letter to Rogation concerning the deacon who had rebelled against his bishop, Cyprian advises him to depose this deacon or suspend (abstinere) him.[25] If a norm can be taken from later legislation, it would seem that the word *abstinere* is apparently used as a synonym for *suspendere*. In the councils which will be cited, a time element enters into the penalty; hence it precludes any possibility of excommunication and also deposition. Thus the council of Epaon, celebrated in the year 517, de-

Catholic and Apostolic Church, the Great and Holy Snyod decrees that they who are ordained shall continue as they are in the clergy. Wheresoever, then, whether in villages or in cities, all of the ordained are found to be of these only, let them remain in the clergy and in the same rank in which they are found. But if they come over to where there is a Presbyter or a Bishop of the Catholic Church, it is manifest that the Bishop of the Church must have the Bishop's dignity; and he who is named Bishop by those who are called Cathari shall have the rank of Presbyter, unless it shall seem fit to the Bishop to admit him to partake in the honor of the episcopal name, . . ."—Fulton, *Index Canonum*, p. 127. Cfr. Mansi, 1, 671.

24 Pontificale Romanum, tit. *Ordo Suspensionis* . . . etc., III, 176; Fanning, "Suspension," *Catholic Encyclopedia*, XIV, 345.

25 Migne, *Patrologia Lat.*, IV, 347; Hinschius, however, claims that the word *abstinere* used by St. Cyprian designated a total exclusion from the Church.—*Kirchenrecht*, IV, 371, note 9.

crees that for a certain crime a bishop had to suspend himself from communion for three months; and in the case of a priest, the latter had to suspend himself for two months.[26] Similarly the council of Agde, held in the year 506, prescribes that a priest should suspend himself for two months.[27] Gratian, too, speaks correspondingly in the same way.[28] Kober[29] maintains that the word *abstinere* of the early centuries is indicative of suspension. Again Cyprian refers to suspension in his IX Epistle. He uses the word *admonitio* which according to Baronius, as the *Pontificale Romanum* declares, is to be interpreted to mean the same as the censure of suspension.[30] The expression found in Cyprian's letter reads: "Utar ea admonitione quae me uti Dominus jubet."

It can therefore be stated that the third and fourth centuries apparently saw a tendency to suspension in its present form notwithstanding the fact that there was lacking a uniform and accurate terminology. In considering these early penalties, there is always present some degree of uncertainty as to the real nature of the penalty, because even though one does rationalize to arrive at a conclusion, nevertheless all doubt is not removed as to whether the penalty under consideration is suspension or not. The terminology found among the early conciliar laws and the writings of the Fathers, because of its generality, indefiniteness and ambiguity make one hesitate to decide conclusively and with any degree of finality, that such and such a penalty falls into the category of suspension as it exists in the Code.

A penalty of this period which occasioned considerable contention as to its proper classification, was the so-called *communio*

[26] Canon IV: "Si Episcopus est, tribus mensibus se a Communione suspendat duobus presbyter abstineat."—Mansi, VIII, 559. A clearer manifestation that *abstinere* means suspension may be seen from c. 2,3, X, *de clerico percussore*, V, 25. Here the expressions are respectively *ab administratione Missarum abstinere* and *a celebratione Missarum abstinere.*

[27] Canon LV: "Presbyter duobus mensibus se abstineat."—Mansi, VIII, 334.

[28] C. 2, D. XXXIV.

[29] *Die Suspension*, p. 19.

[30] Migne, *Patrologia Lat.*, IV, 253 and also 254, note IV; Pontificale Romanum, tit. *Ordo Suspensionis* . . . etc., III, 176.

peregrina.[31] This penalty, according to some authors[32] appeared for the first time in the third canon of the council of Riez, celebrated in the year 439. As to its proper nature, Hinschius[33] points to Kellner as being of the opinion, that this penalty was a partial suspension, namely a suspension *a beneficio.*. On the contrary, Hinschius himself denies that this *communio peregrina* was a suspension at all. He says that it has the nature of a total exclusion from the Church and also the nature of deposition.[34] The precise nature of this penalty, namely, whether it was an excommunication or a strict suspension is hard to determine. On the one hand, it differs from lay communion; for in effect, reduction to lay communion obliged the penalized cleric to receive Holy Communion with the laity, reduced him perpetually to the lay state and deprived him of the *privilegium fori.*[35] On the other hand, according to Kober[36] *communio peregrina* is less strict than deposition but stricter and severer than a simple suspension. The reason for this, he says, is because the effects of this penalty prohibited the exercise of functions proper to one's office, forbade attendance at divine services and separated the cleric temporarily from the communion of the faithful. It seems, therefore, that the much disputed *communio peregrina* could be placed in the category of a mild form of excommunication, inflicted on a cleric, depriving him at the same time of everything but his clerical status and sustinence. Consequently it can hardly be classified among the suspensions.[37]

The reason for this statement is the fact that when there is question of a suspension, the legal rights founded on Baptism, called the *bona communia,* are never curtailed. The suspension merely re-

31 Hollweck, *Die kirchlichen Strafgesetze,* p. 132; Kober, *Die Suspension,* p. 9.

32 Hinschius, *Kirchenrecht,* IV, 734, note 5; Hefele, *Consiliengeschichte,* II, 290.

33 *Kirchenrecht,* IV, 734, note 5.

34 *Kirchenrecht,* IV, 735.

35 Pontificale Romanum, tit. *Ordo Suspensionis . . .* etc., III, 198.

36 *Die Suspension,* p. 15.

37 Kober, *Die Suspension,* pp. 14-16; Hollweck, *Die kirchlichen Strafgesetze,* p. 132.

stricts those rights which flow from a valid ordination or from the valid possession of an office or a benefice, called the *bona clericalia.*[38] Such a restriction in the exercise of clerical rights dates back as far as the council of Ancyra which was celebrated in the year 314.[39] This council directs that priests who had sacrificed to the idols could retain their sacerdotal dignity and consequently associate with the other clerics, but it forbids these priests to preach, to say Mass or perform other sacerdotal functions. A similar provision may also be found in the eighth canon of the first council of Nice (325), where, at the prudent discretion of the bishop, a cleric is permitted the use of his clerical rights, whose exercise had heretofore been forbidden.[40]

Before concluding this period, mention can be made of a practice which later developed into the suspension *a beneficio.* This was a penalty depriving a delinquent cleric of his revenues.

For the first five centuries, the bishop, as father of all the faithful sustained the clerics from the common fund, which was called the *Patrimonium Christi.*[41] This was only natural, for the Cathedral church as the sole church was coextensive with the diocese, so that the offerings and revenues which came to the priests had to be given to the Cathedral church.[42] This remained in force even at the beginning of the rural parishes. However, later, when these parishes had a resident priest, part of the offerings went to the priest for his support and part went to the bishop.

Not infrequently the resident priest became delinquent in the administration of his office and even at times occasioned grave scandal. In these cases, the bishop would either depose the cleric, and in that instance sometimes permit the enjoyment of part of the revenues,[43] or deprive the cleric merely of the revenues without any deposition.

[38] Kober, *Die Suspension,* p. 24; Hollweck, *Die kirchlichen Strafgesetze,* p. 133; c. 1, *de sententia et re judicata,* II, 14, in VIo.

[39] Canon I—Mansi, I, 514.

[40] Mansi, I, 671.

[41] Thomassinus, *De Beneficiis,* VII, 1.

[42] Thomassinus, *De Beneficiis,* VII, 28.

[43] Kober, *Die Suspension,* p. 21, note 1.

Even in St. Cyprian's time, there is an evidence of a deprivation of revenues. In his twenty-eighth letter, these words are found: *Interim se a divisione mensurna tantum contineant non quasi a ministerio ecclesiastico privati esse videantur, sed ut integris omnibus ad nostrum praesentiam differantur.*[44] Likewise the IV Synod of Carthage, celebrated in the year 398, insists on a deprivation of the *stipendia.*[45]

From the Sixth to the Twelfth Century

Although the terminology became more accurate and uniform in the sixth century,[46] yet the penalty of suspension lacked that complete crystallization into a distinctive and formal method of expression, which so characterized the twelfth century. Various modes of expression are still resorted to, as previously, to established penalties which in some cases appear to be real suspensions and in others leave its nature in doubt or again point to what is now known as the interdict ab *ingressu ecclesiae.*

In general, it may be said that the time from the sixth to the twelfth century furthered considerably the development of suspension and gradually cleared the field for the canonical institute as it exists today. For besides the numerous total suspensions which limited the exercise of all the ecclesiastical functions and rights flowing from an office and the occasional partial suspensions which temporarily deprived one of the exercise of an individual right or function, there appeared also the administrative penalty of suspension and the suspension definitely divided into *ferendae* and *latae sententiae.*[47]

Roman Law is not without its evidences of this penalty of suspension. The few phrases gleaned from the *Novellae* of Justinian point to the restriction of rights akin to that engendered by a sus-

44 Migne, *Patrologia Lat.*, IV, 302.

45 Canon XLIX:—"Clericus qui absque corpusculi sui inaequalitate vigiliis deest stipendiis privetur."—Mansi, III, 995.

46 Wernz, *Ius Decretalium*, VI, n. 203; Ayrinhac, *Penal Legislation in the New Code of Canon Law*, n. 148; Cocchi, *Commentarium*, V, n. 99; Hinschius, *Kirchenrecht*, IV, 734-736.

47 Hinschius, *Kirchenrecht*, IV, 734-736.

pension. Thus the *Novellae* ordain that in certain instances clerics are to be separated for one year from the sacred ministry, or they are to be prohibited for one year from the sacred ministry, or for three years they are to be prohibited all religious ministrations.[48] With such statements as these, one apparently has proof that the sixth century saw the rise of the present day canonical institute.

Conciliar legislation, too, points to suspension despite the fact that the terminology in use today is at times wanting. The second canon of the third council of Orleans, celebrated in the year 538, speaks of a separation from office for three months.[49] Similarly its sixth canon orders a delinquent to be separated from the exercise of offices.[50]

During this period, the word *suspendere* came into more frequent use, although it is not at all certain that it had the same signification as it has today. At times, it appears to have embodied all that is contained in present day excommunication; sometimes it seems to be equivalent to the interdict *ab ingressu ecclesiae.*

The fourth canon of the council of Epaon, held in the year 517 has this to say: "If the cleric is a bishop he should suspend himself for three months from communion for keeping falcons and hunting dogs."[51] Furthermore, the twenty-second canon of the third council of Orleans (538) prescribes similarly, that a cleric should be suspended from communion for taking things belonging to the church and other priests.[52]

On the other hand various canons of different particular coun-

[48] Novels, (123.1) 2: ". . . per unum annum separari a sacro ministerio"; Novels, (123.2) pr.: ". . . per unum annum a sacro ministerio prohibeatur . . ." Novels, (123.10) I: ". . . jubemus eum per tres annos ab omni religioso ministerio prohiberi et in monasterium immitti."

[49] "Ipse Episcopus ad agendam poenitentiam tribus mensibus sit a suo officio sequestratus."—Mansi IX, 12.

[50] "A celebrandis officiis sequestratur."—Mansi, IX, 13.

[51] "Episcopis . . . canes ad venendum et accipitres habere non liceat . . . si episcopus est tribus mensibus se a communione suspendat."—Mansi, VIII, 334.

[52] "Si quis res Ecclesiae debitas vel proprias sacerdotis horrendae cuspiditatis instinctu occupaverit . . . tam diu a communione ecclesiastica suspendatur."—Hefele, *Conciliengeschichte,* II, 277.

cils using the term *suspendere*, make it obvious that the cleric is to be deprived of the exercise of certain functions proper to office or orders, thereby manifesting a decided relationship between suspension then and today. For instance, the tenth canon of the fourth council of Orleans, celebrated in the year 541 refers to a suspension *ab officio sacerdotii.*[53] Similarly the fifth canon of the fifth council of Orleans (549) demands a suspension from the honor and office which had been received.[54] The thirteenth canon of the council of Vern (755) uses the expression *ab officio suspendantur.*[55] Then again, one sometimes finds an expression like *suspensio a divinis mysteriis.*[56]

This tendency of the terminology to accuracy and definiteness of signification clearly shows a decided turn in the field of development. Perfection, however, was not reached until the twelfth century, when the idea of a total or partial restriction in the exercise of office or order became circumscribed within the one word *suspendere*, whether qualified or not.

During this period, according to Hinschius,[57] the nature of suspension consisted in this, namely, that unlike deposition, which completely took away the office, suspension deprived the cleric of the enjoyment of the rights peculiar to the office. Furthermore not only were the rights proper to the office restricted, but at the same time also the rights flowing from orders, because offices and orders were closely connected. The sole basis for this was the fact that in the early Church down to the twelfth century, no cleric could be ordained unless he had previously obtained some office. Thus if the cleric suffered a suspension from office, he at the same time suffered a suspension from orders, because of their intimate connection.[58] Moreover the fact that a cleric was suspended from office did not there-

[53] Mansi, IX, 114; Hefele, *Conciliengeschichte*, II, 781.

[54] "Ab honore et officio suscepto suspendantur."—Mansi, IX, 130.

[55] Mansi, XII, 583.

[56] Council of Rome (862), canon 4—Mansi, XIV, 1003. Hinschius interprets this as a suspension from celebrating Mass.—*Kirchenrecht*, V, 67.

[57] *Kirchenrecht*, IV, 731.

[58] Hinschius, *Kirchenrecht*, V. 67; Hollweck, *Die kirchlichen Strafengesetze*, p. 2, note 1.

by imply a loss of sustenence. There seems to have continued even at this time the special punishment in this regard, known as the privation from the enjoyment of the revenues. Clear evidence of such a penalty is found in the council of Narbonne (589).[59] Likewise canon thirteen of this same council speaks of depriving those of revenues who would not amend.[60]

It was also in the sixth century that another form of suspension took its place among the penalties destined exclusively for clerics. It is a suspension that may be classified neither as a vindictive nor a medicinal penalty, but assumes the unique status of a provisional or administrative penalty.[61] Its aim tends to prohibit the exercise of certain rights and functions during the process of an investigation so as to prevent any scandal and to safeguard any possible prejudice that might ensue from the fact that a cleric is under suspicion. By this enactment, the superior had full power to suspend a cleric, who had fallen under suspicion, temporarily from office, that is, during the time of the investigation. Should the gravity of the crime warrant a severer measure, the ecclesiastical superior could curtail the enjoyment of the revenues accruing from the suspect's office or benefice, in which case the superior had to substitute a vicar.[62] The earliest indication of this unique form of suspension emanates from the council of Lerida, which was celebrated in the year 524.[63] It is to this council that Gratian refers as the source whence he took the law now incorporated in his *Decretum*.[64] The law, thus cited by Gratian, prescribes that if a priest has fallen into ill-repute among his flock and there are no means whereby the bishop can obtain

[59] C. 10: "Non solum a stipendio sed uno anno a communione privetur." —Cabassutius, *Notitia Ecclesiastica,* p. 302.

[60] Cabassutius, *Notitia Ecclesiastica,* p. 302.

[61] Kober, *Die Suspension,* p. 28.

[62] Kober, *Die Suspension,* p. 29; Barbosa, in reference to this penalty says, that the suspect should also be suspended *ab officio* until he vindicated himself, still because of the gravity of the crime he may be suspended *ab officio et beneficio,* even though there is no one accusing him.—Lib. V, tit. XXXIV.

[63] Chapter X, (Fragmenta)—Mansi, VIII, 616.

[64] C. 13, C. 11, q. 5.

probatory testimony, then to avoid scandal the suspect priest should be suspended until he has made satisfaction.[65]

The administrative or provisional penalty continued in subsequent centuries. Gregory the Great, about the year 600 makes allusion to such a method of procedure in his letter to Januarius, bishop of Caralis.[66] Urban III, in the year 1186 also made a similar provision.[67]

The origin of suspension as a censure is disputed. Hinschius[68] claims that the fifth century is possibly the time when the medicinal suspension appeared. Wernz, on the other hand, points to the sixth century as the more probable date.[69] Since, however, evidence leans more to the opinion of Wernz, this phase of suspension shall be treated in the period under consideration.

Up to this time, it seems, that the penalties of the Church were vindictive in nature. There was no sharp distinction between medicinal and vindictive penalties as they exist today,[70] for the penalties in the early Church served principally to repair the social order which had been violated by the crime, since it was the public aspect of the Church rather than the individual pursuits of the members, that was stressed in those days.

The medicinal suspension was the outgrowth of these vindictive penalties.[71] The reason for this change can not be established at the present day. Possibly, as Hinschius asserts, the reason was as follows. It happened that deprivation from office or the prohibition to exercise certain ecclesiastical functions and rights proved inefficient at times, because after a lapse of the required time, the culprit could again exercise his office and rights, even though his con-

[65] A foot-note in the Richter-Friedberg edition of the *Corpus Iuris Canonici* specifies this suspension as *ab officio*—nota in c. 13, C. 11, q. 5. This is an insertion made by the *Correctores Romani.*

[66] Lib. 9, Epist. I:—Migne, *Patrologia Lat.*, LXXVII, p. 939.

[67] C. 3, X, *de crimine falsi,* V, 20.

[68] Hinschius refers to suspension as a censure while speaking of the penalties inflicted on clerics in the first centuries of the Church.—*Kirchenrecht,* IV, 756.

[69] *Ius Decretalium,* VI, n. 203.

[70] Hinschius, *Kirchenrecht,* IV, 748.

[71] Hinschius, *Kirchenrecht,* IV, 756.

duct remained disedifying and scandalous. To deprive the delinquent of his office and rights afresh demanded another penalty. Consequently to take care of a situation like this, the Church established a penalty which would remain until contumacy ceased or sufficient guarantees were given to assure amendment for the future. This penalty was the medicinal suspension.

Wernz's opinion that suspension as a censure appeared for the first time about the sixth century seems to be the better view, because the sixth century is not without its evidences of such penalties. However, it must again be remarked that the penalties cited from the councils of this period leave one in doubt as to their nature. The most that can be said is that medicinal penalties were not unknown and consequently when suspensions were inflicted, they may have been not only vindictive in character but also may have had the effects of a censure, whose sole purpose is to break down contumacy.

That the councils intended such penalties to break down contumacy may be seen from the council of Lerida, which was celebrated in the year 524. Its fifteenth canon ordained that if a cleric, after the first and second admonition, failed to amend, he was to be deprived of the dignity of his office as long as he persevered in his state.[72]

Certitude concerning suspension as a censure, however, can only be reached after the twelfth century, especially at the time of Innocent III. His response in the year 1214 clearly states "that not only should interdict be considered a censure, but also suspension and excommunication."[73]

Although legislation of the first period seems to point to suspension *latae sententiae*, still one can not in truth maintain that this is really a penalty. Thus for example, the sixth canon of the council of Chalcedon says that if any bishop should dare to ordain a person without an office, "the Holy Synod decrees to the reproach of the

[72] ". . . post primam et secundam commotionem si emendare neglexerit, donec in vitio perseverat officii sui dignitate privetur; (quod in vitio perseverat officii sui dignitate privetur) quod si se De juvante correxerit, sancto ministerio restauretur."—Mansi, VIII, 614.

[73] C. 20, X, *de verborum significatione*, V, 40.

ordainer, that such an ordination shall be inoperative and shall nowhere have effect".[74]

Kober[75] asserts that this declaration of the council of Chalcedon is a clear indication of suspension *latae sententiae.* It is true, the effects here stated connote suspension,[56] still when one views this kind of suspension in the light of the present day penalty, as a punishment for personal crimes of clerics, one can conclude that the suspension referred to by the council of Chalcedon is not a penalty. At most it may be called an impediment,[77] since it took effect even though the one ordained had received orders in good faith, contrary to the prescriptions of the law.

The first indication which apparently points to suspension *latae sententiae* as a penalty is found in the XIII council of Toledo (683). The council declares that those who harbor fugitive clerics and monks are to consider themselves excommunicated and deprived of their offices as long as such remain under their powers.[78]

In concluding these periods, it may be stated that all total suspensions are undoubtedly suspensions *ab officio.* This follows naturally from the fact that suspension as a penalty evolved from the severer penalty of deposition. Furthermore, in the early Church the acceptance of an office was all important, so much so that a cleric could not receive orders until he had first obtained some kind of an office.[79] Consequently where there was question of a penalty, it always affected the office. And if occasionally orders were specifically mentioned in stating the extent of the punishment, as the nineteenth canon of the third council of Orleans (538) exemplifies,[80]

[74] Fulton, *Index Canonum,* p. 173.

[75] *Die Suspension,* p. 46.

[76] "According to the existing law, absolute ordinations as is well known are still illicit, but yet valid, and even the council of Chalcedon has not declared them to be properly invalid, but only as without effect by permanent suspension."—Hefele, *History of the Councils,* III, 392.

[77] Wernz, *Ius Decretalium,* VI, n. 206; Kober, *Die Suspension,* p. 50.

[78] C. XI: "Transgressor institutionis paternae tanto tempore excommunicatum et remotum se a suis officiis noverit esse, quanto eum qui fugiit sub sua potestate contigerit remorasse."—Mansi, XI, 1074.

[79] Kober, *Die Suspension,* p. 26.

[80] "Ab ordine depositum"; Mansi, IX, 17.

this restriction was looked upon as affecting the office also, because of the close connection between office and orders.

FROM THE TWELFTH CENTURY TO THE COUNCIL OF TRENT

Before the twelfth century, ordination was forbidden unless a cleric at the time of the reception of orders was destined for a determined ecclesiastical office.[81] Orders and the acceptance of the office were complementary aspects of the same thing, and therefore were considered as forming one act. In fact, one might say that the exercise of one's orders and the administration of one's office were, indeed, synonymous.[82]

However, a change came in the twelfth century. The third council of the Lateran, celebrated in the year 1179, took a definite stand regarding the title of ordination. It separated the reception of orders from the acceptance of any office. Henceforth, after the establishment of this law prescribing absolute ordinations, clerics could receive orders without previously having obtained an ecclesiastical office.[83]

The advent of this new legislation affected a change also in the field of suspensions. Heretofore, the powers attaching to orders and office were considered as one. Now they came to be viewed as separate and distinct entities.[84] Consequently, clerics delinquent in the exercise of their duties and obligations were henceforward to be

81 "Neither Presbyter, Deacon, nor any of the ecclesiastical order shall be ordained, without a charge nor unless the person ordained is particularly appointed to a church in a city or village or to a Martyry or to a Monastery. And if any shall be ordained without a charge, the Holy Synod decrees, to the reproach of the ordainer, that such an ordination shall be inoperative, and shall nowhere have effect." Canon VI of the council of Chalcedon—Translation from the Greek text by Fulton, *Index Canonum*, p. 179.

82 Kober, *Die Suspension*, p. 26.

83 C. 16, X, *de praebendis et dignitatibus*, III, 5: "Licet autem praedecessores nostri ordinationes eorum, qui sine certo titulo promoventur, in injuriam ordinantium irritas esse voluerint et inanes: nos tamen benignius agere cupientes, tamdiu per ordinatores vel successores eorum provideri volumus ordinatis, donec per eos Ecclesiastica beneficia consequantur."

84 Kober, *Die Suspension*, p. 26.

punished, not exclusively with a suspension *ab officio,* but as circumstances warranted, even with a suspension *ab ordine.*

Then, too, about the same time, the beneficiary system of the Church reached the peak of its development. Here again, the Church added to her list of penalties another suspension, which in effect would extend to this canonical institute of benefices. This was the suspension *a beneficio,* a penalty whose effects curtailed not only the enjoyment of the emoluments flowing from the benefice itself, but also the economic administration of its goods, for example, buying and selling.[85]

The suspension *a beneficio* did not arise spontaneously. Its growth was gradual with the development of benefices. It has already been shown how in the early centuries, the clerics obtained revenues from their offices. It has also been shown how the delinquent possessor of one of the parishes was punished with a privation of his revenues or offerings. It was from this practice that the present suspension *a beneficio* took its rise.

The twelfth century ushered in an element of accuracy and clarity in reference to suspension which had heretofore been wanting. There was the special and exclusive significance attached to the penalty in the use of the word *suspendere.* Then, too, there was the uniform division of the effects of suspension according to a recognized and well defined triple category. These factors contributed much not only to engender a degree of certainty as to the effects of suspension, but especially to render the nature of this penalty better discernible.

The threefold category within which the effects of suspension were grouped, embraced the suspension *ab officio,*[86] the suspension *ab ordine,*[87] and the suspension *a beneficio.*[88] From these three

[85] Ferraris, "Suspensio", art. I, n. 4; Glossa in c. 25, X, *de electione et electi potestate,* I, 6, v. *Admiserant;* Glossa in c. 16, *de electione et electi potestate,* I, 6, in VIo, v. *Beneficiis;* Alterius, *De Censuris,* II, Disp. V, c, 2; Hollweck, *Die kirchlichen Strafgesetze,* p. 135.

[86] III Lateran (1179), canon 25—Harduin, VII, 1683: It was incorporated in c. 3, X, *de usuris,* V, 19.

[87] III Lateran (1179), canon 2—Harduin, VII, 1674. It was incorporated in c. 1, X, *de schismaticis,* V, 8.

sprang as from a root all future penalties of suspension, even the combined penalty of suspension *ab officio et beneficio.*[89] These same three are the immediate progenitors of all partial suspensions, because the latter merely particularized their constitutive elements.[90]

After the twelfth century previously existing notions of suspension became fully clarified. The change came about, when together with new legislation, the countless laws of particular councils and papal documents were brought together into one codified unit, the *Corpus Iuris Canonici.* The most preeminent works were those of Gregory IX and Boniface VIII. However, the law on suspension, as it appeared in these authentic works needed clarification. This was done by the commentators who gathered the principles contained therein and formulated with but a few exceptions, the present idea of suspension.

According to the new law, suspension from office restricted the rights flowing from an office, whether or not these were founded on orders or jurisdiction and as a censure bound the culprit everywhere.[91] This was a departure from the previous legislation. It has been noted before in reference to the advent of the absolute ordinations, that if a cleric had been suspended from orders, this also included the suspension from office and vice versa.[92] Now, however, a cleric could be suspended from orders and thus the suspension would only affect the orders and not the office. On the contrary, if there was a suspension from office this included also a suspension from orders. This is true because, if a cleric thus suspended exercised any functions pertaining to orders, he immediately in-

88 III Lateran (1179), canon 3:—Harduin, VIII, 1675. It was incorporated in c. 7, 3, X, *de electione,* I, 6. See also Hinschius, *Kirchenrecht,* V. 66, 67, 70.

89 C. 33, X, *de testibus,* II, 20; c. 1, X, *de secundis nuptiis,* IV, 21; c. 2, X, *de calumniatoribus,* V, 2; c. 11, X, *de calumniatoribus,* V, 2; c. 11, X, *de privilegiis et excessibus,* V, 33.

90 Hinschius, *Kirchenrecht,* IV, 734.

91 Reiffenstuel, lib. V, tit. XXXIX, n. 159; Glossa in c. 53, X, *de appellationibus,* II, 28, v. *Subtrahuntur.*

92 Kober, *Die Suspension,* p. 26.

curred an irregularity.[93] Moreover, if one had been suspended from office the right to receive the sacraments was not curtailed, because the reception of the sacraments was not considered as being in any way connected with ecclesiastical offices.[94]

Furthermore, although the suspension *ab officio,* included orders and jurisdiction, it did not curtail the rights proper to a benefice,[95] namely, the administration and enjoyment of the revenues. The glossa[96] states, that suspension *ab officio* can not be extended to a benefice. A similar distinction is implied by Innocent III about the year 1240. He said that although the ecclesiastical constitution teaches that a cleric be suspended *ab officio,* he would not disapprove of this same cleric being suspended *a beneficio,* if the gravity of the crime should warrant such an action.[97]

Whether or not the suspension *ab officio* prior to the twelfth century restricted the use of revenues is difficult to say. Possibly it did, owing to the fact that the suspension *ab officio* is a mild form and the out-growth of deposition. Hinschius[98] is inclined to think that there was no total deprivation. He offers the nineteenth canon of the third council of Orleans (538) as proof for his statement.[99] Whatever the previous law had enjoined, with the advent of the twelfth century the situation became quite definitely settled.

[93] C. 1, *de sententia et re judicata,* II, 14, in VIo: "Si quis autem iudex ecclesiasticus, . . ., famae suae prodigus et proprii persecutor honoris, contra conscientiam et contra justitiam in gravamen partis alterius in iudicio quicquam fecerit per gratiam vel per sordes, ab exsecutione officii per annum noverit se suspensum . . . si suspensione durante damnabiliter ingesserit se divinis, irrgularitatis laqueo se involvit secundum canonicas sanctiones. . ."

[94] Suarez, *De Censuris,* V, Disput., XXVI, sect. III, n. 10.

[95] Reiffenstuel, lib. IV, tit. XXXIX, n. 159. Hollweck, *Die kirchlichen Strafgesetze,* p. 134.

[96] Glossa in c. 1, *de sententia et re judicata,* II, 14, in VIo.

[97] C. 10, X, *de purgatione canonica,* V, 34.

[98] *Kirchenrecht,* IV, 731.

[99] "Si quis [clericus ut supra in c. XVIII] superbia elatus officium suum indignatione quaecumque implere noluerit juxta statuta priora circa communione contentus, ab ordine depositus tamdiu habeatur, quamdiu digna, sicut scriptum, poenitentia et supplicatione satisfecerit praesidenti pontifici, tamen regulariter et cautalem integram, et quaecumque illis stipendiorum juxta consuetudinem redhibentur pro qualitate temporis ministerii."—Mansi. IX, 17.

Thus the ecclesiastical institute of suspension reached the perfection of its development. In fact no further room for doubt could be had after the response of Innocent III was issued in the year 1214. The response settled for all times the precise status of suspension as a penalty. When asked what must be understood by a censure, the Pontiff replied: "We answer that not only should the interdict be considered a censure but also suspension and excommunication".[100]

At this stage the definition of suspension could then be formulated from the interpretations of various commentators.[101] It was considered a censure or a vindictive penalty, by which a cleric is deprived of the use or exercise of ecclesiastical functions, relative to orders, offices or benefices.

With the division of suspension into suspensions *ab officio*, *ab ordine* and *a beneficio*, no further development took place on this score, save perhaps the combined suspension *ab officio et beneficio*. Some commentators are wont to consider this species of penalty in the same class as the total suspension.[102]

Another important development during this period is the appearance of innumerable partial suspensions. A complete list of these suspensions would be practically impossible. An attempt therefore, is made merely at mentioning a few, to give the reader some idea as to their species.

Among the suspensions *ab ordine* can be mentioned the following partial penalties: suspension from the exercise of pontificals;[103] suspension from the Presbyterate;[104] suspension from the right to ordain;[105] suspension from the right to consecrate other bishops;

[100] C. 20, X, *de verborum significatione*, V, 40.

[101] Barbosa, lib, V, tit., XXVII, c. IV; Joannes Andreae, *Comment. super V Decretal.*, "de clerico excommunicato", cc. IV-X; Hostiensis, *In Quintum Decretalium Librum Commentarium*, "de clerico excommunicato ministrante", c. IIII, n. 4; c. X, n. 2.

[102] Reiffenstuel, lib. V, tit., XXXIX, n. 162.

[103] C. of London (1268), c. 33—Mansi, XXIII, 1247. See also Gratian in c. 32, C. XXIII, q. 8.

[104] C. 11, X, *de officio et potestate iudiciis delegati*, I, 29; c. 2, *de officio et potestate iudiciis delegati*, I, 14, in VIo.

[105] C. 45, X, *de simonia*, V, 3; c. 15, X, *de temporibus ordinationum*, I, 11.

[106] suspension from the right to confer the Presbyterate or Diaconate;[107] suspension from the right to give the Tonsure;[108] suspension from the right to offer the Sacrifice of the Mass;[109] suspension from the right to preach;[110] suspension *a divinis.*[111]

Among the suspensions *ab officio* may be enumerated the following: suspension from the right of granting a benefice;[112] suspension from the right to vote;[113] suspension from the administration of spiritual and temporal matters;[114] suspension from the use of the pallium;[115] suspension from the right of confirming bishops;[116] suspension from the right of granting indulgences;[117] sus-

[106] C. 2, X, *de translatione episcopi,* I, 7.

[107] C. 13, X, *de temporibus ordinationum,* I, 11.

[108] C. 4, *de temporibus ordinationum,* I, 9, in VIo.

[109] C. 28, C. VII, q. 1.

[110] C. 3, *de poenis,* V, 8, in Clem.

[111] C. of Exeter (1287), c. 41:—Mansi, XXIV, 823. The penalty *a divinis* is found copiously in particular sources.—Hinschius, *Kirchenrecht,* V, 596, note 1. A penalty similar to this suspension *a divinis* was the suspension *ab ingressu ecclesiae.* The latter penalty was employed quite frequently by the early particular councils, for example the council of Paris (1429), c. 8:—Mansi, XXVIII, 1100. According to Hinschius, this penalty of suspension *ab ingressu ecclesiae* was, in effect, nothing more than a personal interdict rather than a suspension *a divinis.*

[112] C. 7, 3, X, *de electione et electi potestate,* I, 6; c. 29, X, *de praebendis et dignitatibus,* III, 5; c. unc., *ne sede vacante,* III, 8, in VIo. It is well to remark here that jurisdiction and orders were considered separate powers. This is evident from a case found in the Glossa in c. 15, X, *de electione et electis potestate,* I, 6. The case has reference to an appeal made against a bishop who had suspended a cleric. This bishop, although lawfully constituted had not received consecration and the appeal was based on this fact. In response the pope maintained, that since the bishop had accepted his election, he could fully exercise his powers—" He who has been elected and confirmed possesses jurisdiction and if consecrated possesses also dignity."

[113] C. 2, *de aetate et qualitate et ordine praeficiendorum,* I, 6, in Clem.

[114] C. 2, X, *de solutionibus,* III, 23.

[115] Urban II, Decretum de Primatu Lugdunensi:—Harduin, VI, II, 1729.

[116] C. 2, X, *de translatione episcopi,* I, 7; c. 44, *de electione et electi potestate,* I, 6, in VIo.

[117] Council of Aquileiia (1334):—Mansi, XXV, 1119.

pension from the right to receive new members into a religious Order.[118]

Finally, there can also be mentioned a few partial suspensions *a beneficio*. They are: the suspension from part of the revenues;[119] the suspension from one of several benefices.[120]

With reference to the simple unqualified suspension which appeared in the previous period, this kind of a suspension still continued. An example of such a suspension may be found in the acts of the Synod of Salzburg, which was held in the year 1418.[121]

Worthy of note in this period is the suspension inflicted on moral persons. It was not an uncommon practice after the twelfth century to suspend the exercise of rights which a moral person possessed in its corporate capacity. This included a suspension *ab officio*[122] or *a beneficio*.[123] Never was it considered possible to inflict a suspension *ab ordine* on a community, because orders belonged to the individual, the restriction of whose rights demanded a personal crime.[124]

When a suspension had fallen on a moral person, it was always understood that the individuals forming the community were bound,

118 C. 2, *de regularibus*, III, 14, in VIo.

119 C. 2, *de aetate et qualitate et ordine praeficiendorum*, I, 6, in Clem.

120 C. 37, *de electione et electi potestate*, I, 6, in VIo.

121 Canon IV—Mansi, XXVIII, 983. According to Reiffenstuel, such an unqualified suspension is to be considered as embracing both the effects of the suspension *ab officio* and *a beneficio*. The reason he gives is, because an indefinite proposition is equivalent to a universal.—Lib. V, tit. XXXIX, n. 159.

122 C. un., *ne sede vacante aliquid innovetur*, III, 8, in VIo: "Si ad episcopum et capitulum communiter pertineat collatio praebendarum, mortuo episcopo vel a collatione beneficiorum suspenso, poterit capitulum vacantes conferre praebendas, etiamsi episcopus interesse habeat in collatione hiusmodi ut praelatus. Idem poterit episcopus, si capitulum ab ipsa collatione suspendi contingat, vel singulariter omnes in capitulo majoris excommunicationis vinculo innodari."

123 C. 1, *de electione*, I, 3, in Extravag. com.: "Capitula vero, conventus ecclesiarum et monasteriorum ipsorum et alii quicunque, ipsos absque hujusmodi dictae sedis literis recipientes vel obedientes eisdem tamdiu sint a beneficiorum suorum perceptione suspensi, donec super hoc ejusdem sedis gratiam meruerint obtinere."

124 Suarez, *De Censuris*, V, Disput., XXVIII, sec. III, n. 3.

even though they were innocent, in questions where the moral person as a corporate unit exercised its rights.[125] In other cases, each member of the clerical body could not be deprived of rights which he possessed as an individual by a suspension inflicted on the community.[126]

These provisions of law authorizing the suspension of a moral person's corporate rights which had their rise during this period served as the legal foundation for the present legislation in the Code of Canon Law.[127]

Before bringing this period to a close, mention may be made of suspension as a *latae sententiae* penalty. As to its existence in this period, there can be no doubt, since examples of this type of suspension are found in the common law. Gregory IX,[128] Boniface VIII,[129] and Clement V[130] attest to this fact.

125 Wernz, *Ius Decretalium*, VI, n. 152.

126 C. un., *ne sede vacante aliquid innovetur*, III, 8, in VIo: "Si ad episcopum et capitulum communiter pertineat collatio praebendarum, mortuo episcopo vel a beneficiorum collatione suspenso, poterit capitulum vacantes conferre praebendas, etiamsi episcopus interesse habeat in collatione huiusmodi ut praelatus. Idem poterit episcopus, si capitulum ab ipsa collatione suspendi contingat . . ." Cfr. also c. 1, *de electione*, 1, 3, in extravag. comm.; c, 40, *de electione et electi potestate*, I, 6, in VIo.

127 Canon 2285, § 1: "Si communitas seu collegium clericorum delictum commiserit, suspensio ferri potest vel in singulas personas delinquentes vel in communitatem, uti talem, vel in personas delinquentes et communitatem. § 2: Si primum, serventur huius articuli canones. § 3: Si alterum, communitas prohibetur exercitio iurium spiritualium quae ipsi, uti communitati, competunt. § 4: Si tertium, effectus cumulantur."

128 C. 2, X, *de solutionibus*, III, 23: "Firmiter inhibemus, ne quis praesumat [*de cetero*] ecclesiam sibi commissam pro alienis gravare debitis, aut literas alicui seu sigilla concedere, quibus possent ecclesiae obligari, decernentes, si secus [*quod non credimus,*] fuerit attentatum, ad solutionem talium debitorum ecclesias non teneri. Si quis autem contra praemissa de cetero venire praesumpserit, ab administratione spiritualium et temporalum noverit se suspensum." Cfr. also c. 7, § 3, X, *de electione et electi potestate*, I, 6.

129 C. 40, *de electione et electi potestate*, I, 6, in VIo: ". . . Decernimus ut ii qui praemissa de caetero praesumpserint, (si vacante cathedrali, regulari vel collegiata ecclesia bona a praelato dimissa occupant) eo ipso sint et tamdiu maneant ab officio et beneficiis quibuscunque suspensi. . ." Cfr. also c. 1, *de sententia et re judicata*, II, 14, in VIo.

Finally, mention must be made of the unique form of punishment called the suspension *ex informata conscientia,* because the law establishing this method of procedure has its origin in the early part of this period. The law emanates from Lucius III. It was a response given to the Archbishop of Tours in 1183 in answer to a question concerning Regulars,[131] in which the Pope replied that the Regular Prelates could prohibit their subjects from being advanced to higher orders on account of secret crimes. Although the law does not very clearly establish itself as an exception to the general law of the Decretals,[132] nevertheless by virtue of legal interpretation, it received that meaning and served as a precedent for the Tridentine law.

Prior to the council of Trent, no occult crime could be legally punished because, from its very nature, an occult crime precluded any judicial proof. Even though a bishop had been personally and morally convinced of the existence of the crime, which forced him to decide against the worthiness of the cleric for orders, he could not hinder this cleric from ascending to orders. Moreover the bishop could not forbid the exercise of an order already received.[133] Perfectly powerless was the bishop to touch the occult crimes of his ecclesiastics.[134] His power rested merely in admonishing the culprit privately and at the same time threatening him with divine anger and God's judgments.[135] Oftentimes, however, such exhortations,

130 C. 1, § 4, *de haereticis,* V, 3, in Clem.: "Quodsi odii, gratiae vel amoris, lucri aut commodi temporalis obtentu contra iustitiam et conscientiam suam omiserint contra quemquam procedere, ubi fuerit procedendum super huiusmodi pravitate, aut obtentu eodem, pravitatem ipsam vel impedimentum officii sui alicui imponendo, eum super hoc praesumpserint quoquo modo vexare: praeter alias poenas, pro qualitate culpae imponendas eisdem, episcopus aut superior suspensionis ab officio per triennium, alii vero excommunicationis sententias eo ipso incurrant." Cfr. also c. 1, *de decimis, primitiis, et oblationibus,* III, 8, in Clem.

131 C. 5, X, *de temporibus ordinationum,* I, 11.

132 C. 4, X, *de temporibus ordinationum,* I, 11; C. 17, X, *de temporibus ordinationum,* I, 11.

133 C. 4, X, *de tempore ordinationum,* I, 11.

134 Kober, *Die Suspension,* p. 66.

135 C. 17, X, *de tempore ordinationum,* I, 11.

such threats fell upon deaf ears. Consequently, the sanctuary became the abode of unworthy and unscrupulous clerics. This was the situation, before the council of Trent extended the law of Lucius III and definitely empowered bishops to suspend clerics for occult crimes. What the council of Trent enacted in this regard will be given consideration under the following heading.

From the Council of Trent to the Code of Canon Law

At the time of the council of Trent, the nature of suspension was accurately determined. Consequently, except for the suspension *ex informata conscientia,* the council contributed nothing new in this regard. The council confirmed and restated suspensions of previous laws[136] and directly instituted new ones.[137]

It is well to note here that among the penalties of suspension en-

[136] Some examples of suspensions which the council of Trent restated and confirmed are the following: C. 2, *de temporibus ordinationum,* I, 9, in VIo decrees a suspension from giving the tonsure. This the council restates in Sess., XXIII, *de ref.*—Mansi, XXXIII, 143.

The council confirmed the Decretal law of X, *de cohabitatione clericorum,* III, 2 in Sess., XXV, *de ref.,* c. 14.—Mansi, XXXIII, 189.

In Sess., XXIII, *de ref.,* c. 4, the council indirectly referred to the measure enacted by c. 4, *de temporibus ordinationum,* I, 9 in VIo, namely a suspension from giving the tonsure.—Mansi, XXXIII, 142.

Finally, in Sesss., XIV, *de ref.,* c. 6, the council explicitly states that it renews the constitution of Clement V, published in the Council of Vienne, beginning *Quoniam.*—Mansi, XXXIII, 105. This law may also be found in the *Corpus Iuris Canonici* in c. 2, *de vita et honestate,* III, 1, in Clem.

[137] An example of a new suspension established by the Council may be found in Sess., XXIII, *de ref.,* c. 10—Mansi, XXXIII, 144. The council changed the old Decretal law which permitted abbots to give tonsure and minor orders not only to their subjects but also to those who came to their convent and over whom they had episcopal or quasi-episcopal jurisdiction.—c. 3, *de privilegiis,* V, 7, in VIo. Besides forbidding for the future the giving of tonsure to those who are not their subjects and to seculars, the council instituted the suspension *ab officio et beneficio* which was to be incurred *ipso facto* upon the violation of the prohibition.

Other new suspensions instituted by the council may be found in the following sessions: Sess., VI, *de ref.,* c. 5—Mansi, XXXIII, 46; Sess., VII, *de ref.,* c. 10—Mansi, XXXIII, 57; Sess., XIV, *de ref.,* c. 2—Mansi, XXIII, 103.

acted by the council of Trent, there is one which deals with laymen. Suspension as a penalty can only be inflicted for the personal crimes of clerics,[138] but, in the Tridentine law, provision is made to curtail the exercise of certain rights which a layman enjoys by virtue of his office. In doing this, the council is merely following the practice of the middle ages. In its twenty-fifth session[139] the council decrees that to prevent a bishop from being ignorant "as to the time of profession, the superioress of the convent shall be bound to give notice thereof a month beforehand; but if she does not acquaint him therewith, she shall be *suspended from office,* for as long a period as the bishop shall see fit."[140] Such a suspension is implied in a decree of the Congregation of Bishops and Regulars. It indirectly speaks of a suspension of this kind emanating from the Vicar General.[141]

The opinion of eminent commentators throws light on this form of suspension. Reiffenstuel asserts that such a penalty implied merely a suspension from the office of administration together with the acts pertaining thereto.[142] Leurenius claims that the abbesses and the prioresses of the early Church did not enjoy ecclesiastical jurisdiction properly so called and therefore, suspension from the jurisdiction must be taken in the broad sense.[143]

The most important innovation brought about by the council of Trent was the fact that the council established the power previously given by Lucius III for religious only, also for the secular clergy. But the words of the decree enacting this legislation were vague and inaccurate.[144] So vague was this law, that frequently questions

138 Wernz, *Ius Decretalium,* VI, n. 206; Kober, *Die Suspension,* p. 50.

139 *De reg.,* c. 17:—*Concilium Tridentinum,* Tom. IX, pars VI, 1083.

140 Translation by Waterworth, *Canons and Decrees of the Council of Trent,* p. 248.

141 "Tollendam esse suspensionem emanentam a Vicario generali Episcopi contra Abbatissam, et alias officiales."—S. C. Ep. et Reg., *Placentina,* 3 oct. 1611—*Fontes,* n. 1651.

142 Lib. V. tit. XXXIX, n. 164.

143 Lib. I, tit. XI, n. 222.

144 Sess., XIV, *de ref.,* c. 1: "Cum honestius ac tutius sit subjecto, debitam praepositis obedientiam impendendo in inferiori ministerio deservire, quam cum praepositorum scandalo, graduum altiorum appetere dignitatem ei,

were sent to the Holy See to clarify certain points. Also various instructions were issued to this same effect.[145] But these decisions did not wholly clear the situation. A need for a complete statement of the law was felt. To answer this need the Sacred Congregation of the Propagation of the Faith issued an Instruction on October 20, 1884 in which it clearly and concisely gave the complete legislation concerning the suspension *ex informata conscientia.*[146] The Code, with but slight modifications, has taken over this legislation as contained in the Instruction.[147]

After the council of Trent, the nature of suspension seen in its effects remained the same. Whatever legislation appeared, it had nothing to do with the nature of suspension, but only abrogated previously existing forms of suspensions or instituted new ones. At no time was there a departure from the species of suspension which arose after the twelfth century.

Before proceeding to the enumeration of the legislation affecting suspension after the council of Trent, it would be well to consider a matter of interpretation relative to the suspension *ab ordine.* It is given this consideration here because the glossa undertakes to interpret a law which had its origin in the thirteenth century.[148] Whether the interpretation given by the glossa was recognized in the thirteenth century is difficult to ascertain. In reference to this law, the glossa makes it clear that a cleric who has been suspended from a minor order could not exercise the functions flowing from major

cui ascensus ad sacras ordines a suo praelato ex quacumque causa, etiam ob occultum crimen, quomodolibet, etiam extrajudicialiter, fuerit interdictus, aut qui a suis ordinibus seu gradibus vel dignitatibus ecclesiasticis fuerit suspensus, nulla contra ipsius praelati voluntatem concessa licentia de se promoveri faciendo aut ad priores ordines, gradus, dignitates sive honores restitutio suffragetur."—Mansi, XXXV, 357.

145 Instr. S. C. Ep et Reg., 11 iun. 1880, art. 9—*Fontes,* n. 2005; *ASS,* XIV (1880), 292; S.C.C., *Lucionen.,* 8 apr. 1848—*ASS,* XIV (1880), 299; S.C. Ep. et Reg., 24 aug. 1894—*ASS,* XXVII (1894), 430; S.C.C., *Nullius,* 3 feb. 1593 —*Fontes,* n. 2254; S.C.C., *S. Severini,* 17 sept. 1778—*Thesaurus Resolutionum,* XLVII, 47.

146 *Coll. S.C.P.F.,* n. 1628; *Fontes,* n. 4907.

147 Murphy, *Suspension Ex Informata Conscientia,* p. 37.

148 C. 2, *de temporibus ordinationum,* I, 9, in VIo.

orders.[149] From the principle thus formulated, there followed this extended interpretation, which commentators[150] say is based on Roman Law,[151] namely, that a suspension from a lower order, for the time in which the penalty continued, prevented a cleric from ascending to a higher order. Suarez[152] maintains that a cleric thus suspended from a minor order is prohibited from the reception of a major order, because the character of the inferior order is, as it were, a moral faculty to receive a higher order. Benedict XIV speaks of this indirectly, when he says that a cleric taking such a step would, indeed, commit a sacrilege but would not incur an irregularity.[153]

The first official document to affect suspension after the council of Trent was the Constitution of Pius IX, *Apostolicae Sedis*, which was issued on October 12, 1869.[154] The purpose of this Constitution was to moderate and mitigate the whole code of *latae sententiae* censures, including suspensions, and to establish such penalties as were thenceforward to have the force of general law. Consequently, in dealing with suspensions, the Constitution enumerated seven suspensions reserved to the pope, confirmed some of the suspensions of previous laws and abrogated all others.[155] These suspensions became new law and remained in force until the Code.

149 Glossa in c. 2, *de temporibus ordinationum*, I, 9, verb. *Ordinum*.

150 Hollweck, *Die kirchlichen Strafgesetze*, p. 134, note 2; Kober, *Die Suspension*, p. 114; Hinschius, *Kirchenrecht*, V, 599, note 4.

151 D., (48.22) 7.22:—"Est enim perquam rediculum, eum, qui minoribus poenae causa prohibitus sit, ad majores adspirare."

152 "Et confirmatur simul et ampliatur nam suspensus ab ordine inferiori consequenter est suspensus seu prohibitus, ne superiorem ordinem possit recipere, si illum non habet . . . quia character inferioris ordinis est veluti facultas moralis ad suscipiendum ordinem superiorem; unde receptio superioris ordinis aestimari et dici potest veluti usus quidam characteris inferioris ordinis, qui licet videatur magis passivus, quam activus, tamen inter functiones clericales numerari potest; qui ergo suspensus est ab usu ordinis inferioris, consequenter est suspensus a receptione ordinis superioris. Estque haec communis sententia. . ."—*De Censuris*, V, Disput., XXVI, sect. III, n. 8.

153 *De Synodo Dioecesana*, lib. XII, C. 3, n. 7.

154 *Fontes*, n. 552.

155 Leech, *A Comparative Study of the Const. "Apostolicae Sedis" and the Codex Iuris Canonici*, p. 125.

The Constitution confirmed the law and penalty laid down by the Congregation of the Council under date of September 21, 1624, which decreed that dismissed religious who remained outside of their religious house were *ipso facto* suspended from the exercise of orders.[156] It also restated the suspensions affecting ordaining prelates as prescribed by Gregory IX,[157] excluding however the suspension prescribed for those receiving orders.[158] Likewise with the law of Innocent XII,[159] the Constitution retained the suspension referring to the ordaining prelate but abrogated it for the recipient.[160] Then, too, the Constitution confirmed the law wherein clerics ordained in Rome were suspended from the exercise of orders illicitly received and bishops suffered suspension for one year from the exercise of pontifical acts.[161]

156 "Praetera statuit . . . ut eiecti extra Religionem degentes sint perpetuo suspensi ab exercitio Ordinum . . ."—S.C.C., decr. 21 sept. 1624, § 9, § 10.—*Fontes,* n. 2454.

"Suspensionem perpetuam ab exercitio Ordinum ipso iure incurrunt religiosi eiecti, extra religionem degentes."—Pius IX, const., *Apostolicae Sedis,* 12, oct. 1869, § V, 5.—*Fontes,* n. 552.

157 C. 45, X, *de simonia,* V, 3: "Si quis ordinaverit seu ordinem praesentaverit aliquem, promissionem vel iuramentum ab illo recipiens, quod super provisione sua non inquietet eundem, ordinator a collatione, praesentator vero ab exsecutione ordinum per triennium, et ordinatus ab ordine sic suscepto, donec dispensationem super hoc per sedem apostolicam obtinere meruerint, noverint se suspensos."

158 "Suspensionem per triennium a collatione Ordinum ipso iure incurrunt aliquem Ordinantes absque titulo beneficii vel patrimonii cum pacto ut ordinatus non petat ab ipsis alimenta."—Pius IX, const., *Apostolicae Sedis,* 12 oct. 1869, § V, 2.—*Fontes,* n. 552.

159 ". . . volumus, ut si quid in iisdem praemissis, seu eorum aliquo secus fiat, Ordinans quidem a collatione Ordinum per annum, Ordinatus vere a susceptorum Ordinum executione . . . eo ipso suspensus sit . . . etc."—Innocentius XII, const., *Speculatores,* 4 nov. 1694, § 8.—*Fontes,* n. 258.

160 "Suspensionem per annum ab ordinum administratione ipso iure incurrunt Ordinantes alienum subditum . . . etc."—Pius IX, const., *Apostolicae Sedis,* 12 oct. 1869, § V, 3.—*Fontes,* n. 552.

161 Edict of the Card. Vicar under Clem. VIII, nov. 24, 1603; decree of S.C.C., sept. 21, 1624 under Urban VIII; edict of the Card. Vicar under Benedict XIV, mart. 20, 1743.—Leech, *A Comparative Study of the Const., "Apostolicae Sedis" and the "Codex Iuris Canonici",* p. 136, note 39.

Other laws affected by the Constitution *Apostolicae Sedis* were the following. Boniface VIII[162] prohibited bishops, abbots and other prelates elected by the Holy See, under pain of suspension, from assuming the administration of their offices, or benefices without having Apostolic letters. Chapters and monasteries were forbidden under pain of suspension from revenues, to give or receive obedience before the newly appointed incumbent presented his Apostolic letters. The Constitution changed this law by restricting the penalty to the chapters and monasteries.[163] Furthermore the Constitution confirmed the previous law of Pius V concerning the ordination of secular and religious clerics who had not sufficient means for sustenance.[164]

Finally the Constitution *Apostolicae Sedis* confirmed the Tridentine suspensions. This is evident from the text of the Constitution itself which clearly states this fact.[165]

[162] C. 1, *de electione*, 1, 3, in extravag. comm.

[163] "Suspensionem ipso facto incurrunt a suorum Beneficiorum perceptione ad beneplacitum S. Sedis Capitula et Conventus Ecclesiarum et Monasteriorum, aliique omnes, qui ad illarum seu illorum regimen et administrationem recipiunt Episcopos aliosve Praelatos de praedictis Ecclesiis seu Monasteriis apud eamdem S. Sedem quovis modo provisos, antequam ipsi exhibuerint Litteras apostolicas de sua promotione."—Pius IX, const., *Apostolicae Sedis*, 12, oct. 1869, V, n. 1.—*Fontes*, n. 552.

[164] "Nos igitur, qui singulorum Dei ministrorum honorem, et decus, quantum in Nobis est . . . decretum praedictum [conc. Trid., sess., XXI, *de ref.*, c. 2] de Clericis saecularibus loquens, ad omnes, et singulos, etiam cuiuscumque Ordinis Clericos Religiosos, sive saeculares more Religiosorum viventes in communi, non professos, harum serie extendimus, et ampliamus . . . ut ad sacros Ordines promoveri, necnon omnibus, et singulis venerabilibus fratribus nostris . . . Episcopis, . . , ut Ordines ipsos huiusmodi Religiosis personis impendere, nisi observata forma dicti decreti Nos virtute sanctae obedientiae, et sub indignationis nostrae poena, interdicimus, et prohibemus, ac contrafacientes per annum a praestatione talium Ordinum ipso iure suspendimus."—Pius V, const., *Romanus Pontifex*, 14 oct. 1568, 3.—*Fontes*, n. 129.

"Suspensionem per annum a collatione ordinum ipso iure incurrit qui, excepto casu legitimi privilegii, Ordinum sacrum contulerit absque titulo beneficii vel patrimonii clerico in aliqua Congregatione viventi, in qua solemnis professio non emittitur, vel etiam religioso nondum professo."—Pius IX, const., *Apostolicae Sedis*, 12 oct. 1869, § V, 4.—*Fontes*, n. 552.

[165] "Denique quoscumque alios Sacrosanctum Concilium Tridentinum sus-

Besides the Constitution *Apostolicae Sedis* new suspensions were enacted by the Constitution *Romanus Pontifex* which was issued on August 28, 1873. This Constitution decreed that if any of the dignitaries who had conceded or transferred the administration of their church to any person without the required Apostolic letters were bishops, they incurred *ipso facto* suspension from the exercise of pontificals.[166]

On the 25th of May 1893, the Sacred Congregation of the Council issued a decree which declared a suspension *a divinis* is to be incurred *ipso facto* by all priests, who engaged in trafficking with Mass stipends. Besides this, it instituted a suspension *ab ordine* for those not yet promoted to the priesthood.[167]

An Apostolic Letter, *Orientalium Dignitas,* of November 30, 1894 enacted another suspension. Leo XIII in this letter forbade any missionary priest of the Latin rite, whether secular or religious, to induce Orientals to transfer from their rite to the Latin rite. The penalty to be incurred *ipso facto* upon the violation of this provision was the suspension *a divinis.*[168]

Finally another new suspension was enacted by a decree of the Sacred Congregation of the Council, *In Perturbationibus,* under date of July 12, 1900. In this decree Leo XIII condemned the actions of those clerics who involve themselves in political disturbances,

pensos . . . ipso iure esse decrevit. Nos pari modo suspensioni . . . eosdem obnoxios esse volumus et declaramus."—Pius IX, const., *Apostolicae Sedis,* 12 oct. 1869, § VI, 2.—Fontes, n. 552. Cfr. Pennacchi, *Commentaria In Constitutionem Apostolicae Sedis,* II, 432.

[166] "Si vero aliqui ex praedictis Episcopali charactere sint insigniti, in poenam suspensionis ab exercitio pontificalium . . ."—Pius IX, const., *Romanus Pontifex,* 28 aug. 1873, § 11.—*Fontes,* n. 565.

[167] "Si quis ex sacerdotali ordine contra enunciata decreta deliquerit, suspensioni a divinis, S. Sedi reservatae et ipso facto incurrendae, obnoxius sit; clericus autem sacerdotio nondum initiatus eidem suspensioni quoad susceptos Ordines simpliciter subjaceat, et inhabilis praeterea fiat ad superiores recipiendos . . ."—S.C.C., *Vigilanti studio,* 25 mai. 1893, § 4.—Fontes, n. 4286.

[168] "Missionarius quilibet latinus e clero saeculari vel regulari, qui orientalem quempiam ad latinum ritum consilio auxiliove inducat, praeter *suspensionem a divinis,* quam *ipso facto* incurret . . ."—Leo XIII, litt. ap., *Orientalium,* 30 nov. 1894, I.—*Fontes,* n. 627.

in violation of the admonitions given by the council of Trent. He forbade the clerics to put aside their clerical garb or to leave their residence for the purpose of participating in civil war. They were to have no part at all in these civil contentions. Any cleric violating these prescriptions of the pope incurred thereby a suspension *ipso facto* from the exercise of orders and from all offices or benefices that the cleric might possess.[169]

These official acts of the Holy See complete the general law of the Church with reference to suspension prior to the Code.

With the promulgation of the Code of Canon Law in 1918, all general penal legislation not contained in the Code itself lost its binding force. This meant that those suspensions which were not expressly contained in the new law were to be henceforth considered as abrogated. To the list of suspensions which the Code incorporated from the old law, seven entirely new ones were added. These form the Code's contribution to the catalog of ecclesiastical penalties exclusively reserved for clerics.[170]

169 ". . . Leo PP. XIII . . . statuit atque decernit, ut in posterum quisquis ex clero ut intestinis bellis et publicis contentionibus opem utcumque ferat propriam residentiae locum absque justa causa, quae a legitima ecclesiastica auctoritate recognita sit, deseruerit; vel clericales vestes exuerit, quamvis arma non sumpserit et humanum sanguinem minime fuderit et eo magis qui civili bello sponte sua nomen militiae dederit, aut bellicas actiones quomdocumque dirigere praesumpserit, etsi ecclesiasticum habitum retinere pergat, ab ordinum et graduum exercitio et a quolibet ecclesiastico officio et beneficio suspensus illico et ipso facto maneat . . ."—S.C.C., decr., *In Perturbationibus*, 12 iul. 1900—*Fontes*, n. 4311.

170 Canon 2341: ". . . demum si, non obtenta ab Ordinario loci licentia, [quis contra praescriptum can. 120 ausus fuerit ad iudicem laicum trahere] aliam personam privilegio fori fruentem, clericus quidem incurrit ipso facto in suspensionem ab officio reservatam Ordinario . . ."

Canon 2366: "Sacerdos qui sine necessaria jurisdictione praesumpserit sacramentales confessiones audire est ipso facto suspensus a divinis; qui vero a peccatis reservatis absolvere, ipso facto suspensus est ab audiendis confessionibus." It must be noted that this law contains two suspensions.

Canon 2371: "Omnes, etiam episcopali dignitati aucti, qui per simoniam ad ordines scienter promoverint vel promoti fuerint aut alia Sacramenta ministraverint vel receperint, sunt suspecti de haeresi; clerici praeterea suspensionem incurrunt Sedi Apostolicae reservatam."

Canon 2386: "Religiosus fugitivus ipso facto incurrit in privationem officii, si quod in religione habeat, et in suspensionem proprio Superiori majori reservatam, si sit in sacris . . ."

Canon 2400: "Clericus qui in manus laicorum officium, beneficium aut dignitatem ecclesiasticam resignare praesumpserit, ipso facto in suspensionem a divinis incurrit."

Canon 2402: "Abbas vel Praelatus *nullius* qui contra praescriptum can. 322, § 2, benedictionem non receperit, est ipso facto a jurisdictione suspensus."

CHAPTER II.

THE NOTION OF SUSPENSION

The concise definition of the Code, with regard to the ecclesiastical punishment of suspension, merely presents in admirable form the best notions of the old authors.[1] With but a few exceptions, the same rights now proper to clerics suffer similar restrictions as formerly. These rights are fourfold.[2] First, there are the rights flowing from orders, known as spiritual rights. These are forbidden either cumulatively or disjunctively, according to the effects of the specific suspension incurred or inflicted. Secondly, there are the essentially spiritual rights which constitute an ecclesiastical office in the strict sense.[3] Thirdly, temporal rights are also affected by a suspension, in as far as they are annexed to a benefice. Finally, by reason of the fact that a cleric may enjoy an office and a benefice at one and the same time, the exercise of these two rights, both spiritual and temporal, may likewise be curtailed by a suspension.

But, before entering upon a definition of suspension, it would be well to make this fact clear, that the term *suspension* has different meanings, and therefore, care must be taken in dealing with this subject, to distinguish the canonical penalty from the simple prohibition. The general term *suspension* may be viewed in a broad sense, in a less broad sense and in a strict sense.

[1] Innocent III speaks of the censure in c. 20, X, *de verborum significatione*, V, 40. Barbosa speaks of suspension from offices and benefices. Lib. III, tit. VIII, c. IV; lib. V, tit. XXVII, c. IV. Joannes Andraae refers to suspension from offices and benefices in Comment. super V Decretal., *de clerico excommunicato*, cc. IV-X. Schmalzgrueber treats at length the suspension *ab ordine* in lib. V, tit. XXXIX, n. 291 seq. Reiffenstuel speaks of the suspension *ab officio et a beneficio simul* in lib. V, tit. XXXIX, n. 162; Pennacchi, *Commentaria In Constitutionem Apostolicae Sedis,* II, 333.

[2] Blat, *Commentarium Textus Codicis Iuris Canonici,* V, n. 106.

[3] Canon 145, § 1.

In a broad sense, suspension is a pure prohibition or impediment, merely forbidding any person whatsoever, male or female, the exercise of a right, or rendering such incapable of eliciting a certain determined function, as for example, the suspension *ab officio* of a superioress or an irregularity *ex defectu* or *ex delicto*. In the less broad sense, a suspension may also be considered as an impediment or prohibition, with the added element, however, that it is restricted solely to clerics. Thus, even though a cleric had committed no crime, yet he may be suspended from the orders he has received.[4] Likewise, a superior may have heard some derogatory accusations against one of his clerics, and hence, to avoid scandal, he may make use of an administrative measure and suspend the cleric with a suspension *ad cautelam*, which is neither vindictive nor medicinal.[5] Finally, suspension in the strict sense is really a canonical penalty. It implies more than a mere prohibition. It may be defined as a penalty, either medicinal or vindictive in its nature, by which a cleric guilty of a crime is temporarily forbidden (prohibetur), in whole or in part, the use or exercise of rights which he possesses, either by reason of his orders, or by reason of his office or benefice considered separately, or by reason of his office and benefice taken conjointly.[6]

In its terminology, the Code clearly brings out the prohibitive nature of suspension by the use of the verb *prohibetur*. It excludes any idea of an invalidating effect *per se*. Only under certain conditions, expressly determined in the Code, is there mention, in the

[4] Canon 2372: ". . . qui vero bona fide a quopiam eorum [i.e., ab excommunicato vel suspenso vel interdicto post sententiam declaratoriam vel condemnatoriam] sit ordinatus exercitio careat ordinis sic recepti donec dispensetur."

[5] "Nonnumquam suspensio datur ad cautelam . . . et tunc dicitur decretum inhibitorium."—*S. Romanae Rotae Decisiones seu Sententiae*, V, Dec. XLVI, n. 10.

[6] Canons 2278, § 1; 2255, § 2; 2298, n. 2; Temporary is used to distinguish from the perpetual effects of deprivation, deposition and degradation, where there exists little hope, if any, of recovering lost rights. It also indicates the time during which the reason or cause for the suspension endures. It is not meant to exclude the perpetual suspension.

law, of invalidity attaching to acts performed by a suspended cleric.[7]

Furthermore, it must be remembered, that the prohibition confines itself to the temporary use or exercise of the power of orders or jurisdiction, or the exercise of spiritual or temporal rights accruing to an office or benefice. Suspension, in no way permanently takes away these rights nor deprives the delinquent cleric of his title.[8]

SUSPENSION DIFFERS FROM EXCOMMUNICATION. Besides the fact that suspension can be either medicinal or vindictive in its nature, whereas excommunication is never other than a censure (medicinal penalty), there are other factors which clearly bring out further differentiations. The practical difference between these two punishments is important when they touch individuals. An excommunication affects both clerics and laymen alike; suspension is restricted exclusively to clerics. Similarly, an excommunication, when it is meted out to a moral person can not touch the moral person as such, but only the guilty individuals constituting the corporate body; suspension, on the other hand, can prohibit the exercise of every function and right which the moral person enjoys as a unit.[9] Every member of that corporation, whether innocent or guilty, must then observe the effects. These effects prohibit the cleric the active use and exercise of his rights and privileges but not the passive use.[10] When a cleric is suspended for some crime, even though the suspension be total and absolute and not merely partial, he may participate in and receive those impetratory and satisfactory values which accrue to the good works and prayers of all the faithful as members of the Mystical Body of Christ. He may also assist at divine services, receive the sacraments and sacramentals and likewise Christian burial, for he possesses all these rights and privileges, not as a cleric but as a member of the Church through Baptism.[11] He

[7] Canons 2283; 2284.

[8] De Meester, *Compendium Iuris Canonici et Iuris Canonico-Civilis,* III, pars 2a, n. 1779.

[9] Canon 2255, § 2.

[10] Lehmkuhl, *Theologia Moralis,* II, n. 900.

[11] Wernz, *Ius Decretalium,* VI, n. 201.

may not, however, administer the sacraments or sacramentals; nor may he enjoy the fruits of his benefice, or exercise any ecclesiastical jurisdiction, except when in view of special attending circumstances, the law permits such an exercise or administration for certain designated cases.[12] Excommunication, on the other hand, concerns itself primarily with the personal spiritual benefits and favors of an individual and only secondarily with all other rights and privileges, so that no excommunicated person, whether lay or cleric, may either actively or passively participate in certain rights and privileges which result from Baptism, whilst an excommunicated cleric is in addition barred from the active and passive enjoyment of certain rights and privileges consequent upon the clerical state. When an excommunication is incurred or inflicted, its effects fall with all their indivisible force, so that a separation of these effects by way of greater or lesser penal consequences, is at no time admissible. The evident reason for this is found in the fact that excommunication severs the individual completely from full communion with the rest of the faithful, and thus touches the rights and privileges he previously possessed as a member of the Church. The effects of suspension are not of this indivisible type. They are as divisible as are the varied rights which admit of separate and partial prohibitions.[13] Thus, a cleric suspended *a divinis* may exercise purely jurisdictional acts and vice versa a cleric suspended *a jurisdictione* may exercise every act of orders which does not entail an act of jurisdiction.

SUSPENSION DIFFERS FROM INTERDICT. There is also a marked distinction between the penalties of interdict and suspension. Both punishments, it is true, are alike in this that they may be either vindictive or medicinal.[14] Furthermore, both penalties allow a division relative to their effects, for the particle *etiam* at the beginning of canon 2278, § 2,[15] in which there is express mention of the divisibility of the effects of suspension, establishes a link of com-

[12] Canons 2284; 2261.
[13] Canon 2278, § 2.
[14] Canon 2255, § 2.
[15] "Etiam suspensionis effectus separari queunt."

parison with the effects of the interdict delineated in the immediately preceding canons. But, by way of differentiation between them, the effects of suspension are not so extensive as those of the interdict. The interdict affects not only persons, whether cleric or lay, moral or physical, but also places, whilst suspension can never affect places, but only persons, and these latter only when they are clerics.[16] Both the suspension and interdict alike may be visited upon persons either as physical individuals or as members of a corporate moral personality. With regard to the personal rights which a cleric enjoys as a cleric, these, too, form a basis for a distinction between suspension and the interdict. A cleric under suspension is forbidden the active use of sacred rights because of his clerical status, but, should this same cleric be personally interdicted, his rights would not only be affected actively but even passively, in the sense that he would be barred from the reception of the sacraments, because it is the nature of the personal interdict to curtail rights which a person possesses as a member of the Church.[17]

SUSPENSION DIFFERS FROM DEPOSITION AND DEGRADATION. It is true, deposition and degradation like suspension are restricted in their application to clerics alone, yet there is the greatest difference between them. In its effects, deposition is always permanent. Without, however, depriving the cleric of his privileges and obligations, it always brings with it a suspension *ab officio* and renders the cleric legally incapable of acquiring certain offices, dignities and benefices, even though the cleric had been ordained on such a title. It not merely prohibits the exercise of rights but takes them away completely.[18] Furthermore, deposition is never incurred as a penalty *latae sententiae* nor does it ever have the nature of a censure, but is always vindictive in character and can be inflicted only in a condemnatory sentence by a tribunal of five judges.[19] It must be remembered that the penalty of deposition may never be inflicted, except when the law prescribes it as a preceptive penalty *ferendae*

16 Canon 2255, § 2.
17 Canon 2275, n. 2; De Meester, *Compendium,* III, pars 2a, n. 1779.
18 Canon 2303, § 1.
19 Canon 1576, § 1, n. 2.

sententiae,[20] and once inflicted, it can only be remitted by the Holy See.[21]

Degradation is the severest of all ecclesiastical penalties proper to clerics. Its effects include suspension, deposition, perpetual privation of the ecclesiastical garb and reduction to the lay state.[22] Like deposition, degradation is vindictive in character and never medicinal and can only be inflicted *ferendae sententiae* by a tribunal of five judges, in such cases alone wherein the law mentions it as a preceptive or at least a prospective punishment.[23] Once inflicted its permanent effects can not be dispensed by any one, save the Holy See.[24]

In view of the foregoing considerations, with reference to suspension, the disparity is clearly evident. Suspension is temporary, even though no time limit is specified. It merely prohibits the exercise of rights and does not take them away completely. It is either medicinal or vindictive; and also it may be either *latae* or *ferendae sententiae.* Nor is it required by law that a suspension be inflicted only upon due procedure in court, since circumstances may justify its infliction by precept.[25] With regard to its cessation, the penalty of suspension may cease as a censure by absolution alone, and as a vindicitive penalty either by dispensation or at the expiration of a definite time or upon the fulfillment of a condition. The absolution and the dispensation are not always restricted to the Holy See. Even if there be a reservation of this kind, the law grants faculties, under certain conditions to remove the suspension.[26] This is not the case with regard to deposition and degradation.

SUSPENSION DIFFERS FROM AN IRREGULARITY. An irregularity is

20 Canons 2303, § 3; 2314, § 1, n. 2; 2320; 2322, n. 1; 2328; 2350, § 1; 2354, § 2; 2359, § 2; 2379; 2394, n. 2; 2401.

21 Canon 2236, § 3.

22 Canon 2305, § 1.

23 Canons 1576, § 1, n. 2; 2314, § 1, n. 3; 2343, § 1, n. 3; 2354, § 2; 2368, § 1; 2388, § 1.

24 Canon 2236, § 3; Ayrinhac, *Penal Legislation in the New Code of Canon Law,* n. 175; De Meester, *Compendium,* III, pars 2a, n. 1799.

25 Canons 2225; 1933, § 4.

26 Canons 2236; 2237; 2252; 2254; 2289; 2290.

a perpetual quasi-penal canonical impediment which by its nature directly and primarily prohibits the reception of orders and also their use.[27] Suspension, on the contrary, is not an impediment, but a real penalty and as such is not confined to orders and their exercise. It also affects the exercise of jurisdiction and the enjoyment of temporalities annexed to things spiritual. Furthermore, suspension can only be inflicted on a cleric for a personal crime, whereas an irregularity can be incurred even though the cleric is innocent of any offense. Then again, suspension pertains only to clerics. An irregularity can be incurred even by a layman, either as, an irregularity *ex defectu* or *ex delicto*. Finally, as regards their cessation, the irregularity requires a dispensation; suspension, on the other hand, requires absolution or dispensation, or a lapse of time or a fulfilled condition, according to the medicinal or vindictive nature of the punishment.

This comparative investigation has now established, through a series of contrasts, a negative notion of suspension. From this can be drawn the positive statement, that suspension is a real canonical penalty, inflicted medicinally or vindictively upon clerics alone, to punish them for crimes which they have committed as individuals or as members of a moral corporate personality, acting in their moral capacity.

[27] Canons 984; 985.

CHAPTER III

THE DIVISION OF SUSPENSION

BY REASON OF THE OBJECTS. The definition of suspension in the strict sense offers a fourfold division, according to the object affected by the punishment. In this regard, suspension may, therefore, be divided into the suspension *ab ordine*, the suspension *ab officio*, the suspension *a beneficio* and the suspension *ab officio et beneficio simul*. The Code, however, furnishes merely a three-fold division, because it includes the suspension *ab ordine* among the component parts of the suspension *ab officio*.[1]

As to the elements which constitute the suspension *ab officio*, these may be divided into various partial suspensions, depending on the specific clerical rights to be inhibited by the suspension. Thus, in canon 2279, § 2, the Code enumerates nine different partial suspensions *ab officio*. They may be referred to as the suspension *a iurisdictione*, the suspension *a divinis*, the suspension *ab ordinibus*, the suspension *a sacris ordinibus*, the suspension *a certo et definito ordine exercendo*, the suspension *a certo et definito ordine conferendo*, the suspension *a certo et definito ministerio*, the suspension *ab ordine pontificali*, the suspension *a pontificalibus*. The proper effects of these partial suspensions shall not be given consideration here. A detailed explanation shall be undertaken in a subsequent chapter.

BY REASON OF THE AMBIT OF THE EFFECTS. According to the ambit of its effects, suspension may also be divided in the *General* and *Particular* or *Special* Suspension. The general suspension is one, at whose infliction, no qualification or limitation is expressly stated; and, therefore, embraces all the effects of the suspension *ab officio* and *a beneficio* combined.[2] Examples of this type of suspension may be found in canon 2370[3] and canon 2371.[4] The par-

[1] Canons 2278, § 1; 2279, § 1.

[2] Canon 2278, § 2.

[3] "Episcopus aliquem consecrans in Episcopum, Episcopi vel, loco Episcoporum, presbyteri assistentes, et qui consecrationem recipit sine apostolico

ticular or special suspension, on the other hand, is restricted in its effects to the specification determined in the law or mandate of the superior. Thus, for example, the suspension *ab officio,* when placed side by side with the general suspension can be called a particular or special suspension.

The particular suspension may be further divided into total and partial. But, it seems that this division is not to be restricted solely to this type of suspension, for a general suspension can and may warrant a similar division. When the penalty remains unqualified in a general suspension, all the effects spoken of above become operative and the suspension falls into the class of a total suspension. On the other hand, when the specific effects are determined, as in the suspension *ab officio,* this type of penalty, when compared with the general suspension, becomes partial. Here is where a confused terminology may arise. The suspension *ab officio* may also be termined total. Thus, the suspension *ab officio* may be referred to as both partial and total, at one and the same time, depending on whether it is spoken of in connection with the general suspension or not. To obviate difficulties and for the sake of clarity, it would be well to limit the use of the terms total and partial to all suspensions outside of the general suspension, depending on whether the object affected by the suspension is total or partial.

By Reason of the Superior's Purpose in Inflicting. By reason of the purpose in the mind of the superior at the moment of infliction, suspension may be either *medicinal* or *vindictive.* The superior may have in view primarily the amendment of the cleric or the atonement of the crime, and therefore, according to this intent the suspension is, respectively, either a censure or a vindictive penalty.

In considering suspension in this light, one must be on his guard against an erroneous impression. For, it would be wrong

mandato contra praescriptum can. 953, ipso iure *suspensi* sunt, donec Sedes Apostolica eos dispensaverit."

[4] "Omnes etiam episcopali dignitate aucti, qui per simoniam ad ordines scienter promoverint vel promoti fuerint aut alia Sacramenta ministraverint vel receperint sunt suspecti de haeresi; clerici praeterea *suspensionem* incurrunt Sedi Apostolicae reservatam."

to suppose that in inflicting a vindictive suspension the Church excludes altogether the reformation of the delinquent cleric, or that, vice versa, in pronouncing a suspension of a medicinal character, she does not intend to atone for the crime and aim to terrify others from the commission of crimes and maintain respect for her laws. In all her punishments, the Church always has a twofold end in view;[5] first to cause the offender to repent and amend; second to deter others from crimes. It is the good of the individual and the common good at stake always.

Suspension as a censure, therefore, looks primarily to the amendment of the individual and secondarily to the atonement of the crime. Ordinarily, then, the censure can not be inflicted for a past crime, when the cleric has repented and amended his ways. It can only fall upon a past crime, when the contumacy, which produced the crime in the past, continues in the present. Without the presence of a contumacious will, there can be no censure,[6] because it is the nature of the censure to break down that contumacy, and to force the cleric to a better life. By contumacy is meant, a formal or interpretative contempt of the censure. It is judged from the fact that the offending cleric, fully aware, through admonitions and other means,[7] that something is prohibited under censure by law or mandate, nevertheless goes contrary to the prohibition, or that he refuses to make reparation for scandal.

Suspension as a vindictive penalty has as its primary motive atonement for the crime and as its secondary aim the reformation of the culprit. Unlike the censure, it concerns itself with a past crime, even if the delinquent is sincerely repentant, because every crime disturbs the social order, and it is the principal purpose of

[5] C. 1, *de officio iudicis ordinarii,* I, 9, in Clem.: ". . . Eisdem episcopis districte iniungimus, quatenus sic circa correctionem clericorum huiusmodi vigilanter intendant, et diligenter sui officii debitum exsequantur, quod et iidem clerici metu poenae a suis arceantur insolentiis, et alii, eorum exemplo perterriti, prosilire ad similia merito pertimescant."

[6] Canon 2242, § 1:—"Censura punitur tantummodo delictum externum, grave, consummatum, cum contumacia coniunctum . . ."

[7] Canon 2233, § 2; 2242, § 3.

the vindictive penalty to reestablish this order and to bring it back to normal by the removal of scandal.[8]

An added distinction between the censure and the vindictive penalty of suspension is the time element. It is the common opinion, that a censure is always inflicted indefinitely. This statement in no way derogates from the fact, that every suspension's effects are temporary. The censure is based on contumacy; and certainly, no one knows how long it will take for a cleric to come to his senses and depart from his evil ways. Consequently, the indefinite nature of the censure is essential. It must last as long as the incorrigible will continues. With the vindictive penalty, it is different. Since this type of punishment is to make atonement for a crime and to repair the scandal given, this will take a longer or shorter time, according to circumstances, and hence the duration of the penalty must be determined accordingly, whether it is to be for a month or a year or perpetually or dependent on the superior's discretion, *ad beneplacitum nostrum.*[9]

In case of a doubt, when it is difficult to determine from the law or the wording of the decree of the superior, whether the suspension; inflicted or to be incurred, is a censure or a vindictive penalty, the presumption of the law leans toward the censure.[10] The reason is, because a censure is more dificult to incur and more easy to cast off, since first of all to incur it the culprit must really be contumacious, and secondly the absolution presupposes on the part of the delinquent a cessation of his contumacious will, for as soon as absolution is sought, upon evident signs of repentence, the penitent is in all justice entitled to demand and receive absolution from his cen-

[8] Canon 2286: "Poenae vindicativae illae sunt, quae directe ad delicti expiationem tendunt ita ut remissio e cessatione contumaciae delinquentis non pendeat." Cocchi, *Commentarium,* V, n. 98; De Meester, *Compendium,* III, pars, 2a, n. 1779.

[9] Canon 2298: "Poenae vindicativae quae clericis tantum applicantur sunt: 2.o Suspensio in perpetuum vel ad tempus praefinitum, vel ad beneplacitum Superioris." Cerato, *Censurae Vigentes,* n. 102; Wernz, *Ius Decretalium,* VI n. 146.

[10] Canons 1825; 2255, § 2.

sure.[11] Because of this fact, the censure is said to be the milder of the two punishments, and therefore, according to penal interpretation the accused is to be favored.[12]

It must not be forgotten that the censure of suspension differs from the vindictive penalty also in the manner of its cessation. The censure can only cease with absolution,[13] whereas the vindictive penalty is remitted in various ways, either by dispensation, the expiration of the required time, or the fulfillment of a condition, or when the superior in his judgment considers the scandal fully repaired.[14]

The difference between the medicinal and vindictive suspension may also be seen from certain invalidating effects which follow as a legal consequence of an act performed by a cleric in defiance of his suspension.

Throughout the Code, the legislator seems to restrict the invalidating effects which are consequent upon a declaratory or condemnatory sentence exclusively to the censure. Thus, according to the provision of canon 167, § 1, n. 3, those cast an invalid vote who are under a censure after the issuance of a declaratory or condemnatory sentence.[15] Likewise canon 873, § 3 makes a similar assertion with regard to those under a censure of suspension *ab officio* after the pronouncement of a declaratory or condemnatory sentence. The canon states that such clerics lose their ordinary jurisdiction.[16] Although this canon does not use the word *censure,* yet because of its content, and because of its relationship with canon 2284, there is no doubt that the law refers to the censure alone. Canon 2284, in speaking of this same matter, provides that, if a censure of

11 Canons 2241, § 1; 2248, § 2; Vermeersch-Creusen, *Epitome,* III, n. 456; Blat, *Commentarium,* V, n. 80; Cocchi, *Commentarium,* V, n. 83.

12 Canons 19; 2219, § 1.

13 Canons 2236; 2248, § 2.

14 Canons 2236; 2289.

15 "Nequeunt suffragium ferre . . . censura vel infamia iuris affecti, post sententiam tamen declaratoriam vel condemnatoriam . . . si quis ex praedicti admittatur, eius suffragium est nullum . . ."

16 "Haec iurisdictio cessat . . . post sententiam condemnatoriam vel declaratoriam . . . suspensione ab officio . . ."

suspension prohibits an act of jurisdiction, this act is invalid when placed after the pronouncement of a declaratory or condemnatory sentence.[17] Then again, in speaking of a person enjoying the *ius patronatus*, the Code states that such an individual is forbidden the exercise of every right and privilege, if a censure has been declared by sentence and also if a condemnatory sentence has been pronounced. And should he nevertheless use his right, by virtue of canon 2265 his act of presentation would be invalid.[18] Under the same chapter, the law declares that the *ius patronatus* can not be validly granted to an excommunicate after a declaratory or condemnatory sentence.[19] An excommunication, as the law expressly states, can only be a censure.[20]

It seems clear, therefore, that the law reserves all invalidating effects, when a declaratory or condemnatory sentence has been pronounced, to the censure and not to the vindictive penalty.

Going over to suspension, therefore, the law is uniform in its demands. It is the censure of suspension alone, which suffers these invalidating effects, under similar conditions, and not the vindictive penalty. In two instances, namely, in canons 2283 and 2284, the law attaches its nullifying force to the censure alone. Canon 2283 implicitly excludes the vindictive penalty, because the law compares the suspension with excommunication, which is always a censure. Canon 2284, on the other hand, makes explicit mention of the term *censure,* and thereby, again, implicitly excludes the vindictive penalty.[21] In both cases, acts placed after a declara-

[17] "Si incursa fuerit *censura* suspensionis quae prohibet actum iurisdictionis in foro seu interno seu externo, actus est invalidus . . . si lata sit sententia condemnatoria vel declaratoria . . ."

[18] Canon 1470, § 4: "Censura aut infamia innodati post sententiam condemnatoriam vel declaratoriam, usquedum censura vel infamia perdurant, nequeunt ius patronatus exercere eiusque privilegiis uti."

[19] Canon 1453, § 1: "Ius patronatus personale transmitti valide nequit . . . ad quoslibet excommunicatos post sententiam declaratoriam vel condemnatoriam."

[20] Canon 2255, § 2.

[21] Canon 2283: "Quae de excommunicatione can. 2265 statuuntur, etiam suspensioni sunt applicanda." Canon 2284:—"Si incursa fuerit *censura* . . . si *censura* suspensionis . . ." Blat, *Commentarium,* V, n. 113.

tory or condemnatory sentence has been pronounced, are rendered invalid. Moreover, it is stated, that every pontifical rescript relative to prohibited acts, received by a cleric under the censure of suspension, which has been declared or inflicted by a condemnatory sentence, is null and void, unless there has been express mention of the status of the individual.[22] Since penal laws are to be interpreted strictly,[23] it is licit to conclude that the censure alone and not the vindictive penalty of suspension nullifies certain acts, after the pronouncement of a declaratory or a condemnatory sentence.

The reason for this remarkable distinction can possibly be found in the very purpose of these two types of punishment. As has been stated before, the basis for the censure is the contumacious will. All will admit, therefore, that a delinquent cleric who permits himself to go to the extent of having a sentence declared or pronounced against him, is, indeed, contemptuously contumacious, and, consequently, deserving of the worst effects, which the Church can bring down upon him, outside of deposition or degradation, namely, to invalidate his acts and to render him legally incapable of obtaining certain privileges. The vindictive penalty, on the other hand, ordinarily but not necessarily presupposes contrition and amendment. Its main purpose is to repair the disturbed social order. It would, therefore, seem to be an uncalled-for severity, to have a cleric, laboring under a vindictive suspension, suffer the same drastic punishment, which the law metes out to the cleric under censure. The law does not even visit an added punishment upon the cleric vindictively suspended, because he has no choice in the matter. The duration of the penalty depends on the superior. But, the law does inflict an added punishment upon those clerics, who remain under the censure of suspension for six months, after they have been warned. They are to be deprived of their benefices or offices.[24] Moreover, the same disparity of treatment on the part of the law regarding the censure and the vindictive penalty may be seen from the fact that they incur *ipso facto* the interdict *ab in-*

[22] Canons 36, § 2; 2265; 2283.
[23] Canon 19.
[24] Canon 2340, § 2.

gressu ecclesiae, who despite the presence of a declaratory or a condemnatory sentence, knowingly admit clerics laboring under a sentence of this kind, to the exercise of those divine offices which the specific *censure* of suspension curtails.[25]. No punishment is meted out to those, who undertake to admit to the celebration of divine offices, those clerics who have been suspended by a vindictive penalty.

When speaking of the invalidating effects which flow from a declaratory or a condemnatory sentence, it must be remembered that acts of orders are excluded. This power is outside of the jurisdiction of the Church, in as much as orders have been conferred through a sacrament.[26] Hence, if all the conditions are placed, even though conferred by one suspended in a declaratory or a condemnatory sentence, all orders are validly conferred and received.[27]

BY REASON OF THE ORIGIN AND OF THE MANNER OF INCURRING. The ecclesiastical punishment of suspension, when considered in view of its enactive origin and relative to the manner in which it is incurred may be divided into the suspension *a iure* or *ab homine*, and into the suspension *latae sententiae* or *ferendae sententiae*. Since these suspensions are, at times, so closely related, it was deemed advisable to give them a joint consideration.

A suspension *a iure* is one determined in the law itself. But, relative to the manner of incurring it, the suspension *a iure* may be one or the other of two penalties, namely, *latae* or *ferendae sententiae*. The latter terminology is dependent on whether the suspension established by the law or the special mandate of a superior is incurred immediately upon the commission of the crime, or whether its infliction is commanded by the law or is left to the discretion of the judge or superior.[28] When the suspension is incurred immediately upon the violation of the law or precept, it is called *latae sententiae;* when the infliction of the suspension is commanded or left to the discretion of the judge or superior, it is called *ferendae sententiae*.

[25] Canon 2338, § 3.
[26] Kober, *Die Suspension*, p. 103.
[27] Augustine, *Commentary*, VIII, 191.
[28] Canons 2217, § 1, n. 2; 2223, §2, § 3.

If a suspension is imposed by a particular precept or by a condemnatory sentence, it is *ab homine*. If imposed by a particular precept, a penalty *ab homine* is *ferendae sententiae*. In the case in which a penalty *ferendae sententiae* is added to the law, the penalty is only *a iure* before the condemnatory sentence is passed; after the sentence, it is both *a iure* and *ab homine*, but is considered as *ab homine*.[29]

The Code always considers a suspension in the light of a penalty *ferendae sententiae*, unless the law or precept expressly declares that the punishment is incurred as a penalty *latae sententiae*, or *ipso facto* or *ipso iure*. This, however, is not an exhaustive enumeration. Other words of similar meaning may also be used, as for example, *subiaceat suspensioni*, or *subsunt*, or *suspendimus*, or *qui hoc fecerit reatum talis poenae incurrat*, or *suspensus maneat*, etc. [30]

Could a suspension *latae sententiae* imposed by a precept be *ab homine*? This is a most important question with regard to absolution. Its consideration here is not deemed out of place, since the treatise, thus far, is attempting to set down certain classifications. To answer the query, one must first of all consider the basis for an *ab homine* punishment. Its foundation, according to canon 2217, § 1, n. 3 is a particular precept or a judicial condemnatory sentence. *Prima facie*, from these constituent elements, it would seem that a *latae sententiae* suspension imposed by a particular precept, can be looked upon as *ab homine*—an opinion which Collison upholds in his dissertation.[31] But, with Roberti[32] and Michiels,[33] the opposite is the case because their interpretation is restricted to

29 Canon 2217, § 1, n. 3.

30 Canon 2217, § 2; Ayrinhac, *Penal Legislation in the New Code of Canon Law*, n. 35; Cerato, *Censurae Vigentes*, n. 5.

31 "Similiter et pari cum reverentia theoriam erudite elaboratam a Cl. Roberti et aliis proponentibus censuras l. s. praecepto particulari adnexas non esse ab homine non admittimus, quia vim infert supponit mutationem antiquae divisionis ["ab homine si feratur per modum praecepti" intellecta fuisse de censuris latae et ferendae sententiae".—Lega, *De Delicits et Poenis*, p. 111.] effectam non per determinatam praecisamque classificationem in codice, sed ope alicuius parallelismi imperfecti. Nostro iudicio, ad summum tantum aliquod dubium potest oriri ex parallelismo allato (potius ex auctoritate propon-

the wording of the Code itself. The Code is speaking solely of a precept *ad instar sententiae,* namely, the law designates that the punishment is inflicted *per modum praecepti.*. The very text and context of the canon favor this statement.

The Code, at times, is not uniformly consistent in its use of expressions. When it speaks of instituting penalties, it uses verbs, such as *statuta,*[34] *constituat.*[35] When it wishes to express the force of the verb *to inflict,* the Code employs verbs such as *in poenis decernendis,*[36] *in poenis applicandis,*[37] *poena inflicta,*[38] *infligi.*[39] But, to denote the establishing of a penalty, the Code employs the very same verb *infligendi poenas,* which is evident from the context of canon 2220. Then, again, in canon 2252, there can be no doubt, that the verb *tulit* signifies *inflixit.* In view of these facts, therefore, one can not insist with any degree of finality, that the verb *feratur* of canon 2217, § 1, n. 3 is alone confined to the meaning of establish. In fact the context of the canon militates against any assumption of this nature. The phrase *per sententiam judicialem condemnatoriam* belongs equally to the verb *feratur* as does the phrase *per modum praecepti.* And, since there is no doubt that the former expression designates the moment of application, the same can be said of the latter, because of the parity of relationship between the two phrases to the verb *feratur.* The moment of infliction must apply, therefore, equally to the precept as to the condemnatory sentence.

entium) de mutatione in re nominum censurarum. At 'in dubio num aliquod praescriptum cum veteri iuri discrepet, a veteri iure non est recedendum'."—"Non Omnis Censura Ab Homine Est Reservata", *Dissertatio ..... Apud Pontificium Institutum Angelicum,* Romae, 1935, p. 89.

32 "An Censura l. s. per praeceptum constituta sit reservata", *Apollinaris,* VI (1933), 341.

33 "De Reservatione Censurae l. s. praecepto peculiari adnexae", *Ephemerides Theologicae Lovanienses,* IV (1927), 180.

34 Canon 2224, § 3.

35 Canon 2231.

36 Canon 2218, § 1.

37 Canon 2223, § 1, § 3, n. 1.

38 Canon 2219, § 2.

39 Canons 2227, § 1; 2233, § 1.

Furthermore, the part of canon 2217, § 1, n. 3, which begins with the words *quare poena ferendae sententiae*, serves to confirm the opinion, that the precept spoken of here is *ad instar sententiae*. The canon goes on to say, after giving the elements of a penalty *ab homine*, "wherefore all penalties mentioned in the law, *ferendae sententiae*, before a sentence, are *a iure*". Consequently, since the verb *feratur* means to inflict and pertains equally to the precept and the condemnatory sentence, and since the subsequent part of the canon, just referred to concerns itself with the situation before and after sentence, it seems right to conclude, that the legislator is consistent in the context of the canon; and hence, what applies to the condemnatory sentence applies also to the precept. It is the *ferendae sententiae* penalty, therefore, the legislator is referring to and not the *latae sententiae*. Hence, it can be said, that the precept here is *ad instar sententiae*. Since this is the case, it appears that the only kind of penalty threatened by a precept which can be *ab homine*, is the one contained in the precept *ad instar sententiae*.

Furthermore, to indicate, that a *latae sententiae* penalty has fallen upon a delinquent, the terminology commonly used is "to incur" rather than "to inflict." It is the violation of the law threatening the penalty, which brings into effect immediately the force of the punishment. It is not the superior directly inflicting the penalty but the law or the precept. Consequently, the precept threatening the *latae sententiae* suspension would not be *ad instar sententiae* but rather *ad instar iuris*, and therefore, such a suspension threatened by precept, is only *a iure* and not *ab homine*.

The probable reason why the Code does not mention the precept when it gives the notion of an *a iure* penalty is because, strictly speaking, laws are not constituted by a particular precept. However, since a precept takes the place of a law, its threatened penalty, although it can not be strictly called *a iure*, nevertheless can be considered *quasi a iure*. For this reason, then, and prescinding from every idea of application or infliction, which would render a precept *ad instar sententiae*, a *latae sententiae* penalty, threatened by a precept can not be considered *ab homine*.

Nor can a suspension *latae sententiae*, incurred in violation of a particular precept or even of a law in the strict sense, be looked upon as *ab homine*, when a declaratory sentence has been pronounced.[40] Canon 2217, § 1, n. 3 leaves no doubt regarding this. It is explicit in stating, that the only sentence to make a penalty *ab homine* is the condemnatory one. And, therefore, a suspension *latae sententiae* which has received a declaratory sentence remains solely *a iure*.

By Reason of the Curtailment of Jurisdiction in the One who may Remit the Penalty. The most frequent manner in which jurisdiction is restricted is in the form of reservation. Reservation is merely the withholding or withdrawal of jurisdiction over certain cases by a superior, so that with the restriction of power, the penalty can not be remitted. In so far as jurisdiction is restricted or not, suspension may be considered as reserved or non-reserved. In speaking of the reservation of censures, note must be taken of the fact, that such a reservation differs from the so-called reservation of sins. The former is a negative act, whereby jurisdiction is not given to remove the punishment in question, whereas with regard to the latter, there is posited a positive act by the superior, by which he takes away the jurisdiction of the confessor over certain sins.[41]

The fifth Book of Code offers certain norms to determine when a suspension is reserved. Some of these norms regard the *ferendae sententiae* suspension, whilst others regulate for the *latae sententiae* suspension.

Relative to the *ferendae sententiae* suspension, the Code restricts itself to the *ab homine* penalty, namely, one inflicted by a particular precept or a condemnatory sentence. When either of these two conditions has been verified, the suspension is reserved to the one who issued the precept, or who passed the sentence, or to the superior, the successor, or the one delegated by either.[42]

With regard to the *latae sententiae* suspension, there is to be no reservation, unless the superior states expressly in the precept or

[40] A Coronata, *Institutiones Iuris Canonici*, IV, n. 1690; Cappello, *De Censuris*, n. 76.

[41] D'Annibale, *Summula*, I, n. 338, note 16.

[42] Canons 2217, § 1, n. 3; 2245, § 2; 1933, § 4.

law that he reserves the penalty to himself.[43] Should there be a doubt as to whether the suspension under consideration is reserved or not, or should there be a doubt as to whether the conditions required by law to induce a reservation are conformable to the circumstances in a given case of suspension, the Code definitely declares there is to be no reservation.[44] Subsequently, when absolution is petitioned from a censure of suspension, whose reservation is in doubt, it need not be given *ad cautelam;* nor would it be necessary to have recourse; nor would it be necessary to obtain absolution later on should the fact be established that the suspension was reserved.[45]

The provision of canon 2245, § 4, that a penalty *latae sententiae* is not reserved unless express mention is made of this fact, has occasioned considerable dispute, especially, when compared with the second paragraph of this same canon. Those who hold that every precept is *ab homine* without distinguishing between the precept *ad instar sententiae* meet an apparent contradiction, when comparing the two paragraphs. Canon 2245, § 2 states that every *ab homine* penalty is reserved; § 4 provides that no *latae sententiae* penalty is reserved unless the reservation is expressly specified in the precept. Attempts to arrive at a satisfactory explanation and reconciliation have provoked various opinions.

Cocchi,[46] Vermeersch-Creusen,[47] Cappello [48] are of the opinion, that in the old law, a censure *ab homine,* namely, by precept either *latae* or *ferendae sententiae* or by sentence was always considered reserved. This, they say, has been confirmed by the new law in the Code. Then again, the old law distinguished the particular precept and the common precept given to a community. The law today, they claim, implicitly accepts this distinction between par-

[43] Canon 2245, § 4.

[44] Canon 2245, § 4.

[45] Cappello, *De Censuris,* n. 71.

[46] *Commentarium,* V, (De Delictis et Poenis), n. 71.

[47] Epitome, III, n. 443; Creusen, "De reservatione censurae precepto latae", *Ius Pontificium* (1924), pp. 26-29; "La réserve des censures ab homine", *Nouvelle Revue Theologique* (1928), p. 436.

[48] *De Censuris,* n. 68.

ticular and common precepts. The particular precept is treated in canon 2217, § 1, n. 3, the common precept is given consideration in canon 2245, § 4. By maintaining this hypothesis, namely, that the general precept is meant in canon 2245, § 4, the discrepancy, according to these authors, is solved.

It is difficult to see where the Code today confirms the statement of the pre-Code authors, that every *ab homine* penalty, whether *latae* or *ferendae sententiae* is reserved. From what has already been stated, it would seem that only that precept is *ab homine* which is *ad instar sententiae;* therefore, if there is question of a *latae sententiae* precept which is always *ad instar legis,* canon 2245, § 4 provides that reservation is in order only then when this fact is expressly mentioned.

Furthermore, to say that the precept mentioned in canon 2245, § 4 is general rather than particular does not seem to be a satisfactory solution. Nowhere in the Code, neither in canon 2245, § 4 nor elsewhere does the law make a distinction between a common and a particular precept. Hence, it is hard to see, how the authors can put forward this view to explain away the apparent contradiction. If, as they say, a general precept is a law, this fact would have been taken care of by the words *in lege.* Hence, the expression *vel praecepto* would be superfluous. The better opinion considers the precept of canon 2245, § 4, indeed, particular, but particular *ad instar legis,* and the precept constituting the *ab homine* penalty in canon 2245, § 2 as a particular precept also, but a precept *ad instar sententiae.*

Salucci explains the difficulty by stating that, by virtue of canon 2245, § 2 *ferendae sententiae* censures are reserved to him who inflicted the penalty or pronounced the condemnatory sentence; and by virtue of canon 2245, § 4 *latae sententiae* censures are not reserved unless the fact of the reservation is mentioned expressly in the law or precept, either general or particular. In canon 2245, § 2, he continues, there is question of a *ferendae sententiae* censure either *a iure* or *ab homine.* The Code uses this general term *ab-homine* simply to indicate that a *ferendae sententiae* censure, even if it is *a iure* becomes *ab homine* and hence reserved after a sentence. In § 4, it is clear that the canon speaks only of *latae senten-*

tiae censures, either *a iure or ab homine.* However, because they are considered more odious than the *ferendae sententiae* censure, reservation is not ordinarily attached to them.[49]

Salucci's opinion carries with it some truth, but it does not satisfactorily solve the difficulty. If one holds that every precept is *ab homine,* how will one reconcile this fact with § 4 of canon 2245, where no *latae sententiae* precept is reserved unless it contains express mention of the reservation?

Sole's view-point on this matter is, that *ab homine* censures which are inflicted by a judicial sentence are reserved, and *latae sententiae* censures which are either *a iure* or *ab homine* as a result of a precept, are not reserved unless this fact is expressly stated in the law or precept. He argues from the old law. He says that, from c. 29, X, *de sententia excommunicationis,* V, 39, *a iure* censures were not specifically reserved, and hence anyone could absolve from them. This implied that, unless special mention was made of a reservation, anyone was at liberty to impart absolution. This rule of Innocent III concerning the *a iure* censure, he continues, finds its counterpart in canon 2245, § 4 relative to *latae sententiae* censures which are *ab homine* in virtue of a precept.[50]

This opinion too, appears to present no satisfactory solution. The difficulty still remains; for as canon 2245, § 2 rules—the *ab homine* censure is reserved.

After considering these various attempts at explaining away the apparent contradiction between § 2 and § 4 of canon 2245, let it be said that there is at least a doubt of law, and hence, unless a precept which threatens a *latae sententiae* censure contains some phrase indicating reservation, the censure is not reserved. Thus for example, should a bishop say to a cleric, "If you visit this person again, you are suspended by that very fact", even though this is a particular precept pure and simple, and according to some, *ab*

[49] *Il diritto penale secondo il codice di diritto canonico,* (Subiaco, 1926), I, 198, note 1.

[50] *De Delictis et Poenis,* p. 122. Collison holds the same opinion.—"Non Omnis Censura Ab Homine Est Reservata", *Dissertatio . . . Apud Pontificium Institutum Angelicum,* Romae, 1935, p. 90.

homine, the suspension which is incurred upon the violation of this precept, is not reserved, because the fact of the reservation was not expressly mentioned. To induce a reservation, the bishop would have to say, "If you visit this person again, you are by that very fact suspended, and the suspension is reserved to me". This will obviate all doubts and secure the desired reservation. Of course, it must be remembered, that the precept spoken of here is presumed to have legal force in the external forum. It is presumed that, in accordance with the provision of canon 2225, the issuance of the precept together with the threat of suspension was done in writing, or if orally, pronounced before at least two witnesses. The precept would then be formal and before the ecclesiastical court would stand the test of unquestionable legality.[51]

BY REASON OF THE INVALIDITY OF EFFECTS CONSEQUENT UPON THE ISSUANCE OF A SENTENCE. Occasionally in the old law, authors distinguished the suspended cleric, as *suspensus vitandus* or *suspensus toleratus*.[52] Today, however, with regard to suspension this differentiation is not found in the law. The Code restricts the use of the terms *vitandus* and *toleratus* solely to excommunication. For suspension it employs the phraseology *ante* or *post sententiam declaratoriam vel condemnatoriam*. According to these two categories suspension is classified. According to these two categories, the validity or invalidity of acts consequent upon the violation of a given suspension is determined.[53]

[51] Michiels, *Normae Generales*, I, 519.

[52] Konings, *Theologia Moralis*, II, n. 1690, quaes., 6.

[53] It may be said that after a declaratory or condemnatory sentence, a suspended cleric is considered *quasi-vitandus*, because, while he is not severed from communion with the rest of the faithful, he is nevertheless not qualified to validly perform certain acts, for whose exercise ecclesiastical jurisdiction is necessary. On the other hand, before a declaratory or condemnatory sentence, a suspended cleric is similar to an excommunicated person, whom the law designates as *toleratus*, relative to questions regarding the administration of the sacraments and other acts which fall within the sphere of suspension. While it would not be wrong to use the terms *vitandus* and *toleratus* in reference to suspension, such use would engender misunderstanding, first of all because the Code does not use these expressions when referring to suspension, and secondly, these terms imply effects, which can not be applied in full to the penalty

of suspension. Hence for the sake of clarity and uniformity, it would be better to confine the use of this terminology to the censure of excommunication alone.

CHAPTER IV

THE EFFECTS OF SUSPENSION

As an introductory remark to this chapter, it may be stated, that when a suspension has been validly inflicted or incurred, all the effects, which the Code determines for the various kinds of suspensions become operative immediately. There is no further external agency or execution required. As Kober[1] says, the penalty is self-executory.

THE GENERAL SUSPENSION. Unless the contrary is evident, this suspension, decreed absolutely and without qualifications, embraces all the effects of the suspension *ab officio* and the suspension *a beneficio.*[2] Besides these major effects, there are others, which are equally included in the general suspension. Thus, a cleric, laboring under a suspension of this type, according to the better opinion,[3] may not elect, present or nominate another to an ecclesiastical office; nor may he obtain dignities, offices, benefices or pensions; finally, he is forbidden to ascend to a higher order. Should he, notwithstanding these prohibitions, undertake to contravene the provisions of the law, his act would be illicit but not invalid, provided no sentence had been declared or pronounced. If, on the other hand, he should disregard the above mentioned prohibitions, after a declaratory or condemnatory sentence, his act would not only be illicit but also invalid. This would also include the cleric's use of favors and dispensations granted by a papal rescript, even if no mention is made of the suspension; for all papal rescripts are invalid, if obtained by one suspended after a sentence.[4] The reception of a higher order would not be rendered invalid, because once the essential conditions for the valid conferring and receiving of orders have been fulfilled, the Church can not but recognize the

1 *Die Suspension*, p. 88.

2 Canon 2278, § 2.

3 Chelodi, *Ius Poenale*, n. 45; Cappello, *De Censuris*, n. 502.

4 Canons 2283; 2265, § 2; 36, § 2.

validity of the orders conferred. The Church is simply powerless to set up any regulations affecting the validity of orders through the intervention of a purely ecclesiastical enactment.

The penalty of invalidity attaches to the above mentioned acts only from the moment the suspension has been made manifest by a declaratory sentence. The acts are not affected in their validity during the interim between the incurring of the suspension and the ultimate declaration consequent thereto. This conclusion is fully warranted despite the general legislation of the Code that a declaratory sentence relative to a given penalty makes such a penalty operative from the moment the delict was committed.[5] This legal regulation means nothing more than that the declaratory sentence does not in any way inhibit or diminish the effects of the penalty already present in view of the violation of the penal law to which the penalty was *ipso facto* attached. For, unless a penalty was already incurred, there could not follow what is merely the declaration of it. The declaration engenders the additional effect that such acts which were prohibited before, and therefore, rendered illegal if undertaken, will thenceforth become invalid besides. This is substantiated not only by the comparison of canon 2283 with canon 2265, § 2, in the latter of which, the acts forbidden to an excommunicate are branded as null and void *post sententiam declaratoriam* (*vel condemnatoriam*), but also with the text of canon 2284, in which a prohibited act of jurisdiction is pronounced invalid only if a declaratory (or a condemnatory) sentence has been rendered.

De Meester[6] and Claeys-Bouuaert-Simenon[7] claim that the effects of canon 2265 pertain to those clerics laboring under a general suspension as well as those partially suspended. Vermeersch-Creusen[8] are of the same opinion. They maintain that in recon-

[5] Canon 2232, § 2: "Sententia declaratoria poenam ad momentum commissi delicti retrotrahit." As to what was stated on the above paragraph Augustine appears to hold the contrary. He seems to confuse the *judicial* declaration which alone induces the invalidating effects stated by the law, with the mere extrajudicial declaration of the fact that a penalty has been incurred.—Cfr. *Commentary*, II, 130.

[6] *Compendium*, III, pars 2a, n. 1783, 3o, note 1.

[7] *Manuale Iuris Canonici*, n. 1294.

[8] *Epitome*, III, n. 486.

structing canon 2283 on the lines of canon 2265, the wording of the canon is *Omnis clericus suspensus prohibetur.*

It is true, that canon 2283 refers to all the prescriptions of canon 2265. It is true likewise, that the latter canon begins *Quilibet excommunicatus.* But, would it not be too strict an opinion to hold that for the word *excommunicatus* could be substituted *suspensus,* so that the canon would read *quilibet suspensus?* It appears, the Code does not intend such an interpretation, because in canons 2279 and 2280, the law clearly and definitely determines what shall be the effects of the various suspensions. It would, therefore, seem altogether superfluous to enumerate the effects of the partial suspensions and at the same time presume that the provisions of canon 2265 are also included. Where the Code speaks of the general suspension, it is all embracing, in referring to the effects. It says, that all the effects enumerated in the third article, namely, the effects *ab officio* and *a beneficio,* follow the infliction of this suspension. Such a provision makes this penalty, indeed, most severe. This fact would harmonize more with the prescription of canon 2283, which states, that what is predicated of excommunication in canon 2265 is also to be predicated of suspension. Thus, suspension is placed side by side with the Church's severest penalty, excommunication. Consequently, the effects of a most severe penalty would be out of proportion for any suspension other than that called the general suspension. To hold the opposite opinion would be demanding more than the law does, since the Code undertakes to state specifically what are to be effects of the partial suspensions. Furthermore, the essential difference between excommunication and suspension, namely, that the effects of the former unlike the effects of the latter are inseparable, is an added reason why the content of canon 2265 as directed by canon 2283 should be exclusively restricted to the general suspension. Besides, since penalties must be interpreted benignly, and if the text is obscure, a mild interpretation must be assumed, then the opinion which holds that the general suspension alone is accompanied by the effects mentioned in canon 2265 is the more tenable one.[9]

[9] Augustine, *Commentary,* VIII, 230; Woywod, *A Practical Commentary,* II,

It is the nature of the general suspension to affect all those legitimate ecclesiastical acts, which are concerned with the exercise of orders or jurisdiction and the right to enjoy the revenues of a benefice. Since, therefore, a general suspension includes an office in the strict and broad sense, a cleric thus suspended may not administer the goods of the Church, nor may he exercise the office of judge, auditor, realtor, defender of the bond, promoter of justice, notary, chancellor, beadle, courier, advocate and arbiter. Furthermore, such a cleric would be forbidden to vote, and if he had the *ius patronatus*, the exercise of this right, too, would be forbidden him, since there would be question of presenting another, an act which is forbidden by canon 2265. All these acts, if undertaken, would be illicit, unless there is an excusing cause, as for example, the legitimate request of the faithful. Roberti[10] says, that in questions of ecclesiastical trials, this is nearly always the case. Cappello asserts that these acts are illicit but valid.[11] Those which in any way touch upon jurisdiction are invalid if placed after a declaratory or condemnatory sentence.[12] The provision of canon 1654 as such, which prohibits an excommunicate laboring under this penalty after a sentence, from bringing and defending a suit in an ecclesiastical court, does not apply to the case of a general suspension, because the nature of these two penalties is different. Excommunication severs the culprit from communion with the church, which would affect his right, therefore, to bring a case before an ecclesiastical court. Suspension, on the other hand, does not affect the rights which the delinquent enjoys as a member of the Church, but merely restricts certain rights proper to his state. Consequently, a suspended cleric, who had a sentence declared or pro-

2124; Chelodi, *Ius Poenale*, n. 45; Haring, J., *Grundzüge des Katholischen Kirchenrechts*, p. 952, note 2; Blat, *Commentarium*, V, n. 112; A Coronata, *Institutiones Iuris Canonici*, IV, n. 1815; Ayrinhac, *Penal Legislation* (ed. 1936), n. 152, (b). Cocchi, *Commentarium* (De Delictis et Poenis), V, n. 101 and Cappello, *De Censuris*, n. 502 do not give a contrary opinion. Before the Code, it was Wernz's opinion, that every suspension did not produce the effects now mentioned in canon 2265. Cfr. *Ius Decretalium*, VI, n. 209.

10 *De Processibus*, I, n. 175.

11 *De Censuris*, n. 150.

12 Canons 2265, § 2; 2284; 1931.

nounced against him would not be excluded from an ecclesiastical trial, because the law of canon 1654 speaks solely of excommunication; and therefore, since penal laws must receive a strict interpretation, the suspended cleric has full right, in view of canon 1654, to appear in court.

When the general suspension has been inflicted by a particular diocesan statute or by precept, its legal force extends only to those offices and benefices within the jurisdiction of this diocesan law or to those offices and benefices alone which the suspended cleric had obtained from the superior, who gave the precept or issued the condemnatory sentence.[13] This same norm can not be applied to the general suspension incurred *ipso facto* by common law or which the common law commands the superior or judge to inflict or which it leaves to their discretion to inflict or not.[14] The general principle governing a situation of this kind is, that all the offices and benefices which the cleric enjoys anywhere in the Church fall within the prohibitions of the suspension.[15] The ordinary rule is, that those who are subject to the general laws of the Church are everywhere subject to the penal sanctions attached to these laws, unless they are expressly exempted. Consequently, once any one of these sanctions has been inflicted, the cleric is bound everywhere in the Church, unless the contrary is stated.[16]

One might question the case, where a superior or judge inflicts a suspension already established by the Code, arguing that such a suspension would be limited solely to the jurisdiction of the superior or judge. It must be remembered, that the penalty has been established by the common legislator, and therefore, pertains to his jurisdiction which is universal. The fact that a lower superior or judge inflicts or applies this suspension does not limit the universal effect of this punishment. Such a superior or judge is merely acting with vicarious power, as it were, pronouncing sentence in the name and authority of the Church.

[13] Canon 2281.

[14] Canon 2223, § 2, § 3.

[15] Canon 2282.

[16] Canon 2226, § 4.

General Suspension and Papal Rescripts. Before the Code, the *Ordo Servandus* for the Sacred Congregations, Tribunals and Offices of the Roman Curia which was published in conjunction with the *Sapienti Concilio* forbade only those persons from validly obtaining a papal rescript who were excommunicated *nominatim* or whom the Holy See suspended *nominatim a divinis.*[17]

The Code is in harmony with the *Normae.* It excludes those against whom a declaratory or condemnatory sentence has been pronounced. For, if *nominatim* is meant to designate the individual so definitely that he can not be confounded with other suspended persons, certainly by a declaratory or condemnatory sentence such designation is accomplished. Hence, after such sentences, according to the interpretations of the present law, no cleric has a legal capacity for a papal rescript, if he is under a general suspension, unless in the papal rescript mention is made of the censure, implying therefore, that the concession is made in spite of it, or unless an absolution from censures, called *ad effectum,* be inserted in the rescript for the purpose of securing its validity. From the arguments already adduced, it is evident that it is the general suspension alone which comprises the effects enumerated in canon 2265, among which is found this provision concerning the use of papal rescripts.[18]

The favors which such a suspended cleric is forbidden to ask are not limited to such favors as are special or proper to the clerical state, but to any and all favors in general. Canon 36, § 2 makes it clear, that no favor or dispensation can be obtained or validly re-

17 "Servatis, tum quae superiore *num.* 4° statuta sunt circa rescriptorum executionem, tum necessariis conditionibus ad sacras indulgentias lucrandas; a die III mensis Novembris MDCCCCVIII, quo die incipient vim legis habere praescripta in Constitutione *Sapienti consilio,* gratiae ac dispensationes omne genus a Sancta Sede concessae, etiam censura irretitis, ratae sint ac legitimae, nisi de iis agatur qui nominatim excommunicati sint, aut a Sancta Sede nominatim pariter poena suspensionis a divinis multati."—*Ordo servandus in Sacris Congregationibus Tribunalibus Officiis Romanae Curiae,* Pars Altera, Normae Peculiares, Cap. III, art. I, n. 6.—*AAS,* I (1909), 64.

18 Canons 2265; 2283; Chelodi, *Ius Poenale,* n. 45; Blat, *Commentarium,* V, n. 112; Ayrinhac, *Penal Legislation in the New Code of Canon Law,* n. 121.

ceived from the Holy See after a declaratory or condemnatory sentence.[19]

A doubt may arise as to whether canon 2265, § 2 includes privileges and dispensations.[20] Canons 36, § 2 and 62 give rise to this doubt. The former expressly distinguishes between a favor and dispensation, while the latter expressly distinguishes between a simple favor on the one hand, and a dispensation and privilege on the other. It seems certain, however, that canon 2265, § 2 has reference not only to simple favors, but likewise, to privileges and dispensations. The words *gratiam ullam pontificiam* indicate this, for privileges and dispensations are commonly included under the name of favors.

Furthermore, not only are rescripts of favor included but also rescripts of justice. This is evident from the general terminology used by canon 36, § 1.[21] The canon uses the word *rescripta* which would include, therefore, not only rescripts of favor but also rescripts of justice.

To understand these two rescripts, it would be well to define them. A rescript of favor is one which grants a favor that is generally *praeter* or *contra* the common or the particular law. It in no way touches upon the affairs of a tribunal. A rescript of justice, on the other hand, tends to the administration of justice and therefore grants favors to those concerned with a trial, which are regularly *secundum ius*. A rescript of this kind may be one which grants delegation to extraordinary judges etc.[22]

Canon 36, § 1 states that any one may receive a rescript from the Holy See who is not prohibited. Paragraph two of this same canon designates all those who are prohibited, namely, all those who are excommunicated, suspended or interdicted after the pronouncement of a declaratory or condemnatory sentence. Since, therefore,

[19] "Gratiae et dispensationes omne genus a Sede Apostolica concessae etiam censura irretitis validae sunt, *salvo praescripto* can. 2265, § 2, 2275, n. 3, 2283."

[20] Cappello, *De Censuris*, n. 157.

[21] "*Rescripta* tum Sedis Apostolicae tum aliorum Ordinariorum impetrari libere possunt ab omnibus qui expresse non prohibentur."

[22] Michiels, *Normae Generales*, II, 169.

§ 1 uses the general term *rescripta,* it may be stated that those who are suspended by means of a declaratory or condemnatory sentence are forbidden to obtain not only a rescript of favor from the Holy See, but also a rescript of justice.

Augustine[23] maintains that, according to all authors, even a cleric suspended by a declaratory or condemnatory sentence is allowed to ask for a rescript revoking the suspension. If this privilege were legally denied, he claims, the way of justice would be precluded to him.

Even though there is no danger of losing one's good name and even though the suspension were incurred for a notorious crime, namely, one publicly known and committed in such circumstances that it can be neither concealed nor excused, a cleric may, nevertheless, obtain a papal rescript, because the general rule is that any one may ask for a papal rescript who is not expressly forbidden. The only ones forbidden are those who are suspended after a declaratory or condemnatory sentence has intervened. The notoriety of the crime in no way prevents a cleric from asking for a papal rescript. The law of canon 2232, § 1 states that a suspension for a notorious crime can be enforced in the external forum. The notoriety of the crime does not invalidate the rescript. For practical purposes, however, the external forum is safeguarded by the customary procedure of the Curia, which requires, at least, a letter of recommendation from the Ordinary, in all petitions for papal favors pertaining to the external forum. If, in the case of a notorious crime, the Ordinary should inadvertently sanction with approval the petition of a cleric for a favor from the Holy See, he would have a right by law to withhold the execution of the rescript granted *in forma commissoria,* on the ground that the recipient was unworthy. In doing this, however, he must make sure to inform the Holy See of his action.[24]

In the case of a suspended cleric upon whom neither a declaratory nor a condemnatory sentence has been passed, the validity of the papal rescript issued for him is not affected; nevertheless, it would be illicit for him to ask for a favor during the time of his sus-

23 *Commentary,* I, 126.

24 Canon 54, § 1.

pension, if the granting of the favor be prohibited because of his suspension. Yet, under these circumstances, the danger of losing his good reputation could render the cleric's plea for the favor a lawful request.

The nullifying effect of suspension, consequent upon a declaratory or condemnatory sentence, asserts its legal force in the case of a rescript granted in *forma gratiosa* at the very moment of concession. On the other hand, in the case of a rescript granted *in forma commissoria*, the nullity of the rescript becomes effective only at the moment of its eventual execution.[25]

When a rescript is granted *in forma gratiosa*, a suspension which is the result of a condemnatory sentence, or which has been declared by sentence, does not invalidate the rescript if it has been remitted at the time of the concession, even though the petition was made when the suspension existed. Should such a suspension be present only prior to and not contemporaneously with the granting of the rescript *in forma commissoria*, the validity of the grant in the rescript is in no way affected. The validity or invalidity of the rescript is dependent upon the absence or presence of the suspension at the time of the execution. Should the sentence, however, be declared or pronounced after the execution, still this circumstance does not affect the validity of the papal favor already received.[26]

GENERAL SUSPENSION AND RESCRIPTS OF ORDINARIES. From papal rescripts, the mind of the reader naturally turns to a consideration of rescripts of favor granted by an Ordinary. It has been seen how papal rescripts are forbidden under pain of nullity to those clerics who are laboring under a censure of suspension consequent upon a declaratory or condemnatory sentence, unless mention is made, in the papal rescript, of the existence of this suspension. With regard to the rescript of an Ordinary, the dispositions of the law differ. No cleric is forbidden to ask for a rescript from his Ordinary, which the latter can grant by his ordinary power, even though there exist a censure of suspension issued through a

[25] Canon 38.

[26] Canon 2296, § 2:—"Iura iam quaesita non amittuntur ob supervenientem inhabilitatem, nisi huic addatur poena privationis."

declaratory or a condemnatory sentence. Canon 36, § 2 correlated with canon 2265, § 2 refers solely to pontifical rescripts.[27]

Limitations and conditions, however, may be determined by a particular law, which a cleric must observe according to the tenor of the law. It certainly is within the province of the Ordinary, who is the custodian of all favors which an Ordinary may grant, to regulate them according to his own ordinances. Whether a suspension after a declaratory or condemnatory sentence has been pronounced will invalidate an Ordinary's favor, will depend on the statutory law, or the will of the Ordinary.

It has been said, that the provision of canon 36, § 2 and canon 2265, § 2 do not pertain to those favors, which the Ordinary can confer by his ordinary power. In how far will they affect rescripts granted by an Ordinary in virtue of faculties delegated by the Holy See? Regarding particular rescripts where the Ordinary is the necessary or voluntary executor, a cleric under suspension, after a sentence has been issued, that is either declaratory or condemnatory, can not receive such papal favors, unless express mention is made of the censure. The question is doubtful, however, in cases when the Ordinary grants favors through his use of an Apostolic faculty or indult. Michiels[28] claims, that when an Ordinary acts by virtue of an indult, he still acts as a delegate, in the name of the Holy See, and hence, from the nature of delegation, must observe the norms determined by the Holy See. These norms, canon 36, § 2 and canon 2265, § 2 clearly determine. Consequently, no papal favor can be validly obtained by a cleric under a suspension after the issuance of a declaratory or a condemnatory sentence, even though an Ordinary can grant it by virtue of an indult, unless there is express mention of the suspension. Ordinaries, however, by virtue of canon 66, § 3 enjoy every faculty required to make effective their power, granted them by an indult. Therefore, they may absolve from the censure of suspension, even though it should be reserved to the

[27] A Coronata, *Institutiones Iuris Canonici,* I, n. 61; Cappello, *Summa Iuris Canonici,* I, n. 142; Ayrinhac, *General Legislation in the New Code of Canon Law,* n. 133.

[28] *Normae Generales,* II, 196 (b).

Holy See, in order that the cleric may enjoy the papal favor requested. This statement, it seems, must be understood in this light, namely, that the Ordinary in granting absolution for the use of a papal favor, which he is empowered to grant through an indult, may not transcend the limits to which the Roman Curia restricts itself in its customary procedure or practice.

THE SUSPENSION *ab officio.* Although the definition of the Code most accurately supplies the fundamental concept of this suspension, it is nevertheless general. The following consideration will endeavor to show, in detail, the essential prohibitions, which are intimately connected with every suspension *ab officio.*

The word *office*, in reference to the suspension *ab officio*, embraces the twofold signification of this term, as expressed in canon 145, namely, in the strict and broad sense.[29] In the strict sense, an office is any personal function, trust or charge permanently established, either by divine or ecclesiastical law, which is conferred by a legitimate superior according to the norms of law, and which enjoys some participation in ecclesiastical power, either of orders or of jurisdiction. It must be a power that is ordinary, that is to say, an endowment of competence which attaches to a person by the very act of his incumbency. Thus, it is distinguished from an office in the broad sense,[30] because offices of this nature convey no power except that delegated by the superior. They are mere duties exercised for a spiritual end, even though they be material in the structure or composition of their performance and fulfillment, such as the office of organist or chanter; or they may be duties of an essentially spiritual character, but only temporary or transient in their duration so as to depend for their continuance entirely upon the uninhibited will of the superior. Offices of this type would be that of confessor or chaplain.

Canon 145, § 2 declares that in the law the term *ecclesiastical office* is to be understood in its strict sense, unless the contrary is apparent from the context. It is, however, apparent from the suspension *ab officio*, that not only the offices in the strict sense are

[29] Blat, *Commentarium*, V, n. 108.
[30] Wernz-Vidal, *De Personis*, II, n. 140.

included but also the offices considered broadly, because from the nature of the case, this suspension touches every exercise of orders and jurisdiction, both of which enter the domain of the latter as well as the former.

By the power of orders is meant, that which refers directly to the sanctification of souls through the exercise of acts of divine worship and through the effectuation and administration of the sacraments and sacramentals.[31] This is, indeed, the meaning of the word *ordo* used in canon 2279, § 1. Furthermore, the same term, according to canon 950, must be said to include, besides episcopal consecration, all the orders enumerated in canon 949,[32] namely, all the major orders and the four minor orders. Tonsure is not included, however, since the canon, in reference to orders, speaks of the power of orders, which is not given at tonsure. Tonsure merely gives one a capacity for orders.

Jurisdiction, spoken of by canon 2279, § 1 is not limited to any one kind but embraces all, both for the internal and external forum, ordinary, delegated, judicial and non-judicial.[33] It may be defined as a public power granted by Christ or His Church, through a canonical mission, of ruling over and administering to the needs and exigencies of the baptized faithful in relation to their eternal destiny.[34]

When, therefore, a suspension *ab officio* is decreed absolutely and without restriction, as for example, if the bishop should say, "I suspend you from office", this implies, not only the prohibition to exercise the rights proper to the office which the addressed cleric possesses, but also the prohibition to exercise any act of orders and

31 Maroto, *Institutiones,* I, 567.

32 "In canonibus qui sequuntur, nomine maiorum vel sacrorum intelliguntur presbyteratus, diaconatus, subdiaconatus; minorum vero acolythatus, exorcistatus, lectoratus, ostiariatus."

Canon 950:—"In iure verba: ordinare, ordo, ordinatio, sacra ordinatio, comprehendunt, praeter consecrationem episcopalem, ordines enumeratos in can. 949 et ipsam primam tonsuram, nisi, aliud ex natura rei vel ex contextu verborum eruatur."

33 Canons 200; 201, Blat, *Commentarium,* V, n. 108.

34 Vermeersch-Creusen, *Epitome,* I, n. 275.

jurisdiction of any kind. Likewise, it forbids the administration proper to the office, and also the administration of ecclesiastical goods, as for instance, the making of investments and the alienation of Church property,[35] because the administration of ecclesiastical goods is an act of jurisdiction.[36] The suspension does not, however, forbid the administration of the goods of one's benefice. Hence, a cleric suspended *ab officio* may retain control over the manner in which the investment shall be made. He also enjoys the right to make repairs, to sign checks, etc. To take away this right of administration, the superior must make express mention of this fact.[37]

According to the above norms, therefore, if the suspended cleric is a pastor, he may not lawfully offer the Holy Sacrifice of the Mass; neither may he preach, nor administer the sacraments, except according to the provisions of canon 2232, § 1, 2284, 2261. He is, however, bound to say his Breviary, to have the *Missa pro Populo* said, etc.

As to the sacrament of Matrimony, since the censure of suspension *ab officio*, prior to a declaratory or condemnatory sentence, merely forbids the administration of the sacraments and sacramentals,[38] the pastor, under such a suspension, may not licitly assist at a marriage. It is true, his assistance at marriage is not an act of administration of the sacrament, since the parties themselves effectuate the sacrament,[39] still it entails an active use of sacramentals which is forbidden according to canon 2261. However, in this case, the prescription of canon 2232, § 1 must not be overlooked, because before the issuance of a declaratory sentence, no one is obliged to observe a *latae sententiae* censure or vindictive penalty, whenever there is danger of losing one's good name.

Under the decree *Ne Temere*, a pastor could assist at a marriage, unless he had been suspended *ab officio* by name or by a

[35] De Meester, *Compendium*, III, pars 2a, n. 1782.

[36] De Luca, *De Rebus Ecclesiasticis*, III, 360.

[37] A Coronata, *Institutiones Iuris Canonici*, IV, n. 1813.

[38] Canon 2284.

[39] Marc-Gestermann, *Institutiones Morales Alphonsianae*, II, n. 1969.

public decree.[40] Today, the law does not demand that the culprit be suspended *nominatim;* nor is it required that the decree be public. In the event, that the censure of suspension remains unknown and is secret, which will hardly ever be the case when a condemnatory or declaratory sentence has been issued, canon 209 could be invoked, and the pastor could validly witness a marriage, on the strength of supplied jurisdiction in common error,—a principle applicable to assistance at marriage which is akin to jurisdiction—because the ignorance on the part of the parties has occasioned their false judgment. The pastor would then be putative as regards his power and as such can validly assist at a marriage.[41]

The general norm is, that after a declaratory or condemnatory sentence has been issued, a pastor loses all legal capacity of valid assistance at marriage.[42] The enumeration of the penalties in canon 1095, § 1, n. 1 definitely includes the suspension *ab officio.* Thus, is indicated the fact that all other suspensions have not this invalidating effect, with regard to the assistance at marriage. This, however, is not to bring about the inference, that the general suspension is excluded. Since the suspension *ab officio* is included in the general suspension, the latter penalty also renders assistance at marriage invalid, if attempted after a declaratory or condemnatory sentence has been pronounced.[43]

Does the suspension *ab officio* deprive the pastor of the right to the stole fee, which is customary at the time of the celebration of marriage. The right to the stole fee is based on the pastor's competence to assist licitly at a marriage. In general, therefore, he alone has full right to receive and retain the stole fee, who has a

[40] "Parochus et loci Ordinarius valide matrimonio adsistunt, a die tantummodo adeptae posesssionis beneficii vel initi officii, nisi publico decreto nominatim fuerint excommunicati vel ab offico suspensi . . . etc."—S.C.C., decre. *Ne Temere,* 2 aug. 1907, art., IV, 1.—*Fontes,* n. 430.

[41] Vermeersch-Creusen, *Epitome,* II, n. 392.

[42] Canon 1095, § 1, n. 1:—"Parochus et loci Ordinarius valide matrimonio assistunt, a die tantummodo adeptae canonicae possessionis beneficii ad normam can. 334, § 3, 1444, § 1, vel initi officii, nisi per sententiam fuerint excommunicati vel interdicti vel suspensi ab officio aut tales declarati . . . etc."

[43] Canon 2278, § 2; Capello, *De Censuris,* n. 146.

right to assist at the marriage. A pastor, under the suspension *ab officio,* whether before or after a sentence, forfeits this right, because the effect of this suspension disqualifies him for assistance at marriage, a right proper to his office.[44] Even though, he should in good faith depute another to assist at a marriage in his stead, still he would not be allowed to benefit by this offering. Consequently, he must restore the perquisites to the next legally competent proper pastor of the contracting parties.

Nor may a pastor suspended *ab officio* delegate another to assist at a marriage. There is no doubt, that those who enjoy an ecclesiastical office, properly accepted, may delegate others to exercise powers granted them by the Code, unless this is expressly restricted. However, the power to assist at the celebration of a marriage is not properly jurisdictional, yet it is attached to the office of pastor, and, according to the law, may be delegated to another.[45] It is a strict right of the pastoral office.[46]

The act of assistance at marriage, while not strictly jurisdictional, is allied to it, because the right to assist at marriage is acquired by virtue of an office, and secondly, this right can be delegated.[47] Moreover, canon 20 will support this contention. For, although the law does not expressly refer to assistance at marriage as real jurisdiction, yet it does demand in parallel questions of jurisdiction, that the same norms be followed, as is evident from legal procedure in this matter. According to the opinion of the Rota, the power by which a faculty is granted is similar to an act by which one confers a privilege or jurisdiction.[48] In another

[44] Canon 462, n. 4.

[45] Canon 1095.

[46] Augustine, *Commentary,* VIII, 190, note 65; Kober, *Die Suspension,* p. 103, note 4.

[47] Cappelo, *De Sacramentis,* III, n. 694.

[48] "Illa porro licentia concessa sacerdoti celebrandi matrimonium est in genere facultatum, seu privilegiorum, aut etiam, lato sensu, delegationum iurisdictionis (licet non sit stricto sensu delegatio iurisdictionis, cum actus, quo parochus interest matrimonio non sit exercitium iurisdictionis). Actus itaque quo conceditur licentia, assimilatur actui, quo conceditur privilegium, seu facultas, seu iurisdictio."—S. R. Rota, in Divionensi (Dijon), 20 Jan. 1911 —*AAS,* III (1911), 285.

part of this same case, the Rota speaks of the one delegating and the one delegated,[49] a terminology which is applied to cases of jurisdiction, where the word *delegate* is always used. Likewise, the Pontifical Commission for the Authentic Interpretation of the Code employs the terminology, which the Code alone reserves to questions of jurisdiction.[50] It, too, speaks of delegation and subdelegation. Since, therefore, it is the mind of the law to look upon the granting of permission to assist at a marriage as similar to delegation, it governs this act by the same principles laid down under the canons relative to this matter.

Every act of delegation is an exercise of jurisdiction. Since the same norms apply to the right to assist at a marriage as to real jurisdiction, it would follow, that whatever renders an act of real jurisdiction illicit or invalid affects the act of assistance at marriage in the same manner. Consequently, should a pastor suspended *ab officio* depute another to assist at a marriage, before a sentence, this act would be illicit. After a sentence, however, the act would not only be illicit but also invalid.[51] Canon 2284 refers to acts of jurisdiction. Therefore, since the granting of permission to assist at a marriage is to be governed by the principles of delegation, and since every act of delegation entails an act of jurisdiction, the effects of canon 2284 take their toll of illicitness or invalidity, in every attempt, on the part of the pastor suspended *ab officio*, to delegate his right to another. The basis for this is the legal principle:

[49] "In hac causa duo proposita sunt capita nullitatis matrimonii: unum ex parte parochi delegantis, qui non dedit licentiam efficacem et sufficientem: alterum ex parte sacerdotis delegati, qui licentiam sibi concessam ante matrimonium ignoravit."—Casu Divionensi (Dijon), 20 Jan. 1911—A.A.S., III, 287.

[50] "An vicarius cooperator, qui ad normam canonis 1096, § 1, a parocho vel loci Ordinario generalem obtinuit delegationem assistendi matrimoniis, alium determinatum sacerdotem subdelegare possit ad assistendum matrimonio determinato?

"An parochus vel loci Ordinarius, qui ad normam canonis 1096, § 1 sacerdotem determinatum delegaverit ad assistendum matrimonio determinato, possit ei etiam licentiam dare subdelegandi alium sacerdotem determinatum ad assistendum eidem matrimonio. R. Affirmative ad utrumque".—Dec. 28, 1927—*AAS*, XX (1928), 61.

[51] Canon 2284; 1095, § 1, n. 1.

Nemo potest plus iuris transferre in alium quam sibi competere dignoscatur.[52]

Authors are divided when they speak of the delegated priest being under the suspension *ab officio.* Wouters,[53] Vlaming,[54] Petrovits[55] claim, that a delegated priest may validly assist at a marriage, even if he is suspended *ab officio,* after the issuance of a declaratory or condemnatory sentence. They maintain, on the one hand, that the law concerning the delegate does not signify the contrary, and on the other, it is not proper to apply to the delegate or extraordinary qualified witness, all those legal disabilities, which the law demands for the ordinary qualified witness. Vermeersch-Creusen,[56] Augustine,[57] De Smet,[58] Cappello,[59] take the better supported view. The decree *Ne Temere*[60] explicitly states, that the delegate is bound by the same rules, with reference to licit and valid assistance, as the delegating Ordinary or pastor. Although the Code does not mention this fact, still, it seems, the same norm obtains at present. It would be strange, if a suspended priest could be delegated to assist at a mariage, when the law is against the validity of such an act on the part of the Ordinary or pastor. Moreover, a priest suspended *ab officio,* either by a declaratory or condemnatory sentence, may not validly exercise jurisdiction, in virtue of canon 2284. Although, as was stated previously, assistance at marriage is not strictly jurisdiction, it is, nevertheless, governed by the same principles. Therefore, every act of assistance at marriage, after a declaratory or condemnatory sentence of

52 Reg. 79, R. J., in VIo.

53 *De Forma Sponsalititiae et Matrimonii,* p. 25.

54 *Praelectiones Iuris Matrimonii,* II, n. 573.

55 *New Church Law on Marriage,* n. 474.

56 *Epitome,* II, n. 396.

57 *Commentary,* V, 286.

58 *De Sponsalibus et Matrimonio,* n. 122.

59 *De Sacramentis,* III, n. 677.

60 "Delegatus autem, ut valide et licite adsistat, servare tenetur limites mandati, et regulas pro parocho et loci Ordinario n. IV, [Parochus et loci Ordinarius valide matrimonio adsistunt], et V, [Licite autem adsistunt], superius statutas".—S.C.C., decr. *Ne Temere,* 2 aug. 1907, art., VI,—*Fontes,* n. 4340.

suspension *ab officio*, is invalid. The Code makes this general statement in canon 1095, § 1, n. 1. Hence, whether as ordinary or extraordinary witness, the same invalidating effect follows.

If a bishop has fallen into a suspension *ab officio* his jurisdictional powers are suspended. Therefore, before a sentence, every attempt to exercise this power would be illicit, unless there is danger of infamy or grave scandal, and, then, if the suspension is *latae sententiae*, either medicinal or vindictive, he can act in the external forum, as if there existed no suspension. He may, therefore, continue to dispense and grant others this right. On the other hand, after a declaratory or condemnatory sentence, any exercise of jurisdiction on his part would be invalid, with the exception of sacramental absolution in danger of death.[61]

Maroto[62] is of the opinion, that the power of the delegate is suspended, when the delegator's power is curtailed. But, this is not true. According to the latter part of canon 207, § 1, he does not lose his power, unless in harmony with the provision of canon 61, the mandate so provides, that the delegation is to end with the death, legal or natural of the delegator, or the case for which the delegation had been given, has not as yet been considered. In judicial matters, all delegation would cease, if there had been no legitimate citation.[63] Consequently, all those with delegated faculties may continue to use them, after the bishop has incurred a suspension *ab officio*, even should this penalty be declared or come by way of a condemnatory sentence. Confessors, too, may without scruple continue to hear confessions, unless there is question of a case which demands a special faculty, and the case has not yet been considered.

With the interdiction of the bishop's powers, by reason of the suspension, follows a similar curtailment on the part of the Vicar General,[64] because vicarious power is conceived as curtailed, whenever it is suspended in the person from whom it is derived. On the contrary, the *Officialis*, who like the Vicar General is also the

[61] Canon 2284; 2232, § 1.
[62] *Institutiones*, I, 854-855.
[63] Canon 1725, n. 3.
[64] Canon 371.

alter ego of the bishop, but only in judicial matters, is not restricted in the exercise of his jurisdiction. The Code itself makes this provision,[65] and permits him to continue in his office, even during an interregnum.[66] If the law does not take away the power of the *Officialis* in this case, *a fortiori* he retains all his powers, when his bishop becomes suspended. To have his jurisdiction revoked, this fact must be clearly and directly intimated to him. Only upon its receipt does the revocation become effective.[67] Hence, he may continue to perform those acts of delegation, which are called for in a judicial trial. With regard to the Promoter of Justice and the Defender of the Bond, they, like the *Officialis*, continue in office, during the bishop's suspension *ab officio*, if they have been elected for the universality of affairs. Again, the law makes this provision.[68] Pastors, too, remain in office, for they have ordinary power, and likewise an office in the strict sense.[69]

This principle must always be borne in mind, that a cleric suspended *ab officio*, before the issuance of a declaratory or condemnatory sentence, may validly delegate others, but not licitly, unless there has been a legitimate request on the part of the faithful, or a grave and just cause urges such an action. Whether one illicitly delegated may lawfully exercise jurisdiction is controverted. Cappello[70] claims, that it is probable such an exercise of jurisdiction would be licit.

Cardinals under the suspension *ab officio* may not exercise their right to grant indulgences, to hear confessions, to absolve and to delegate others to absolve from censures.[71] The only exception is the provision of canon 239, § 1, n. 2. But here it is not the Cardinal giving faculties to the confessor of his choice, but the law.

What has been said of the cardinal applies equally to the bishop. He, too, could not licitly grant indulgences, before a sentence,

[65] Canon 1573, § 6.
[66] Canon 1590, § 1.
[67] Canons 207; 192, § 3, n. 2; Vermeersch-Creusen, *Epitome*, I, n. 270.
[68] Canon 1590.
[69] Canons 183, § 2; 208.
[70] *De Censuris*, n. 155.
[71] Canon 239, § 1, n. 1, 24.

nor validly, after a sentence.[72] He may not hear the confessions of his subjects, except in accordance with the norms of law.[73] Neither may he absolve nor may he delegate others to absolve from censures. He, too, has the right to choose a confessor, who then receives faculties from the law to absolve the bishop and his *entourage* from any censure of suspension.

Another effect of the suspension *ab officio* is the prohibition to exercise the active voice in canonical elections. Those under censure of suspension *ab officio,* after a sentence can not validly cast a vote in a canonical election. Before a sentence a cleric suspended *ab officio* may validly cast a vote and the election can not be annulled. If the electors are thus suspended the election is valid, because suspension as such in no way interfers with one's right to vote. It is only when the suspension is medicinal and there is also present the added circumstance of a declaratory or a condemnatory sentence, that votes by electors laboring under a suspension of this kind, are null. The election is valid unless it is evident that the candidate lacks the required votes to give him a title to the office.[74]

In papal elections, cardinals, suspended *ab officio,* even though after a sentence, may cast a valid vote. But, it must be understood, that this provision holds only for the election itself.[75]

Another important question worth considering is the *Missa pro populo,* which every pastor is bound to say. It is not only a personal but also a real obligation.[76] Under the suspension *ab*

72 Canon 349, § 2, n. 2.

73 Canons 881, § 2; 2284; 2261.

74 Canon 167.

75 "Nullus Cardinalium, cuiuslibet excommunicationis, suspensionis, interdicti aut alius ecclesiastici impedimenti praetextu vel causa a Summi Pontificis electione activa et passiva excludi ullo modo potest; quas quidem censuras et excommunicationes ad effectum huiusmodi electionis tantum, illis alias in suo robore permansuris, suspendimus".—Constitutio Pii pp. X, *Vacante Sede Apostolica,* 25 Decembris 1904, tit. II, c. I, n. 29—*Codex Iuris Canonici,* docum. I.

76 "Certum et extra dubitationem positum esse videtur, Parochus ad applicationem Missae pro suis fidelibus divino iure teneri . . . hujusmodi porro Parochi obligationem personalem esse Canonistae et Theologi tradunt . . ."—

officio, even though it is a censure, the pastor has a reason to depute another to fulfill this obligation for him. However, since the censure depends upon his will for its cessation, in as far as he repents, his change of will becomes even more urgent, in the face of the obligation to say the *Missa pro populo*.

A very helpful principle to obviate difficulties and to secure one's good name, is the provision of canon 2232, § 1. Should the pastor's refraining from Mass be the occasion of scandal or should his good name be endangered, he may under this circumstance lay aside the observance of the suspension *latae sententiae*, whether this be a censure or a vindictive penalty, as long as no declaratory sentence has been pronounced. Furthermore, no one can urge the observance of such a penalty in the external forum, unless the suspension is the effect of a notorious crime.

Before continuing with the presentation of the elements of canon 2279, it is noteworthy to state, that the different species of suspension mentioned in this canon are not exhaustively enumerated. They are the ones most frequently used in the law, but in no way do they exclude other forms of suspension.

Furthermore, it must be remarked that in the use of the forms designated by the Code, the presumption is always, that the superior intends all the effects defined in the law. Whatever formula the superior employs, those effects follow which the Code specifically indicates, no matter what the superior may intend in inflicting a certain defined suspension.

SUSPENSION *a iurisdictione.* A consideration of the partial effects of the suspension *ab officio* lends a better understanding of all the elements of this penalty. Both constituents of the suspension *ab officio* have already been seen. They are concerned with the power of orders and the power of jurisdiction. Accordingly, the Code in canon 2279, § 2 divides the total suspension *ab officio* into the partial suspension *ab ordine* and *a iurisdictione.* The first of these two partial suspensions to be given consideration will be the suspension *a iurisdictione.*

S.C.C., *Claromonten.*, 9 apr. 1881—*Fontes*, n. 4252. St. Alphonsus, *Theologia Moralis*, VI, n. 326; canons 466; 306; 339, § 4.

This type of penalty embraces every species of jurisdiction, whether ordinary, delegated, judicial or voluntary, because the word *iurisdictio* has a general import. For the same reason, too, it may be said that the suspension includes the jurisdiction of both the internal and external forum.[77]

In speaking of the suspension *a iurisdictione* care must be taken to keep in mind the distinction between jurisdiction strictly so-called and administration. The jurisdiction, as embraced by the penalty, affects executive acts alone, namely, the making of laws, the inflicting of penalties, the dispensing from laws, the remitting and absolving of penalties, etc. Yet, one must not infer that administration is totally excluded. There is a kind of administration which is executive by nature, as for example, the alienating of property, the making of investments, etc. This type of administration falls under the bann of this suspension because it is an exercise of jurisdiction. The administration which is excluded, however, does not deal with executive acts, but solely with the exercise of the power of orders. Consequently, a pastor suspended *a iurisdictione,* while he may not administer ecclesiastical property nor hear confessions, because these entail jurisdiction, he may nevertheless baptize and administer Holy Viaticum and Extreme Unction. Similarly, a bishop thus suspended may not confer offices and benefices, approve confessors, grant dimissorial letters, or inflict penalties, because these entail acts of jurisdiction. He may, however, ordain, consecrate and confirm. In a word, he may perform any act which does not demand jurisdiction.

This was a mooted question before the Code. Lega[78] and Suarez maintained, that the obvious concept of jurisdiction adopted by Canon Law embraced all power both executive and administrative, annexed to an office.[79] D'Annibale[80] sponsored the common opinion of today, and held for a distinction.[81]

[77] Canons 196; 197; 201, § 2, § 3; 202, § 1, § 2, § 3.

[78] *De Delictis et Poenis,* editio altera, n. 187.

[79] *De Censuris,* V, Disp. XXVI, c. IV, n. 16: ". . . ubi enim iurisdictio est de substantia actus, ut est in sola absolutione sacramentali, actus erit nullus si fiat cum tali suspensione, quia deest potestas necessaria ad valorem ejus.

The case might arise, where a bishop says to a pastor; "I suspend you from your diocesan faculties". What is the extent of this suspension? At first glance it might seem that after such a suspension the pastor could not hear confessions or grant dispensations over which he has jurisdiction in his pastoral office. This, however, is not the case. It must not be forgotten that the pastor has ordinary power to hear confessions. Hence, this suspension affects only those powers which the pastor does not possess by virtue of his office. Thus, in virtue of his pastoral office which remains intact when he is merely suspended from the diocesan faculties, a pastor can continue to hear the confessions of his subjects within or without his parochial limits, and use his ordinary power for the granting of dispensations.[82] To curtail the pastor's ordinary power the bishop would have to invoke the suspension *ab officio*. This may have been the intention of the bishop in issuing the suspension. But, since penal laws must be interpreted strictly, no matter what the unexpressed intention of the one who inflicts the punishment only those effects, follow which the suspension indicates, neither more nor less.

Again, the matter of assistance at marriage must be considered in connection with the suspension *a iurisdictione*. It has been seen that assistance at marriage is not properly jurisdictional,[83] but

Ubi autem fuerit iurisdictio de iustitia actus (ut sic dicam) erit prohibitus ne licite fiat, factus tamen validus erit. Sic peccabit parochus suspensus quaelibet sacramenta ministrando suis ovibus ut ordinarius pastor, et episcopus suspensus conferendo ordines suis subditis, quia non solum potestate ordinis, sed etiam iurisdictionis utitur . . ."

[80] *Summula*, I, n. 380, note 13: "Quod mihi durum videtur, quia actus huiusmodi [Episcopum suspensum concedere dimissorias ad ordines et parochum solemniter baptizare et ungere aegrotos] lata significatione iurisdictionis esse dicuntur."

[81] Vermeersch-Creusen, *Epitome*, III, n. 483; Chelodi, *Ius Poenale*, n. 43; Cappello, *De Censuris*, n. 499.

[82] Canons 873, § 1; 1245, § 1; 1044; 1045.

[83] Kober, *Die Suspension*, p. 103, note 4:—"Die pfarrliche Assistenz bei Abschliessung der Ehe ist kein Ausfluss der Jurisdiction, daher ist die vor einem suspendirten Pfarrer eingegangene Ehe gültig, aber sowohl für diesen als such die Nupturienten sündhaft, wenn sie vom Vorhandensein der Strafe Kenntniss hatten."

rather an act of a qualified witness. Cappello[84] asks the question: "Who will say that a witness as such exercises jurisdiction?"

The norms given under the suspension *ab officio* can not be applied here for the suspension *a iurisdictione*. By his office a pastor becomes competent to assist at a marriage. Once the rights of the office are suspended, the right also to assist at marriages suffers a prohibition. With regard to jurisdiction it is different. The suspension *a iurisdictione* is concerned with jurisdictional acts properly so-called. Therefore, all acts which are not properly an exercise of jurisdiction do not fall within the prohibition of the suspension. Hence, a pastor suspended *a iurisdictione* can *per se*, according to Cappello,[85] validly assist at a mariage, even after a declaratory or condemnatory sentence has been pronounced. The reason is, because assistance at marriage is not an act of jurisdiction and, also, because canon 1095, § 1, n. 1 explicitly refers only to the suspension *ab officio*. The disjunctive wording of the canon *nisi per sententiam fuerint excommunicati vel interdicti vel suspensi ab officio*, implies that the penalties disqualifying a pastor and others are listed in their completeness. Vermeersch-Creusen[86] and De Meester[87] seem to be of the opposite opinion and claim that the right to assist at a marriage is lost when there is question of a suspension from jurisdiction with the added circumstance of a declaratory or condemnatory sentence. It is, however, difficult to see how a pastor under these circumstances could be guilty of an invalid act when the act itself is not jurisdictional. The opinion of these eminent canonists seems to go beyond the provisions of canon 1095, § 1, n. 1.

An objection might be based on the fact that although assistance at marriage be not an act of jurisdiction, yet it is governed by the principles of delegation. This objection is destitute of intrinsic

[84] *De Censuris*, n. 499.

[85] *De Sacramentis*, III, n. 662.

[86] Epitome, II, n. 392.

[87] *Compendium*, III, pars 2a, n. 1782:—"Invalide assistit parochus suspensus (a iurisdictione) post sententiam condemnatoriam aut declaratoriam, ex can. 1095, § 1, n. 1."

value. The only reason the act of assistance at marriage is governed by the principles of delegation is, because such an act bears some similarity to jurisdiction, in the sense that the capacity for its performance is obtained by virtue of an office and may be transmitted to another.

If a bishop suspended a priest from assisting at a marriage, the latter's violation of this suspension would render the assistance at the mariage illicit, but not invalid. The illicitness would be brought about by the fact that the pastor disobeyed the mandate of the bishop. In reference to this question, Benedict XIV remarks that if the assistance is undertaken, the marriage is valid.[88] When the marriage is celebrated before the pastor, all the requisites prescribed by the council of Trent have been placed, hence there is no question of invalidity. The prohibition of the bishop is for the licitness and not the validity.[89]

The question whether or not preaching falls under the prohibition of a suspension *a iurisdictione* is a disputed one. Cappello[90] and Cerato[91] assert, that a cleric suspended from jurisdiction may exercise his office of preaching. Augustine, on the contrary, denies this.[92] In another section, he claims that preaching is an act emanating primarily from jurisdiction.[93] The better opinion seems to be that preaching is not an exercise of jurisdiction. Ordinarily, jurisdiction is the power to govern. Then again, the right to preach is given to the deacon at his ordination. To exercise this right he needs a positive deputation from a superior, either by a particular faculty or by the grant of an office. This faculty, it appears, is not a grant of jurisdiction, but a kind of authoritative act similar to that granted by a superior to an exorcist in order that he may exercise his right in public. Since, however, the question is disputed and the whole affair is *in odiosis*, therefore, the practical re-

88 *De Synodo Dioecesana*, XII, c. V, n. 2.

89 Gasparri, *Tractatus Canonicus De Matrimonio*, editio nova, II, n. 973; Cappello, *De Sacramentis*, III, n. 662.

90 *De Censuris*, n. 499.

91 *Censurae Vigentes*, n. 104.

92 *Commentary*, VIII, 221.

93 *Commentary*, VIII, 354.

sult is that a priest suspended *a iurisdictione* may continue to preach.

SUSPENSION *a divinis.* Prior to the Code the suspension *ab officio* merely considered the jurisdictional powers of the cleric, whereas today it includes not only jurisdiction but also orders. The suspensions which in the old law pertained to the suspension *ab ordine* are now considered as partial suspensions *ab officio.* The first is the suspension *a divinis.*

The Code brings to an end the uncertainty which existed in pre-Code law concerning the content of the suspension *a divinis.*[94] It was not infrequent, according to Hinschius,[95] that this punishment was confused with the suspension *ab ordine,* which from the fifteenth century was looked upon as signifying a curtailment of all the rights flowing from orders.

Today, the law is definite and accurate concerning the effects of this suspension. All rights flowing from sacred orders received through a valid ordination, and all rights pertaining to an exercise of sacred orders arising from an Apostolic privilege, fall within the scope of the suspension *a divinis.* Rights relative to an act of jurisdiction are not touched by this suspension. Therefore, a cleric suspended *a divinis* may exercise any act of jurisdiction which does not simultaneously require an actual exercise of orders. Hence, a bishop thus suspended may delegate to others the power to absolve from sins, though he himself may not exercise this right.

All exercise of major orders, therefore, is forbidden. Canon 2279, § 2, n. 2 in stating the effects uses the terminology *per sacram ordinationem.* According to canon 949 the words *sacra ordinatio* include in their signification the presbyterate, the diaconate and the subdiaconate. Although the canon makes no reference to the episcopate, there is no doubt that *a fortiori,* the exercise of this order is also included, since the more common opinion of theologians and canonists is that the episcopate is the complement and the extension of the presbyterate.[96] Consequently, any one in episco-

94 Cerato, *Censurae Vigentes,* n. 104.
95 *Kirchenrecht,* V, 596.
96 Gasparri, *De Sacra Ordinatione,* I, n. 23.

pal orders who is suspended *a divinis* may not consecrate bishops, ordain to any order, celebrate the divine Sacrifice or administer any of the sacraments or sacramentals. Likewise, a major cleric is forbidden the exercise of all acts of orders which he enjoys in virtue of an Apostolic indult, such as the conferring of first tonsure or of the minor orders,[97] the administration of Confirmation,[98] the bestowal of reserved blessings, the consecration of chalices, patens and altars.[99]

This Apostolic privilege may be derived either from the grant of a particular indult or from the commitment of the common law itself. By virtue of the privilege conceded by the Code, Abbots who have legitimately received the abbatial blessing,[100] Prefects and Vicars Apostolic, and Prelates *nullius*[101] even though lacking the episcopal character, may, within the limits of their territory, give first tonsure and minor orders to their subjects and others with proper dimissorial letters. Thus, if any of these are suspended *a divinis,* this privilege is denied them.

Since the suspension *a divinis* forbids the administration of the sacraments and sacramentals, the prescription of canon 2261 must be observed. Even though canon 2261 deals with the effects of excommunication, it is nevertheless applicable here, precisely because there is this point in common between an excommunicated priest and a priest suspended *a divinis,* namely, that both are barred from the administration of the sacraments and sacramentals. Before a declaratory or a condemnatory sentence, therefore, a cleric suspended *a divinis* may not licitly administer the sacraments and sacramentals, unless legitimately requested by the faithful. It appears, that this provision does not prohibit the priest to show himself ready to hear confessions on Saturdays and feast days, to celebrate Mass on Sundays and Holy Days, provided there is no scandal. During these days of daily Communion and daily Mass,

97 Canons 294, § 2; 323, § 2; 951.

98 Canon 782, § 2.

99 Canons 294, § 2; 323, § 2; 1147, § 1.

100 Canon 964, n. 1.

101 Canon 957, § 2.

it would seem, that even on days throughout the week, he may show himself in readiness, because the petition of the faithful need not be explicit. An implicit or a reasonably presumed one suffices. Such is had whenever the good of souls demands the celebration of Mass, the administration of the sacraments, or the preparation or administration of the sacramentals and there is present no other minister besides the suspended priest.[102] St. Alphonsus says, that it would even be licit for the faithful to attend the Mass celebrated by a suspended priest, provided there is no scandal.[103] Moreover, if there is danger of losing his good name, a priest who has incurred a *latae sententiae* penalty, whether it be medicinal or vindictive in its nature, may nevertheless in the external forum act as if he were not under such a canonical sanction, as long as a declaratory sentence has not been added.[104] Since this ruling is made in general terms, it includes the case of suspension as well as the other *latae sententiae* censures and vindictive penalties. Hence, a priest suspended *a divinis* may still say Mass, hear confessions and administer the other sacraments and sacramentals, if in his case the danger of a loss of his good name is really to be feared.

After a declaratory or condemnatory sentence has been pronounced, however, only the faithful who are in danger of death may ask from such a suspended priest the benefit of sacramental absolution and also the ministration of the other sacraments and the sacramentals, if qualified priests are not at hand.[105] Even in the latter circumstance, namely, should there be present a non-suspended priest, the one suspended *a divinis*, when requested by the person in danger of death, can exercise his priestly powers.[106]

The general principle is, that since suspension *a divinis* forbids every act of sacred orders, it forbids also acts of jurisdiction intimately connected with the exercise of these orders, such as the act of sacramental absolution. The power of orders and the power of

[102] Hyland, *Excommunication*, p. 93; Cfr. Vermeersch-Creusen, *Epitome*, III, n. 463; Sole, *De Delictis et Poenis*, n. 220; Cappello, *De Censuris*, n. 148.

[103] *Theologia Moralis*, VII, n. 313.

[104] Canon 2232, § 1.

[105] Canon 2261, § 3.

[106] Canons 882; 884.

jurisdiction can not be separated in sacramental absolutions. Consequently, from canon 2284, an act of absolution performed after the issuance of a declaratory or condemnatory sentence is invalid, unless there is present the circumstance of danger of death.

What has been stated thus far concerning the suspension *a divinis* applies equally to the other suspensions which forbid the administration of the sacraments in one way or another. Besides the suspension *a divinis,* the suspensions which produce this effect may be enumerated as follows: the general suspension, the suspension *ab officio,* the suspension *ab ordinibus, a sacris ordinibus,* the suspension from a certain and definite order to be exercised, the suspension from conferring a certain and definite order, the suspension from a certain and definite ministry, when this is concerned with an order, the suspension from the pontifical order, the suspension from a determined office, when in virtue of an office the administration of the sacraments is permitted.

SUSPENSION *ab ordinibus.* The suspension *ab ordinibus* differs from the suspension *a divinis* in this, that it excludes in its prohibition those acts of orders, whose exercise depends on an Apostolic indult. Only those rights are forbidden, which flow from a valid ordination,[107] even though in their exercise, there may be required an act of jurisdiction, as for example, sacramental absolution. Thus, a priest enjoying the privilege to confer Confirmation, even though suspended *ab ordinibus,* may licitly and validly administer this sacrament. Likewise, an Abbot or a Prefect Apostolic, who lacks the episcopal character, may give first tonsure and minor orders, because this is considered an Apostolic privilege conceded by the Code itself.[108]

Since the terminology used by the Code, in reference to this suspension is general, the doubt arises, as to whether minor orders are embraced under the word *ordinibus.* Cerato[109] settles the doubt, in accordance with the general principles of law, when he states, that no distinction is made by the law, and, therefore, not only an

[107] Canon 2279, § 2, n. 3.
[108] Canons 782; 964, n. 1; 957, § 2.
[109] *Censurae Vigentes,* n. 104.

exercise of major orders but also an exercise of minor orders is forbidden by the suspension. A Coronata,[110] D'Annibale,[111] De Meester[112] make a distinction, and claim, that only those acts of minor orders are included, which are exclusively proper to a cleric and which can not be exercised by a layman. Cappello[113] with Cerato has no doubt, that all minor orders are included without exception, from the significant terminology used by the Code, in distinguishing the three kinds of suspension, namely, the suspension *a divinis*, the suspension *ab ordinibus*, the suspension *a sacris ordinibus*. Moreover, he claims, that a cleric is not forbidden the exercise of minor orders as a layman but solely as a cleric because suspension is proper to clerics alone. The opinion of Cappello, from its intrinsic value is, therefore, more probable; hence, it will be licit to conclude, that all the minor orders are included in the suspension *ab ordinibus*.

SUSPENSION *a sacris ordinibus*. Similar to the suspension *a divinis*, this suspension *a sacris ordinibus* forbids every exercise of orders flowing from each of the major orders,[114] namely, the episcopate, the presbyterate, the diaconate and the subdiaconate.[115] It does not, however, forbid the exercise of minor orders or the exercise of delegated ministries; neither does it forbid the exercise of jurisdiction, provided this exercise does not require an act of sacred orders. Furthermore, since the conferring of an order is, without doubt, an exercise of orders, this fact is also forbidden by this suspension and by all others which forbid the exercise of orders.[116] From this it follows that a bishop can not licitly confer an order, not even tonsure, if he is suspended *a divinis, ab ordinibus, a sacris ordinibus, ab ordine pontificali*, or *a pontificalibus*.[117] The con-

110 *Institutiones Iuris Canonici*, IV, n. 1806.

111 *Summula*, I, n. 381.

112 *Compendium*, III, pars 2 a, n. 1782.

113 *De Censuris*, n. 499.

114 Canon 2279, § 2, n. 4.

115 Canons 949; 950.

116 A Coronata, *Institutiones Iuris Canonici*, IV, n. 1806; Cocchi, *Commentarium*, V, (De Delictis et Poenis), n. 103; Cappello, *De Censuris*, n. 499.

117 Chelodi, *Ius Poenale*, n. 43.

ferring of tonsure is forbidden, because *per se* this pertains to one in episcopal orders; this would be, indeed, an exercise of a major order.

A question of interest which might be discussed here is one having reference to the imposition of hands at an ordination ceremony. Could a priest suspended *a sacris ordinibus,* or *a divinis,* or *ab ordinibus* impose hands licitly and validly? Since the imposition of hands of the assistant priests at an ordination ceremony is merely a sign of election and association in the same ministry, as Gasparri claims,[118] and, therefore, has no intrinsic bearing on the conferring of the order, it would seem that a suspended priest may licitly and validly impose hands. Should the knowledge of the fact that he is suspended be the occasion of scandal, then, certainly, he would not be permitted to impose hands. The Church does not regard this ceremony in question even as pertaining to the integrity of the sacrament, so much so that, should the imposition of hands by the assistant priests be omitted altogether, the ceremony is not to be supplied.[119]

SUSPENSION *a certo et definito ordine exercendo.* This suspension, as the terminology indicates, prohibits every act of a specified order, as for example, the acts proper to the priesthood or the diaconate. It forbids one, therefore, to confer the order determined by the suspension. Furthermore, it prohibits the reception of a higher order, for instance, a suspended deacon may not present himself for the presbyterate. Finally, if a suspended cleric should disregard the prohibition and nevertheless receive the higher order, he may not, by virtue of the suspension, exercise this order.[120]

A consideration of the extent of the prohibitions comprised in this suspension naturally raises the question of the lawful exercise

[118] *De Sacra Ordinatione,* II, n. 1080;—" . . . nam presbyteri manus imponunt solum in signum cooptationis et societatis ad simile ministerium . . . etc."

[119] S.C. de Prop. Fide., 6, aug. 1840:—"Utrum supplendae sint caeremoniae impositionis manuum sacerdotum, quae in ordinatione sacerdotali ob distantiam missionariorum omissae fuerunt? Negative."—Coll. S.C.P.F., n. 1195.

[120] Canon 2279, § 2, n. 5; Cappello, *De Censuris,* n. 500; Chelodi, *Ius Poenale,* n. 43.

of an order, which is either higher than the one from which the cleric has been suspended, or lower than that specified by the suspension. According to Gasparri, some of the old authors thought that a cleric suspended from a lower order was also suspended from the higher orders which he possessed. Others taught that one was suspended from the higher orders only when their exercise included an act of an inferior order from which the cleric was suspended.[121] Thus, for example, a priest suspended from the diaconate could hear confessions, administer Extreme Unction and assist at marriages, but he could not celebrate Mass, because in the Mass he must read the gospel, which function is really a part of the office of a deacon.[122]

D'Annibale claimed that this suspension could not be so extended by canon law as to comprise superior orders, but he likewise maintained that in virtue of the natural law, a cleric suspended from inferior orders could not lawfully exercise his superior orders.[123] To the first statement of D'Annibale—that suspension is not to be so extended by canon law as to comprise superior orders—Gasparri lends his support, for a penal law must ever be interpreted strictly.[124] Hence, one suspended from the subdiaconate is not simultaneously suspended from the diaconate or the priesthood. Moreover, when an act of a superior order includes an act of an inferior order from which the cleric has been suspended, for instance, the saying of Mass, wherein occurs the reading of the epistle which properly belongs to the office of a subdeacon, then that act of the superior order is not prohibited by this particular suspension. Whilst the reading of the epistle in Mass is, indeed, an act proper to the office of subdeacon, yet, precisely because it constitutes a part of the celebration of Mass which in its entirety is proper to the office of priesthood, the reading of the epistle in Mass remains as much the function of a priest as of a subdeacon. Consequently, if a priest were suspended from the exercise of the subdiaconate, he

121 *De Sacra Ordinatione*, I, n. 149.
122 Schmalzgrueber, lib. V, tit. XXXIX, n. 293.
123 *Summula*, I, n. 306.
124 *De Sacra Ordinatione*, I, n. 149.

could nevertheless lawfully say Mass, and therefore, read the epistle, for he is suspended only in so far as the office of subdeaconship enters into the celebration of Mass. To the second statement of D'Annibale—that in virtue of the natural law a cleric suspended from inferior orders could not lawfully exercise his superior orders—Gasparri replies that it does not seem absurd for one who is forbidden the exercise of an inferior order still to retain permission to exercise the acts of an order of superior rank. But, he fully concedes the prohibition of the natural law for the reception of a higher order, in line with the statements of the Roman Law Digest,[125] for anyone whose unworthiness is manifest with regard to an inferior order, because such a one reveals a still greater unworthiness in relation to a superior order. He concludes by saying that there is no parity between the exercise of an order already received and the reception of a higher order.

The opinion of Gasparri is the law of the Code today.[126] Wherefore, it can be said, that a cleric suspended from a specified order may exercise all the other orders he possesses, even though these are above or below the order prohibited by the suspension.

A bishop who is suspended merely from the episcopal order may exercise the ordinary functions of the priesthood, as exercisable by a priest, such as, the celebration of Mass without pontificals and the hearing of confessions. He may not, however, licitly consecrate bishops or ordain priests. Should he be suspended from the sacerdotal order, he may exercise and confer all other orders to the exclusion of the priesthood. With regard to a priest who has been suspended from the priesthood, he may not say Mass, hear confessions, or impart those blessings reserved to priests alone. He may, however, give those blessings, which are the privilege of the deacon consequent in some cases upon the permission, at least pre-

[125] D., (1.9) 4: "Qui indignus est inferiore ordine, indignior est superiore." D., (48.22) 7.22: "Est enim perquam rediculum, eum, qui minoribus poenae causa prohibitus sit, ad maiores adspirare."

[126] Canon 2279, § 2, n. 5:—"Suspensio *a certo et definito ordine exercendo*, omnem actum ordinis designati; suspensus autem prohibetur insuper eundem ordinem conferre et superiorem recipere receptumque post suspensionem exercere."

sumed, of the Ordinary or pastor. Thus the suspended priest could bless the paschal candle;[127] he could bless the grave at the time of a funeral;[128] he could distribute Holy Communion,[129] and solemnly administer the Sacrament of Baptism.[130] He may not be promoted to the episcopate; and should he receive the episcopal consecration, he may not perform acts proper to the episcopal order. Then again, should a priest be suspended from the diaconate, he may not sing the gospel at a solemn high Mass. He may, however, expose the Blessed Sacrament and distribute Holy Communion, because, although these acts are proper to a deacon, they belong equally to the priestly order.

The question may now be asked, whether or not the prohibition to ascend to a higher order is restricted to the suspension *a certo et definito ordine exercendo,* or whether it applies also to the suspension *a divinis, ab ordinibus, a sacris ordinibus, ab officio.* It is certain that this prohibition applies in the case of a general suspension, because canon 2283 conjointly with canon 2265, § 1, n. 3 expressly states that such a suspended cleric may not be promoted to orders. As to the other suspensions, Cappello[131] and Chelodi[132] are of the opinion, that there is a doubt. Chelodi, however, would be inclined to think that from intrinsic reasoning the prohibition to ascend to a higher order would apply equally to the suspensions *a divinis, ab ordinibus, a sacris ordinibus* and *ab officio.* But, he maintains, since the rules of strict interpretation in penal matters and the general principle of always favoring the delinquent as expressed in canons 19, 20 and 2219, § 3 may not be overlooked, consequently, the prohibition to ascend to a higher order is the effect of the suspension *a certo et definito ordine exercendo* alone, and any violation of this prohibition would induce an irregularity.[133]

127 *Missale Romanum,* Sabbato Sancto.

128 *Rituale Romanum,* (1929), tit. VI, c. 3 et c. 7 in fine.

129 Canon 845, § 2.

130 Canon 741.

131 *De Censuris,* n. 499.

132 *Ius Poenale,* n. 43.

133 Canon 985, n. 7; Chelodi, *Ius Poenale,* n. 43, p. 56, note 2.

The opinion of Gasparri is the correct one, namely, that suspension in itself does not forbid the reception of a higher order *de iure ecclesiastico,* but, the one suspended is unfit for the reception of higher orders *de iure naturae.* It is because of this latter fact, as he asserts, that every suspension forbids the reception of a higher order.[134]

If all suspensions, with the exception of the general suspension and the suspension *a certo et definito ordine exercendo,* do not specifically mention this prohibition, the practical conclusion from the present law of the Code is that prescinding from the two suspensions which expressly mention the prohibition, a cleric in ascending to a higher order would not incur an irregularity. There is first of all no express mention of this prohibition,—penal laws are to be interpreted strictly—and secondly there arises from the whole question a doubt of law. This fact, however, can not be overlooked, namely, whether or not an irregularity is incurred in the violation of suspensions other than the suspension *a certo et definito ordine exercendo* and the general suspension, the prohibition of the natural law remains—that by virtue of this law a suspended cleric is unworthy to ascend to a higher order, and because of this fact is forbidden.

Superiors are under obligation of not promoting unworthy clerics to orders. Adequate provisions for administrative rather than penal measures are clearly indicated by canons 211, § 2, 330 and 973, § 1, § 3. Canon 2222, § 2 also grants the lawful superior preventive power. It obliges him to make use of this power in the case of a probable crime and of a crime against which criminal action can not be brought on acount of prescription. By a probable crime is meant one which can not be fully proven, yet is testified to by, at least, one credible witness or known to the superior extrasacramentally. The superior must refuse to promote to orders a cleric whose worthiness is not evident. Certainly, there can not be any doubt as to the unworthiness of a cleric who is laboring under a suspension. Hence, superiors must take care not to promote such clerics to orders.

134 *De Sacra Ordinatione,* I, nn. 149-152.

SUSPENSION *a certo et definito ordine conferendo.* The effects, as enumerated by canon 2279, § 2, n. 6 were already considered more probable by Gasparri before the Code.[135] They are confined to a determined order and no other, even though the right to confer this order had been received by a special apostolic indult.[136] It must not be forgotten that the canon speaks of the conferring of a definite order and not the exercise thereof. Therefore, a bishop suspended from conferring the priesthood is not forbidden the exercise of this order.[137]

Should a cleric knowingly receive an order from a bishop who has been suspended, after a declaratory or condemnatory sentence, from conferring it, he incurs *ipso facto* a suspension *a divinis* reserved to the Holy See.[138] As long as the orders were not validly conferred, there can be no question of a suspension *a divinis,* for the reception of invalid orders is tantamount to the reception of no orders, and the non-reception of orders precludes the very presence of powers or faculties against which any kind of suspension might be invoked. The crime of the recipient of orders under the circumstances delineated is constituted not by the passive fact of a valid administration but by the active element of his formal cooperation in the act of receiving orders when forbidden to do so.[139]

SUSPENSION *a certo et definito ministerio vel officio.* A ministry, in the sense of the canon, is the exercise of some obligation or right. The words *office* and *ministry* are convertible and at times are used indiscriminately, because, in the last analysis they generally refer to one and the same duty. Thus, one can speak of the office of confessor and also of the ministry of hearing confessions. It can be stated that it makes little difference which term is

[135] "Episcopus suspensus a conferendo uno ordine, e.g. subdiaconatu, certe potest conferre gradus inferiores; sed probabilius potest quoque conferre gradus superiores, e.g. diaconatum, presbyteratum, etc."—*De Sacra Ordinatione,* I, n. 149.

[136] Blat, *Commentarium,* V, n. 108.

[137] A Coronata, *Institutiones Iuris Canonici,* IV, n. 1809.

[138] Canon 2372.

[139] A Coronata, *Institutiones Iuris Canonici,* IV, n. 2156.

used, because, when there is question of a suspension, only those effects follow which the law prescribes as a definite penalty.

This suspension under consideration interdicts the exercise of all rights proper to a determined ministry, as for example, the hearing of confession, preaching, etc. As to the term *office* which is found in the title, the same norms of interpretation are to be followed which were used when the limits of a suspension *ab officio* were considered above. Consequently, every form of office, whether in the strict or broad sense, is circumscribed by this type of suspension.[140] If a confessor, therefore, is suspended from his office, he may not hear confessions nor may he exercise those acts connected with the hearing of confessions, as the act of commuting vows[141] or of dispensing from matrimonial impediments in occult cases, etc.[142] If a pastor is suspended from his pastorate, he is then forbidden the exercise of all those acts which he can and must place in virtue of his ordinary power.[143] He may not without the proper diocesan faculties hear the confessions of people within his parish or of his parishioners outside of his parish; he may not assist at marriages without a special delegation; he may not preach, baptize solemnly nor dispense from the laws of abstinence and fast in his parish, for all of these ministries are integral and constitutive parts of his rights and obligations as a pastor. But, he may administer his parochial benefice and enjoy the fruits and revenues thereof, if he has vicariously attended to all the pastoral obligations through the employment of a properly designated substitute.[144]

SUSPENSION *ab ordine pontificali.* This type of suspension has as its effects the prohibition to exercise those acts which flow from the episcopal character, as distinct from the exercise of those rights which flow from the sacerdotal order or from episcopal jurisdiction.[145] Consequently, a bishop suspended *ab ordine pontifi-*

[140] Blat, *Commentarium,* V, n. 108.

[141] Canon 1314.

[142] Canons 1044; 1045.

[143] Canons 464; 462; 892.

[144] Cappello, *De Censuris,* n. 500; Cocchi, *Commentarium,* V, (De Delictis et Poenis), n. 103.

[145] Cocchi, *Commentarium,* V, (De Delictis et Poenis), n. 103.

cali is forbidden to confirm, to confer any of the orders, whether major or minor; he may not give first tonsure; nor may he consecrate altars, chalices or patens, etc.[146] He may, on the contrary, hear confessions, institute pastors, confer benefices and approve confessors. He is permitted, furthermore, to celebrate solemn Mass with the use of pontificals and even the pallium.[147]

The extent of the effects of the suspension *ab ordine pontificali* may be seen from an analogy with canon 2279, § 2, n. 3. In the latter canon, which is concerned with the suspension *ab ordinibus,* only those acts are forbidden which flow from a valid ordination to the exclusion of those which one enjoys by privilege. The suspension *ab ordine pontificali* affects acts which also flow from an order. The order, however, is specified as the episcopal order. Consequently, only those acts which are the direct outcome of episcopal consecration alone suffer a restriction in their exercise through this suspension. It can be said, therefore, that the suspension *ab ordine pontificali* does not affect priests and other prelates who lack the episcopal character, although they are empowered through an apostolic indult to perform certain sacred functions which are proper to the episcopal order. The only exception is the case in which a suspension of this kind is personally inflicted *ab homine* upon one who enjoys an apostolic privilege. The action of the superior in this case clearly shows that he wishes to restrict the exercise of the privilege.[148]

SUSPENSION *a pontificalibus.* If Thesaurus and Benedict XIV are correct in their inference that the exercise of pontificals embraces all acts proper to the episcopal order, then, there would be little difference between the preceding suspension *ab ordine pontificali* and the one now being discussed.[149] There is a difference

146 Canons 782, § 1; 950; 951; 1147, § 1.

147 Blat, *Commentarium,* V, n. 108; Cocchi, *Commentarium,* V, (De Delictis et Poenis), n. 103.

148 A Coronata, *Institutiones Iuris Canonici,* IV, n. 1811.

149 Benedict XIV, ep. *Ad audientiam,* 15, febr. 1753 § 8:—"Tertiam denique in collatione Tonsurae et Ordinum minorum, Pontificalia exerceri; id quod inficiari nemo potest, quemasmodum diligenter advertit Thesaurus in suo Tractatu *De Poenis Ecclesiasticis,* part. 2, verbo *Episcopus,* cap. 4, num. 3,

however. Canon 2279, § 2, n. 8 speaks of the episcopal order, and therefore, refers to all those acts which require, at least, *in se* the episcopal character. The present suspension as enuntiated by canon 2279, § 2, n. 9 is limited to the exercise of pontificals alone, according to the norm laid down in canon 337, § 2, where the law gives a definition of what is meant by the exercise of pontificals. It declares that to exercise pontificals is in law to perform sacred functions which according to liturgical rubrics always require the use of pontifical insignia, namely, the crosier and miter.

In speaking of the suspension *a pontificalibus*, one must be careful to distinguish between the exercise and the use of pontificals.[150] The use of pontificals spoken of in law signifies those concessions made to any prelate of wearing in specified functions some of the insignia proper to bishops.[151] These prelates may or may not be in episcopal orders. As long as they enjoy some privilege, whether by a particular indult or by common law, as for example, Cardinals,[152] Papal Legates,[153] Prelates *Nullius* and Abbots,[154] Bishops,[155] Metropolitans[156] and Prothonotaries Apostolic,[157] they may use pontificals.

According to the Constitution *Decet Romanos* of Pius VII under date of July 4, 1823, the pontificals common to all may be enumerated as follows: buskins, sandals, gloves, dalmatic, tunicle, ring

ubi recte observat, Pontificalium nomine, ad effectum, de quo nunc agimus, venire non modo quorumvis Ordinum, etiam Minorum collationem, sed etiam consecrationem Vasorum Ecclesiae, ac Virginum, et Chrismatis, necnon Sacramenti Confirmationis ministrationem, ac indumentorum, et Corporalium benedictionem . . . etc."—*Fontes*, n. 424.

150 Vermeersch-Creusen, Epitome, III, n. 483.

151 Goyeneche, *Commentarium pro Religiosis et Missionariis*, XVII (1936), 28.

152 Canons 239, § 1, n. 15; 240, § 3.

153 Canon 269, § 3.

154 Canon 325.

155 Canon 337, § 1, § 3.

156 Canon 274, n. 6.

157 Motu Proprio, *Inter multiplices*, 21 febr. 1905—*Fontes*, n. 665; Constitution Apostolica, *Ad incrementum decoris*, 15 aug. 1934—*AAS*, XXVI (1934), 497-521.

with one stone, pectoral cross without a stone and the miter.[158] The crosier, however, and the use of the throne and the baldachin, the seven candles and the deacons of honor are excepted.[159]

Canon 337, § 2 refers to the exercise of pontificals in functions which require the use thereof. These functions are: Pontifical Mass and Vespers, assistance at solemn Pontifical Mass and the Choral Office, the blessing of the Holy Oils, the conferring of orders, the consecration of bishops, the blessing of abbots, the blessing and consecration of virgins, the blessing and coronation of kings, the consecration of churches, altars and sacred vessels, the blessing of a corner-stone, a cemetery, and the reconciliation of churches and cemeteries, and the solemn administration of the sacrament of Confirmation.[160]

In order that the suspension *a pontificalibus* be effective, the hypothesis is always that the above mentioned functions are performed in solemn rite.[161] If they are exercised privately, then the rubrics do not insist on the use of pontificals, namely, the miter and crosier; hence, the one laboring under the suspension *a pontificalibus* would not violate the penalty. In order to incur the suspension, the cleric must have the right to use the crosier and the miter. This is the meaning of the suspension under consideration. It is the suspension from the exercise of pontificals at certain functions and not the suspension from the use of pontificals.

Is the use of the pallium also included in the suspension *a pontificalibus?* Although the pallium is a sign of jurisdiction

158 "Sub generico ornamentorum pontificalium nomine, quae ex privilegio Apostolica Sedis insignioribus capitulis quandoque concedit, intelliguntur dumtaxat, ex pluries decisis a sacra congregatione, caligae, sandalia, nec auro, nec argento ornata, sericae item chirothecae, dalmatica, tunicella, annulus cum unica gemma, crus pectoralis sine gemma, mitra simplex et tela alba cum sericis lancinus rubei coloris . . . Hisce omnibus uti poterit solummodo dignitas, canonicus, aut rector solemniter celebrans, nisi forte privilegium non omnis haec, sed aliqua dumtaxat insignia permittat."—*Bullarii Romani Continuatio,* tom. VIII pars 2a, MC., ad art. VII-IX, 2338.

159 Motu Proprio, *Inter multiplices,* I, ad 6—*Fontes,* n. 665.

160 *Caeremoniale Episcoporum et Pontificale Romanum,* I, c. XVII, n. 8; Cfr. S.C.C., *Monopolitana,* 9 febr. 1924—*AAS,* XVII (1925), 245-246.

161 Cappello, *De Censuris,* n. 500

alone,[162] still it is considered as belonging to those things which are classified as coming under the term, pontificals.[163] However, its use by a Metropolitan suspended *a pontificalibus* would not, in virtue of canons 2279, § 2, n. 9 and 337, § 2 induce an irregularity, because these canons refer to the use of the crosier and miter alone.

SUSPENSION *a beneficio*. The effects proper to this suspension are exhaustively enumerated in canon 2280, § 1. Wherefore, a cleric laboring under such a suspension, without losing the title to the benefice and the right to dwell or live in the residence thereof, is deprived of the fruits or income. He is, furthermore, given full liberty to administer the goods of the benefice, namely, to perform all the legal acts required by law for the administration, improvement and safeguarding of the property.[164] Unless a judicial sentence or extrajudicial decree takes away this right of administration and gives it to another, the suspended cleric may lease any lands and houses possessed by the benefice or sell any of its fruits; he may also act, personally or through a procurator, as defendant or plaintiff in court, concerning matters relative to the benefice.

As to the spiritual obligations of the beneficiary, it may be said that despite the suspension *a beneficio* he retains full exercise of his power of orders and jurisdiction. All of these obligations, proper to his office, such as the recitation of Divine Office, residence, care of souls, saying the *Missa pro populo* must be fulfilled by him without any remunerative salary, because the obligations do not arise from the enjoyment of the fruits but from the incumbency in the benefice.[165]

The right of the suspended cleric to live in the residence of the benefice, which he retains even after a declaratory or condemnatory sentence has been pronounced implies certain concessions which

[162] Vermeersch-Creusen, *Epitome*, I, n. 353.

[163] Ballerini-Palmieri, *Opus Theologicum Morale*, VII, n. 506: "Pontificalium nomine intelligitur usus auctoritativus insignium Pontificalium ut mitrae, baculi pastoralis et pallii." Cfr. Gasparri, *De Sacra Ordinatione*, I, n. 367.

[164] Canon 1476.

[165] Cfr. St. Alphonsus, *Theologia Moralis*, VII, n. 316.

are intimately connected with his habitation therein.[166] Whatever may be regarded as contributing to the ordinary conveniences and usual accommodations which make the rectory habitable for its clerical resident may also be safely recognized as included in his continued right to make the beneficial residence his place of dwelling. Such conveniences and accommodations include light, water, fuel, heat, gas, electricity and such furnishings as are necessary and useful for the beneficiary's offices and living rooms.[167] They likewise include the right to furnish his table with the necessary groceries and provisions and to procure the ministrations of a housekeeper to care for the domestic affairs of the beneficial residence.

To meet the expense which the enjoyment of these daily commodities and necessities entails the suspended beneficiary may draw upon the revenues of the benefice. It must be considerd, that such a use does not contravene the nature of the suspension *a beneficio,* which is to prohibit the enjoyment of the beneficial revenues, because the law allows the cleric to live in the residence of the benefice.

Should the sentence or decree take away the right to administer the benefice, then an administrator must be appointed to this office. His support must be drawn from the revenues due to the suspended cleric. What portion of these fruits he is to receive is to be determined by the bishop or the one who inflicted the suspension. As to the remainder of the revenues, according to the Council of Trent[168] and from analogy with canon 2381, n. 1,[169] these must be either given to the Ordinary or placed in the treasury of the benefice or distributed among the poor. There is no provision of law to serve as a norm in a situation of this kind, and therefore, through canon 20, the tenets of canon 2381, n. 1 may serve as a guide. It is not a question of extending a penal law but of setting down a rule of

166 Cfr. Augustine, *Commentary,* VIII, 225.

167 Cfr. Woywod, *A Practical Commentary on the Code of Canon Law,* II, n. 2122.

168 Sess., XXIII, *de ref.,* c. 1.—Mansi, XXXIII, 141.

169 "Eo ipso privatur omnibus fructibus sui beneficii vel officii pro rata illegitimae absentiae, eosque tradere debet Ordinario, qui ecclesiae vel alicui pio loco vel pauperibus distribuat."

jurisprudence. Hence, it would seem that the application of canon 2381, n. 1, in the present analogous case is perfectly in order.

The superior may also divide the total suspension *a beneficio* into various partial punishments, since there is a possibility of having different endowments constituting the dowry of the benefice. Accordingly, therefore, a cleric may be suspended from one class of revenues and be permitted the enjoyment of the rest; he may likewise be suspended from a third or possibly a half of the revenues. Whatever the superior wishes to be affected by the suspension he must clearly and expressly indicate.

With reference to the suspension from the administration of the benefice, in the present law, it seems, one could not correctly consider this a partial suspension *a beneficio,* because the effects of this latter suspension bear upon the enjoyment of revenues to the exclusion of administration. Were a cleric suspended from the administration of the benefice, this would rather be a suspension *a iurisdictione* than a partial suspension *a beneficio,* because administration of ecclesiastical goods is based on jurisdiction.

To become more conversant with the whole import of the suspension *a beneficio,* it would be well, first of all, to consider the definition of a benefice, as contained in the present law. According to canon 1409, a benefice, is a juridical entity, which is established or erected in perpetuity by the competent ecclesiastical authority, and which consists of a sacred office and the right to receive the revenues connected with the office or foundation.

In comparing the status of parishes in the United States with the above definition, it was for a time held uncertain after the promulgation of the Code whether these parishes were real benefices or not. Now, however, the matter is settled, because from a reply of Cardinal Gasparri, head of the Pontifical Commission for the Authentic Interpretation of the Canons of the Code, to the Apostolic Delegate of the United States, concerning the erection and status of parishes, it is clearly deducible that the parishes here in the United States are to be considered ecclesiastical benefices.[170]

[170] A Letter of the Most Rev. Apostolic Delegate to the Bishops of the United States, 10, Nov., 1922:—Bouscaren, *Canon Law Digest,* p. 149.

To the question, what fruits are prohibited by the suspension *a beneficio*, a general answer can not be given. One must consider the benefice and see from the decree of erection and from particular statutes and customs, what revenues *de facto* go to make up the endowment of a given benefice, because the dowries of benefices differ in different countries.

Before the Code, there was considerable dispute as to the exact beneficial revenues. Kober[171] claimed that stipends and stole fees belonged to the accidental revenues of the benefice but were not to be classified as belonging strictly to the beneficial dowry. Others admitted that the offerings of the faithful, imposed as a tax, could be considered as a real revenue of a benefice; but none held that the dowry was constituted of voluntary offerings alone.[172] As to choral distribution, Schmalzgrueber[173] maintained, that if these distributions were taken from the revenues of the benefice, they were included in the fruits of the benefice; not so, if they were taken from some particular foundation of the faithful.

Today, the Code leaves no doubt as to the fruits of a benefice. It considerably augments the notion of a beneficial endowment and includes all those disputed temporalities which were in question before its promulgation. Among these temporalities there can be those which are movable or immovable, corporeal or incorporeal, such as, hereditaments, usufruct, bonds, stocks, securities, leases, rents.[174] In canon 1410 the Code enunciates what fruits may henceforth be looked upon as beneficial revenue. It declares that the endowment of a benefice consists either of goods owned by the benefice itself as a juridical entity, or of a definite obligatory payment of some family or moral person, or of definite voluntary offerings of the faithful which are made with a view to becoming the revenue of the benefice, or of so-called stole fees received according to and within the limits of diocesan taxation or legitimate custom, or of choir distributions, one-third of which are excluded, if the entire revenue of the benefice consists of choral distributions.

171 *Die Suspension*, p. 126.

172 Wernz, *Ius Decretalium*, III, n. 180.

173 Lib. V, tit. XXXIX, n. 302.

174 Cfr. Pistocchi, *De Re Beneficiali*, p. 17, seq.

Stole fees are offerings made to a priest on the occasion of certain priestly functions. As has been already stated, they may be considered as beneficial revenue. But, to be assimilated to the dowry, it is necessary that there be a positive declaration to this effect by the Ordinary in erecting the benefice, because the enumeration of possible sources of beneficial revenue mentioned in canon 1410 is disjunctive rather than conjunctive. Each species of revenue must be explicitly determined. This applies also to the other beneficial fruits spoken of by canon 1410. Vermeersch-Creusen[175] claim that stole fees can only then be made into a source of beneficial revenue when the ecclesiastical property is insufficient of itself to constitute a beneficial dowry. When stole fees, however, are considered part of the dowry, then anything offered voluntarily by the faithful over and above the customary and statutory fee need not be ceded to the benefice.[176] It seems that these offerings would not fall within the prohibition of the suspension *a beneficio*, no matter whether the excess was offered *intuitu personae* or not.

Whilst the question of the choral distributions is without practical import in the United States, yet it must not be overlooked, for such distributions can be and are affected by the suspension *a beneficio* under certain determinable conditions. By choral distributions the Code signifies a certain revenue which is daily available for the members of cathedral or collegiate chapters who are actually present at divine services[177] or who, because they are rightfully excused in their physical absence, are considered in law as present.[178] But, these latter, though lawfully absent from choir, will not share in the distributions which as a very specific category are designated *inter praesentes*, except in the four cases mentioned in nn. 1, 7, 11 and 13 of canon 420, § 1, [179] It is of course understood that this prescription of the Canon law would readily yield to an expressly divergent will of a benefactor in his act of foundation, as expressly allowed in canon 420, § 2.

175 *Epitome,* II, n. 798.
176 *Epitome,* II, n. 743.
177 Canon 418, § 3; by implication also canon 395, § 3.
178 Canon 420, § 1.
179 Canon 420, § 2.

Canon 395, § 1 gives the bishop the right to set aside one-third of the income of all the dignitaries, canons, the incumbents of offices and benefices belonging to the cathedral or collegiate church and convert them into a fund for daily distributions, if there is no such fund in existence or if it is so small that it is of no account. However, since these daily distributions fall to the lot of those who faithfully attend choir and are lost by those who absent themselves, *per se* they do not constitute the dowry of a benefice. Only the remaining two-thirds are to be considered as the dowry under the title of a prebend. This can only be the case, when the whole substance of the benefice consists of distributions. The bishop, then, separates the whole into three parts; the one part constitutes the distribution and the other two parts the prebend, or, in other words, the beneficial dowry.[180] It is evident, therefore, that these distributions become beneficial revenue only when the members of the chapter have no other income. Consequently, when a canon is under a suspension *a beneficio,* the prohibition of the penalty rests on the two parts of the distributions, which go to make up the prebend.

Foundation Masses may also be the sole beneficial endowment. In such a case, a priest under the suspension *a beneficio* may not retain the stipulated sum which ordinarily accrues to him for the saying of a foundation Mass. He must return it, either to the person who established the foundation, or, if there is danger of losing his good name, he would have to give it to some pious cause or to the poor. It should be noted, in this matter, that the deprivation of income by a suspension *a beneficio* does not become convertible into an enforced acceptance of the purchase price of the sacrificial necessities at the beneficiary's own personal expense, especially when the obligation of the celebration and application of the Mass has been assayed in person. If the suspended beneficiary may draw upon the benefice for his habitation, as was stated above, there is more reason why he should not have to incur a direct personal expense. Therefore, it may be licitly concluded, that the beneficiary may retain at least the equivalent of the customary manual stipend to meet his expenses.

180 Pistocchi, *De Re Beneficiali,* p. 23.

If the beneficiary had these foundation Masses said by another, he would have to draw upon the benefice for at least the equivalent of the customary manual stipend, according to the prescription of canon 840, § 2.

Manual stipends are not classed among those fruits, which constitute a beneficial dowry. First of all, they are looked upon merely as personal offerings made to the celebrant for saying the Mass.[181] Secondly, there is lacking that stability which is essentially for a benefice.

In this country, to the exclusion of Christmas and Easter collections, which according to the custom of some dioceses go directly to the pastor, voluntary offerings are definitely meant for the parish and only indirectly for the pastor, in as far as he must seek his set salary from the parish income. Such offerings may come in the form of pew rents, plate collections, subscriptions, yearly dues, Christmas and Easter collections, and the like. But all stole fees are definitely meant for the pastor and only indirectly for the parish in as far as his reception of the stole fees may lighten the parish's duty of support for him.

Neither all the voluntary offerings nor the stole fees are *eo ipso* an accretion for the beneficial revenue. To become part of the dowry of the benefice, there must be a special declaration to this effect in the decree of erection. Therefore, unless the contrary is expressly stated, a pastor suspended *a beneficio* would only suffer the forfeiture of his salary, since this is considered the stable beneficial revenue, and not the loss of the stole fees. To include the stole fees, mention of this fact would have to be made in the decree of erection.

There are certain revenues which, unless expressly mentioned, the suspension *a beneficio* can not touch, because they do not flow from a benefice in the strict sense. Among such are to be cited the financial support accruing from incumbencies in parochial vicariates which lack perpetuity of institution; the income from lay chaplaincies which a cleric possesses independently of ecclesiastical authority; the *congrua fructuum portio* in the case of coadjutor-

181 Vermeersch-Creusen, *Epitome,* II, n. 743.

ships, whether with or without the right of succession, which are held not by personal title but by vicarious right; the emolument arising from personal pensions whose duration may not extend beyond the lifetime of the beneficiary burdened with the cession to the pensioner; the gratuitous allowance connected with the grant of temporary *commendae,* that is to say, honorary offices which provide a source of revenue from some church or monastery during the lifetime of the recipient.[182]

It is evident that a benefice is not had as long as one or the other essential element is lacking. Thus, the parochial vicariates lack perpetuity; lay chaplaincies are erected without the requisite ecclesiastical approval and authority; coadjutorships establish no canonical title for the incumbent; personal pensions are merely a limited apportionment of the fruits of a benefice temporarily conceded; temporary *commendae* are but the settlements of a transient trust upon an honored recipient, for they are grants of income from the revenues of a church or monastry to a cleric, with the accompanying stipulation that at his death the revenues will revert in their entirety to the Church or monastery.

Should a cleric violate the suspension *a beneficio,* the penalty as prescribed by canon 2280, § 2 is that the forbidden revenues must be restored. The delinquent can even be forced by canonical sanctions to make this restitution. The obligation, according to the common opinion, is one of strict justice, binding in conscience even before the issuance of a sentence, because by violating his suspension the offending cleric makes use of something to which he is not entitled.[183]

Chelodi[184] and Cocchi[185] claim, that before the Code this obligation of restitution was by some canonists deemed not altogether certain as long as a decree of the Ordinary or a sentence of the

182 Canons 1412; 477, § 1; 1433; 1429, § 1, § 3; 1298, § 2; Hinschius, *Kirchenrecht,* II, 393; Scherer, *Kirchenrecht,* I, 405.

183 Cappello, *De Censuris,* n. 501; Chelodi, *Ius Poenale,* n. 44; Augustine, *Commentary,* VIII, 225; Woywod, *A Practical Commentary,* II, n. 2122.

184 *Ius Poenale,* n. 44.

185 *Commentarium,* V, (De Delictis et Poenis), n. 102.

judge had not supervened. Canonists, like Hollweck[186] and Kober,[187] however, championed the present-day opinion, namely, that even before a sentence a cleric is bound to restore the revenues he has used during the time of the suspension.

The general rule is that a cleric under a suspension *a beneficio* may not enjoy the revenues of his benefice. However, notwithstanding this serious obligation, he still may make use of canon 2232, § 1, when there is question of losing his good name. Thus, when infamy threatens him, a cleric who has incurred a suspension *latae sententiae* may deport himself in the external forum as if there were present no suspension, as long as no declaratory sentence has been issued. No one is permitted to demand the self-execution of the suspension, unless the crime is notorious. But, in the internal forum the cleric is bound to deprive himself of the use of the beneficial revenues. He is excused from outwardly observing the suspension, only when the observance would bring loss to his good name. Such loss of repute is conceivable only as long as no public sentence has been passed upon him. The passing of a sentence presupposes the forfeiture of his right to a good name, and thenceforth his observance of the penalty finds no escape. On the contrary, his public non-observance of the suspension would not only contribute nothing to staving off infamy to his name, but it would positively aggravate the circumstances which already have sealed and confirmed his ill-repute.

A further question of importance is to determine to whom the restitution must be made. Augustine[188] restricts the restitution to the benefice itself or to the church attached to it, because, he says, the benefice is considered a juridical entity. Precisely because the restitution is due to the benefice, therefore, the suspended cleric has no longer any right to dispose of the forfeited revenues in a manner as he sees fit.[189] There are certain norms to be followed. It has been said, that the norm to be followed is the one taken from an

186 *Die kirchlichen Strafgesetze,* p. 136.

187 *Die Suspension,* p. 120

188 *Commentary,* VIII, 226.

189 A Coronata, *Institutiones Iuris Canonici,* IV, n. 1813.

analogy with canon 2381, n. 1, where the law provides, that the revenues lost through non-residence should be given to the Ordinary, who then places them in the treasury of the benefice or distributes them to the poor. Such a norm, it would seem, applies solely to public cases, where the use of the forbidden revenues has become known, either through a judicial trial or some other circumstance. Positing an occult case, however, a wider latitude of action could be given a cleric, because to force the cleric to restore the used revenues to the Ordinary would be to force him to reveal his crime. Consequently, it seems, in view of the teaching of the Council of Trent[190] and according to the opinion of St. Alphonsus,[191] when speaking of restitution for omitting the canonical hours, that the cleric could satisfy his obligation by giving the revenues to any poor person or to the benefice itself or to the house annexed to it or by putting in order the adjacent grounds belonging to the benefice. He could further satisfy his obligation by applying the fruits of the Mass to the Souls in Purgatory. He could also retain the revenues for himself, if he is poor. It must be understood, however, that this is only permitted when the suspension in question has been inflicted or incurred as a vindictive penalty. All possibility of retaining any part of the fruits is excluded if the suspension has been inflicted or incurred because of contumacy, in other words if the suspension is a censure.[192] But if the suspended priest does his duties conscientiously while he is *occulte suspensus*, he may retain the amount which ordinarily he would have to give to a substitute for fulfilling his duties for him. This recompense is nought else than remuneration for his work and is not to be considered a beneficial revenue.[193]

If the nature of the suspension *a beneficio* is to prohibit the en-

[190] Sess., XXIII, *de ref.*, c. 1: ". . . statuit sacrosancta synodus . . . eum, pro rata temporis absentiae, fructus suos non facere, nec tuta conscientia, alia etiam declaratione non secuta, illos sibi detinere posse: sed teneri, aut, ipso cessante, per superiorem ecclesiasticum illos fabricae ecclesiarum aut pauperibus loci erogare."

[191] *Theologia Moralis*, III, n. 672; IV, n. 128.

[192] *Theologia Moralis*, VII, n. 316, dub. 1.

[193] Aertnys-Damen, *Theologia Moralis*, II, n. 1027.

joyment of the revenues flowing from the benefice, does it mean that the suspended cleric is to be left without any livelihood whatever? An answer to this question calls for a distinction. When the suspension is vindictive in character, then other income should be given the cleric, lest he be obliged to return to secular pursuits, and furthermore, lest his want bring disgrace upon the clerical state.[194]

But, this is not of obligation in justice; it is rather a duty in charity to enable the cleric to live in a manner befitting his state. An analogy may be taken from the provision of the law given in canon 2303, § 2 concerning a deposed cleric. Here the law wishes the Ordinary, in charity, to provide for the cleric, if he has no other means of living or no revenue for decent support, so that he may not be reduced to go begging and thereby bring disgrace upon the clerical state. If the law counsels this for the more severe penalty of deposition, surely the same procedure should be undertaken in regard to the cleric who is laboring under a vindictive penalty of suspension, an ecclesiastical penalty which is less severe than deposition, but rendered similar to it by reason of temporal duration.[195]

In the old law one exception was admitted, namely, when a cleric possessed an income of his own.[196] The present law does not militate against this, and therefore, according to canon 6, n. 2, the same exception will still obtain. This seems to be the mind of the legislator too, because in canon 2303, § 2, the Ordinary is only asked in charity to give the cleric some allowance to avoid any disgrace upon the clerical state. The inference, therefore, is that if the cleric has some means of livelihood, no disgrace will befall the clerical state. Hence, in that case the Ordinary would not have to provide for the cleric.

The law deals more strictly with a cleric under a censure of suspension *a beneficio*. Unless extreme and absolute necessity should

[194] Kober, *Die Suspension*, p. 122; Schmalzgrueber, lib. V, tit. XXXIX, n. 305; Ayrinhac, *Penal Legislation in the New Code of Canon Law*, n. 154.

[195] Reg. 35, R. J., in VIo:—"Plus semper in se continet quod est minus."

[196] Glossa in c. 25, X, *de electione et electi potestate*, I, 6, verb., *admiserunt*:—"Sed si tales suspensi a beneficio haberent patrimonium vel aliud unde vivere possent, tunc ex beneficio nihil habere debent."

urge some consideration, a cleric under the censure may be left temporarily without support, because the censure's purpose is to bring the cleric to his sense of duty, and this can be done in no better way than by depriving him of his source of income completely. Should he choose to remain deprived of his revenues by continuing to be contumacious, he has no one to blame but himself,[197] since he has it within his power to regain his income at the moment of repentance. Once his change of will becomes evident, the superior has an obligation in justice to impart absolution.

As to the revenues forfeited during the time of the suspension, the cleric can never reclaim these, unless the punishment had been inflicted unjustly or invalidly.[198] They are lost forever.[199]

THE EXTENT OF THE BINDING FORCE OF THE SUSPENSION *ab officio et a beneficio.* The Code today authentically settles the controversy which existed prior to its promulgation concerning the extent of the binding force of the suspensions *ab officio* and *a beneficio.* Before the Code the common opinion was that the suspension *ab officio* or *a beneficio* bound the cleric everywhere, even outside of the territory of the one who had inflicted the suspension.[200] Lega[201] countenanced the same opinion. He claimed that the common law has established these suspensions with their effects and hence, even though a local Ordinary inflicted them, they have a universal effect. Wernz's[202] stand in this question coincided exactly with the present Code.

The law today in canon 2281 limits the suspension *ab officio* or *a beneficio* to the territory of the one who inflicts the punishment.[203] All offices or benefices which the cleric holds within this

[197] Reg. 27, R. J., in VIo:—"Scienti et consentienti non fit iniuria neque dolus."

[198] Suarez, *De Censuris,* Disp. XXVII, sec. II, n. 7.

[199] D., (50. 17) 46:—"Quod a quoque poenae nomine exactum est, id eidem restituere nemo cogitur."

[200] Hollweck, *Die kirchlichen Strafgesetze,* p. 133, note 9; Kober, *Die Suspension,* pp. 89 and 118; Suarez, *De Censuris,* Disp. XXVII, sec. I, n. 17.

[201] *De Delictis et Poenis,* (editio altera), n. 191.

[202] *Ius Decretalium,* VI, n. 208, note 405.

[203] Cappello, *De Censuris,* n. 502; Augustine, *Commentary,* VIII, 228.

jurisdiction will be affected by either of these suspensions, unless the superior intends that only a certain definite office or benefice should be included.

The law makes it clear, too, that no local Ordinary has the right to suspend a cleric from a determined office or benefice which the latter possesses in the diocese of another.[204] The reason for this is obvious, because these offices and benefices lie beyond the scope of his jurisdiction.[205] However, if a suspension *latae sententiae ab officio* or *a beneficio*, as constituted and enacted by the common law be incurred, then its binding force is universal according to canon 2282.

There is a difficulty in harmonizing canon 2281 with canon 2279, § 1. The law contained in the latter canon forbids the exercise of any ecclesiastical office, whilst canon 2281 ordains that only those offices are affected by a suspension *ab officio* which the cleric holds in the diocese of the one who suspended him, unless the contrary is apparent.

Woywod[206] bases his solution on canon 2226, § 4. This canon, he maintains, urges the obligation to observe a penalty everywhere, except when the law expressly adduces a contrary provision. Canon 2281 is an explicit prescription to the contrary. It expressly modifies the general principle that a penalty binds everywhere, by restricting the effects of the suspension to the diocese of the Ordinary who pronouncd it.

It may also be maintained that canon 2279, § 1 refers solely to a suspension *ab officio* incurred from the common law, whilst canons 2281 and 2282 govern the extent of the binding force of a suspension *ab officio* which has come by way of a particular law or decree, *ab homine* or *latae sententiae.*

In canons 2281 and 2282 there is also a discrepancy which is based on the general principle that a suspension *ab ordine* binds

[204] Canon 2282.

[205] C. 2, *de constitutionibus,* I, 2, in VIo:—"Statuto episcopi, quo in omnes, qui furtum commiserint, excommunicationis sententia promulgatur, subditi eius, furtum extra ipsius diocesim committentes, minime ligari noscuntur, quum extra territorium ius dicenti non pareatur impune."

[206] *A Practical Commentary,* II, n. 2123.

everywhere. It must be remembered that according to canon 2279, § 1, every suspension *ab officio* has as one of its constituent elements the suspension *ab ordine*. It is this fact that must be reckoned with in the interpretation of the above canons.

Before the Code authors agreed that the suspension *ab ordine* bound the cleric wherever he sojourned, because orders, unlike jurisdiction, adhere to the state of the cleric.[207] The Code itself did not go contrary to this commonly accepted opinion, and hence there is no evident reason why the view of the old authors should be discarded. In fact modern authors adopt the pre-Code view, and maintain that the suspension *ab ordine* binds the cleric everywhere.[208]

If, therefore, the suspension *ab ordine* binds everywhere, then an Ordinary who would suspend a cleric *ab officio* in his own diocese would likewise suspend this cleric from his office in another diocese, if this office carries with it solely an exercise of sacred orders. Hence the law of canon 2281 would be contradicted which states that a suspension *ab officio* inflicted by an Ordinary is limited to those offices alone existing within the jurisdiction of this Ordinary. There would be a similar contradiction regarding canon 2282 where the law forbids the Ordinary to suspend a cleric from an office which the latter possesses in another diocese.

To reconcile these apparent contradictions, it must be asserted, that canons 2281 and 2282 are exceptions to the general principle—the suspension *ab ordine* binds everywhere. There is a general principle of law which states that a more specific derogates from a more general. From the tenor of the law in canons 2281 and 2282

207 Wernz, *Ius Decretalium*, VI, n. 208, note 405; Ballerini-Palmieri, *Opus Theologicum Morale*, VII, n. 502; Suarez, *De Censuris*, Disp. XXVII, sec. I, n. 17; Lega, *De Delictis et Poenis*, (editio altera), n. 191, note 1:—"Statum personarum constituunt ea iura quae faciunt clericum, religiosum seu regularem, civem. Unde hic status non constituitur nisi a iure communi. Quare dum ius commune permittit, per remedia poenalia, status diminutionem, haec personam sequitur ubique locorum."

208 De Meester, *Compendium*, III, pars 2a, n. 1783; Cappello, *De Censuris*, n. 502; Cocchi, *Commentarium*, V, (De Delictis et Poenis), n. 101; Chelodi, *Ius Poenale*, n. 42; Augustine, *Commentary*, VIII, 229.

there can be no doubt that the legislator has, indeed, become more specific in his determination of the binding force of the suspension *ab officio.* In canon 2281, he limits the effects of the suspension to the diocese itself and thus precludes any effects which would militate against the provision of canon 2282, where the law forbids an Ordinary to suspend a cleric from an office outside of his jurisdiction. At least, there is a substantial basis for a doubt of law. Hence, according to canon 15, a cleric would not be bound to observe the suspension *ab officio* inflicted upon him in his own diocese, if this prohibition to exercise orders would interfere substantially with the fulfillment of an office in another diocese.

CHAPTER V

THE INFLICTION OF SUSPENSION

THE AUTHOR OF SUSPENSION. In general, it may be said that they alone have the power to institute the penalty of suspension who have the legal capacity to make laws and to impose jurisdictional precepts.[1] In particular, the following may be classed as enjoying this right. First and foremost of course is the Pope. He has coercive power over the whole Church,[2] and therefore can suspend any cleric, no matter in which part of the world he has been incardinated. The Sacred Congregations, too, enjoy universal power to issue decrees and particular precepts. This power, however, may be exercised solely within the ambit of their competence.[3] An example of such an exercise of jurisdiction is the decree of the Congregation of the Consistory issued on December 30, 1918. The Congregation decrees a suspension *a divinis*, to which all priests are *ipso facto* subject who have rashly and contemptuously emigrated from Europe or the Mediterranean countries to America or the Philippines without having previously obtained the necessary permission in writing. In addition the Congregation reserves to itself the right and power of absolution from this censure.[4] Besides the Pope and the Sacred Congregations, universal power to issue a suspension is enjoyed likewise by Ecumenical Councils.[5]

Suspensions may also be instituted by provincial and plenary councils, provided permission for the celebration of the latter has

[1] Canon 2220, § 1.

[2] Canon 218, § 1.

[3] Canons 247-257.

[4] "Sacerdotes qui, his legibus non servatis, temere arroganterque demigraverint, suspensi a divinis ipso facto maneant: qui nihilominus sacris (quod Deus avertat) operari audeant, in irregularitatem incidant; a quibus poenis absolvi non possint nisi a Sacra hac Congregatione."—*AAS*, XI (1919), 43.

[5] Canon 228, § 1:—"Concilium Oecumenicum suprema pollet in universam Ecclesiam potestate."

been obtained from the Holy Father and provided the approval of the decrees of both have been given by the Sacred Congregation of the Council.[6] In a diocesan synod, the bishop has the right to enact penal laws and to attach to these a suspension.[7] Residential bishops, when they have taken canonical possession of their diocese, even though they should do this before their consecration, enjoy similar jurisdiction to enact suspensions.[8] Vicars General, on the contrary, lack all power to institute suspensions, unless they have received a special mandate from the bishop. They may, therefore, neither legislate nor decree penalties of suspension which are to be incurred *ipso facto,* nor may they apply or inflict a suspension *ab homine.*[9] The cathedral chapter before the election of a vicar capitular, and the vicar capitular himself after his election enjoy coercive power.[10] This same power is enjoyed by the diocesan consultors and the administrator elected by them *sede vacante.*[11] Ecclesiastical judges, too, may apply and inflict suspensions under certain circumstances.[12] All administrators apostolic permanently constituted or even only temporarily appointed,[13] and also all Ordinaries and all prelates enjoying episcopal or quasi-episcopal jurisdiction have the right to issue a suspension.[14] This same power is enjoyed by abbots and prelates *nullius,*[15] vicars and prefects apostolic[16] and also Metropolitans. In the latter case, however, the Metropolitan's right is restricted to the time of visitation, if with the approval of the Holy See, he supplies for a negligent suffragan.[17] Cardinals as such have not the power to inflict a suspension,

[6] Canons 281; 290; 291.

[7] Canons 356, § 1; 362.

[8] Canons 334; 336.

[9] Canon 2220, § 2.

[10] Canon 435, § 1.

[11] Canon 427.

[12] Canons 1640, § 2; 1743, § 3; 2233, § 1, § 2. Cfr. *AAS.*, XXIII (1931), 465, n. 31.

[13] Canon 315, § 1, § 2.

[14] Canons 309, § 2, § 3, § 4; 429 seq; 432, § 2.

[15] Canon 323, § 1.

[16] Canon 294, § 1.

[17] Canon 274, n. 5.

not even upon those attached to their titular church, because they exercise over these clerics merely dominative power.[18] Likewise, with regard to pastors, they possess simple administrative jurisdiction in the external forum, and hence, may not make use of canonical sanctions, even though they have the right to give a jurisdictional precept.[19]

Concerning religious superiors of exempt clerical institutes, there is no doubt that they have the right to make use of the canonical penalty of suspension in dealing with their subjects alone. Superiors who enjoy this right and power are those who are classified as major superiors, such as the Abbot Primate, the Abbot of a monastic congregation, the Abbot of a monastery *sui iuris,* the Supreme Moderator, Provincials and their Vicars and all those possessing power similar to Provincials.[20]

As to the local superiors of exempt clerical institutes the question is open to dispute. Cappello contends that in the old law this faculty was doubtful. With regard to the present legislation, he claims, no one can read into canon 501, § 1, that local superiors possess the power to give a precept to which is attached a penal sanction. Therefore, he says, this power is to be denied them, unless it is expressly conceded by the constitutions.[21] Pejska claims that the power to suspend religious resides with the major superiors.[22] De Meester,[23] Cocchi,[24] Biederlack-Führich[25] deny the power to local superiors to suspend their subjects, unless the constitutions expressly grant the faculty. St. Alphonsus, in speaking of those who have the power to inflict censures, includes local super-

18 Canon 240, § 2; A Coronata, *Institutiones Iuris Canonici,* II, n. 325; Chelodi, *Ius de Personis,* n. 158, b.

19 Canons 461; 469.

20 Canon 488, n. 8.

21 *De Censuris,* n. 11, note 8.

22 *Ius Sacrum C.SS.R.,* p. 336:—"In religione clericali exempta ius suspendendi subditos a sacris exercet Ordinarius proprius seu superior Generalis vel Provincialis non vero superior immediatus seu domesticus."

23 *Compendium,* III, pars, 2a, n. 1711.

24 *Commentarium,* V, (De Delictis et Poenis), n. 29.

25 *De Religiosis,* (Oeniponte, 1919), n. 43.

iors.[26] Konings gives this power to local superiors of religious orders, according to their various statutes.[27] Vermeersch-Creusen claim that local superiors have the power to inflict ecclesiastical punishments according to their constitutions.[28] Cerato asserts that those local superiors have the right to inflict censures who possess the right and office of imposing precepts.[29] Fanfani voices the opinion,[30] that the more probable view seems to be that local superiors of exempt religious institutes may inflict censures. For his reason he relies on the general terminology used by canon 501, § 1 in dealing with superiors.[31] Then, again, the canon says, that superiors of clerical exempt religious institutes have jurisdiction in the external forum. Furthermore, canon 2220, § 1 speaks in general terms of those superiors who may make laws and impose precepts and who are equally qualified for attaching canonical sanctions thereto.[32] From these two canons Fanfani concludes, that although minor superiors have not the power to make laws, they may, however, impose precepts upon their subjects by virtue of the jurisdiction they have in the external forum. Therefore, they may inflict censures within the limits of their jurisdiction.

Which position is in keeping with the whole tenor of the Code? It seems the opinion of Cappello strikes the correct note. It is true, that all superiors of exempt clerical institutes have jurisdiction in the external forum. But, it appears, that the jurisdiction of local superiors is not of a coercive nature, in the sense that they may make use of canonical sanctions, unless this right is conceded to

26 *Theologia Moralis*, VII, n. 10:—"Ordinariam [scil. potestatem] habent: Generales, provinciales et superiores locales religionum respectu suorum subditorum."

27 *Theologia Moralis*, II, n. 1666.

28 *Epitome*, III, n. 411.

29 *Censurae Vigentes*, n. 6, 7o.

30 *De Iure Religiosorum*, n. 55, c.

31 Canon 501, § 1:—"Superiores [omnes] . . . in religione . . . clericali exempta, habent iurisdictionem ecclesiasticam tum pro foro interno, quam pro foro externo."

32 Canon 2220, § 1:—"Qui pollent potestate [ecclesiastica] leges ferendi vel praecepta imponendi, possunt quoque legi vel praecepto poenas [ecclesiasticas] adnectere."

them by the constitutions. In the whole treatise on criminal procedure, the Code restricts all jurisdiction in such matters to the Ordinary.[33] The same may be said of the extrajudicial procedure in the case of the suspension *ex informata conscientia* and the removal of pastors. The Ordinary alone has the right to use coercive jurisdiction in such cases.[34] Furthermore, the only one empowered to issue canonical rebukes and admonitions is the Ordinary. The whole context of the part of the Code treating of these rebukes and admonitions, which also speaks of canonical precepts threatening penal sanctions[35] points exclusively to the Ordinary. Hence, it is hard to see how local superiors who are not Ordinaries, have the right and power validly to inflict a canonical penalty, either jurisdictionally, unless this power is granted them by the constitutions, since they can neither institute a judicial process, nor proceed extrajudicially, because, according to the law, only an Ordinary has the right to issue canonical rebukes, admonitions or warnings and even precepts threatening ecclesiastical penalties and censures.

The only local superior who has the right and power to impose a precept to which is attached a canonical punishment is the superior of a monastery *sui iuris*. But, it must be remembered, he is acting not as a minor local superior, but as an Ordinary, since he is a major superior at the same time.

NORMS FOR THE INFLICTION OF SUSPENSION. Coercive power by which a superior is authorized to inflict penalties is inherent in his office. Therefore, it is within his province to exercise this power himself or through others. But, in this exercise he is not at liberty to inflict or apply censures and penalties at will. He must always act in accordance with the prescriptions of Canon Law, or else he will jeopardize the justice and validity of his act, or at least invite a justified attempt at having it rescinded.

First of all, a superior wishing to enact, inflict or apply a suspension must be free from every legal disability which hinders the valid exercise of his jurisdiction.[36] He can exercise his power over

[33] Canons 1940; 1946, § 3; 1954.

[34] Canons 2142-2194.

[35] Canons 2306-2311.

[36] Canons 2264; 2284.

his subjects even over transients in the particular instances to be discussed later. Within his territory the superior may exercise his jurisdiction to the fullest extent. Outside of his territory he may proceed only in the limited measure provided by the law. In this latter circumstance the superior, in order to secure the avoidance of future crimes, is allowed to inflict a suspension on a cleric-subject of his by means of a statute or a precept, for such an act is not regarded as an exercise of judicial jurisdiction in alien territory from which, under ordinary circumstances, the superior is barred.[37] Ordinarily whilst outside of his territory, a superior may not validly exercise jurisdiction through judicial acts. The only time the law permits this is when the superior has been forcibly detained outside of his territory, or when he is impeded in the lawful exercise of his jurisdiction within his territory. In these instances he may validly and licitly exercise jurisdiction and even pass a sentence, provided, however, he notifies the local Ordinary of the territory in which he resides of his action. This proviso of the law is merely to render his act licit.[38]

In connection with the exercise of jurisdiction outside of the superior's territory, a word should be said in reference to the houses of regulars and the houses of those who enjoy the privileges of regulars. It is more probable that houses of regulars and houses of those who enjoy the privileges of regulars do not enjoy local exemption in the sense that they are considered extra-territorial. A monastery or a convent, as such, is not exempt, but local exemption extends only as far as, and in virtue of personal exemption. Hence, if a bishop should exercise judicial acts in one of these houses, such as the examining of witnesses or the writing of the acts of a trial, these acts would be valid. Whether they would be valid if the entire trial, inclusive of the sentence, were conducted in one of these houses, seems doubtful.[39] If the whole trial was instituted and a

[37] Canon 201, § 2:—"Iudicalis potestas tam ordinaria quam delegata exerceri nequit in proprium commodum aut extra territorium, salvis praescriptis can. 401, § 1, 881, § 2, et 1637."

[38] Canons 201, § 2; 1637; Vermeersch-Creusen, *Epitome*, III, n. 73; Cocchi, *Commentarium*, IV, (De Processibus), n. 54.

[39] Wernz, *Ius Decretalium*, V, n. 315 denies the validity according to a de-

sentence passed, because of the positive and probable doubt, the defect of jurisdiction would be supplied.[40] It is certain, however, that if the whole criminal process were carried out in a place which is itself exempt, as for instance, a territory *nullius*, the proceedings would be invalid.[41]

Ecclesiastical judges among regulars and those enjoying the privileges of regulars must exercise judicial jurisdiction over their subjects in their own houses. Should they undertake to exercise any judicial acts outside of their houses over their subjects, this exercise of jurisdiction does not seem to be invalid, since their jurisdiction is personal.[42]

An Ordinary is given legal competence to examine and to suspend a cleric, even one who is a mere transient, if he is guilty of a real *delictum* within the jurisdiction of this Ordinary.[43] Should the cleric be absent from the territory in which the crime was committed, the Ordinary is empowered to summon the culprit and to pronounce sentence against him.[44]

Besides jurisdiction, whose effectiveness may be impeded by the presence of the censure of suspension after a declaratory or condemnatory sentence has been pronounced, or may be held in abeyance by an appeal, there is another essential element which the superior may not overlook under pain of invalidity. This is the *delictum* or crime.

There must be present a real crime in the sense of canon 2195, § 1, namely, an external and morally imputable violation of a law or precept to which is attached a canonical sanction, at least, indeterminately. Since there is question of the external forum, the act of commission or omission must be perceptible to others beside the culprit himself, because it is only such external acts, as opposed to

cision of the S.C. Ep. et Reg., Sept. 15, 1741; Messmer, *Canonical Procedure*, p. 143 says they are valid. He cites for his argument the S.C. Imm., Jan 21, 1821 and July 14, 1830.

40 Canon 209.

41 Noval, *De Processibus*, n. 232.

42 Roberti, *De Processibus*, p. 292.

43 Canon 1566, § 1.

44 Canon 1566, § 2.

internal ones, which lie within the pale of the Church's penal discipline. The act, moreover, must be morally imputable. By this is meant that the offender freely and deliberately places or omits an act whereby a law or precept is violated, or that there is present in him culpable ignorance or a lack of due diligence in obtaining knowledge concerning the matter in question, or that there is a total disregard of a canonical sanction which the culprit is well aware, at least, in general or in a confused way, will follow the positing of a determined crime.[45] Furthermore, the crime must be such as to constitute a mortal sin, since there is question of inflicting a suspension which is a grave ecclesiastical sanction. The natural law as well as the canon law demands a just proportion between the crime and the penalty.[46] This proportion is maintained only then when the crime is a grave violation of the penal law both objectively and subjectively. If either of these two elements is lacking the enactment and application of penal sanctions is without effect.[47]

Attention must be paid not only to the objective nature of the crime, to the scandal and damage caused, to the gravity of the law violated, but also to the knowledge and mental condition of the cleric. One must also consider his age, his rank in the Church, his purpose in committing the crime, the influences of passion, grave fear, moral duress or physical violence which dominated his act, his promptness in repenting of the evil done, his effort to prevent further evil effects of his misdeed, and other similar conditions attending his act. All of these circumstances and adjuncts present in a case must be prudently investigated and equitably appraised by a superior before he proceeds to the infliction of a suspension, for the practical knowledge of these conditional factors and their consequent modification of the act in which they are involved may constitute an imperative prerequisite for an eventually just, or at least fair determination of the cleric's liability.[48]

Since there must be present a mortal sin before any suspension

[45] Canons 2199; 2202.
[46] Canon 2218, § 1.
[47] Canon 2242, § 1.
[48] Canons 2218, § 1; 2196.

can be inflicted, the superior must see whether or not those elements exist which constitute a mortal sin. There must be a sufficient advertance of the intellect and a commensurate consent of the will. The act must involve a violation in a serious matter which is such either in itself or is made such by reason of its attendant circumstances.[49]

Per se no suspension can be inflicted for a venial offense. *Per accidens,* however, circumstances may be such, that an act which under ordinary conditions is a slight violation of some virtue or law, becomes a serious transgression, and in this case it would be lawful to impose a suspension. Authors prior to the Code intimated that a superior could inflict a suspension for a venial offense. Nearly all maintained that the suspension should not in this case extend over a long period of time.[50] Lega claimed that he would not approve of a bishop suspending one of his clerics for a venial fault; but this, he asserts, does not say that it can not be done. Today, the ecclesiastical punishment of suspension always supposes a grave offense, because to deprive one of something valuable, such as the exercise of certain rights and functions both spiritual and temporal, is indeed a serious sanction;[51] hence, in order that there exist the proportion between the sanction and the crime which justice demands, the crime itself must be serious. Should the superior judge that a slight transgression of a law necessitates some action on his part to bring the guilty cleric to his sense of duty, there are other ways and means to accomplish this without employing a suspension. The law places at his disposal penal remedies and penances. It also counsels him to admonish the culprit and to issue timely rebukes, and at times to set aside days of fast and abstinence and other pious works for the cleric to perform.[52]

To suspend a cleric for listening to a prize fight during the dio-

[49] Cfr. Marc-Gestermann, *Institutiones Morales Alphonsianae,* I, n. 335-336.

[50] Ballerini-Palmieri, *Opus Theologicum Morale,* VII, n. 124; St. Alphonsus, *Theologia Moralis,* VII, n. 30; Wernz, *Ius Decretalium,* VI, n. 156; Lega, *De Delictis et Poenis,* (editio altera), n. 102, note 1; Suarez, *De Censuris,* V, Disp. IV, sec. IV, n. 2.

[51] Canon 2215.

[52] Canons 2306-2313.

cesan retreat, to suspend a cleric for breaking silence during this retreat, to suspend a cleric because he entered the room of another, to suspend a priest for riding in an automobile with a woman or for merely driving an automobile, all of these suspensions would seem to be unjust as long as there was present no grave scandal, because the acts of themselves do not appear serious enough to warrant so serious a penalty. A response of the Congregation of the Council issued on June 11, 1921, stresses the factor of objective gravity in a misdemeanor as a necessary requisite for the infliction of a suspension. The Sacred Congregation declares that, although a bishop may prohibit a cleric from indulging in hunting which is not in violation of canon 138,[53] he should not punish the violation of his prohibition with a suspension *latae sententiae* without special and grave reasons. It advises the bishop to have recourse to the provisions of canons 2306 and 2313 rather than inflict a suspension.[54]

[53] Canon 138:—"Clerici ab iis omnibus quae statum suum dedecent, prorsus abstineant . . . venationi ne indulgeant clamorosam autem nunquam exerceant . . ."

[54] "Idcirco videtur quod Episcopus posset quidem punire clericos venationi clamorosae et tumultuosae vacantes suspensione a divinis etiam *latae sententiae*, tum quia haec venatio est clericis rigorose et absolute a Codice prohibita per illa canonis verba "venationem clamorosam nunquam exerceant" tum quia ipsa omnino dedecet statum clericalem praesertim ob grave periculum occisionis vel mutilationis. Ex adverso sufficere videretur suspensio a divinis *ferendae sententiae* in clericos venationem quietam et frequentem exercentes, quum haec venatio minus rigorose clericos prohibeatur a codice illis verbis "venationi ne indulgeant", atque in singulis casibus quaestio instituenda esset de frequentia vel minus venationis peractae. Denique venatio quieta et moderata, quae nempe raro fit, necessitatis, utilitatis vel etiam animi relaxandi causa, non videretur plecti posse *tali poena quae supponit mortalem culpam,* [italics by the author] quam nemo dixerit singulos actus venationis quietae continere; sed ad rem sufficere remedia poenalia vel poenitentias, quae canonibus 2306 et 2313 statuuntur. Agitur enim in casu de venatione per se licita et nonnisi per accidens prohibita, propter scandalum praesertim fidelium.—Resolutio.—Porro, proposito in plenariis Emorum ac Revmorum S.C. Concilii Patrum comitiis diei 11 iunii 1921, dubio in hanc formulam concepto: "An Episcopus prohibere possit suis clericis venationem etiam non clamorosam, poena suspensionis ipso facto incurrenda"; iidem Emi Patres respondendum censuere:

Scandal, however, is the determining factor whereby a superior is justified in inflicting a suspension upon a cleric for certain acts of misconduct. In its theological sense, scandal is any word or action which has the appearance at least of evil and is the occasion of sin for another. It may be caused directly by being foreseen and intended or indirectly by being foreseen but not intended. In this latter case it arises from ignorance or frailty of him who suffers it or from any malice or hatred entertained toward the person or the state of the one from whom it is taken.[55] The above mentioned acts may seriously weaken discipline and also may give occasion to sins of detraction, calumny and contempt of the clerical state. The judgment of this is of course left to the superior, because the presumption is that the superior is better able, from his knowledge of prevailing conditions and circumstances, to determine the presence of scandal. Whatever is grave or light in the matter of the superior's precept is to be determined not by private judgment but by the authority of the superior. Should there be any doubt at all about the gravity, the ordinance of the superior must be obeyed.[56]

In a circular letter, the Sacred Congregation of the Council under date of July 1, 1926 speaks of grave scandal as a reason for inflicting a suspension. It tells bishops, that they may even threaten clerics who are staying in their dioceses for the sake of health or recreation, with suspension to be incurred *ipso facto,* if they attend public theaters, movies, revues or other profane shows, or if they dress as laymen to visit cities where they are not known and to attend shows that are unbecoming and immoral.[57]

"*Negative,* nisi graves et speciales adsint rationes".—*AAS,* XIII (1921), 500-501.

55 Marc-Gestermann, *Institutiones Morales Alphonsianae,* I, n. 505-506.

56 Canon 2219, § 2; St. Alphonsus, *Theologia Moralis,* VII, n. 32.

57 "Haec Sacra Congregatio Concilii dum postulat ut Ordinarii omnes in hanc rem mentem et animum diligentissime convertant, praescripta quae sequuntur servanda decrevit:—6. b) Ut autem hi sacerdotes facilius in officio contineantur, opportunas poenas constituant quibus afficientur si scandalum dederint, vel si quoquo modo aliquod egerint, quod sacerdotali munere indignum sit. c) Comminari etiam possunt *suspensionem ipso facto incurrendam* si publica theatra, cinematographa, ludos saltatarios ceteraque hujusmodi profana

Should the majority of superiors, contrary to a given few, almost unanimously agree by their negative action, that there is no grave scandal present, still this would not militate against the justice of precepts or statutory laws issued by these dissenting few, because the presumption is that no one knows better than the superior the conditions and circumstances attaching to public actions in his territory or among his subjects. If, in view of the fact that the majority of superiors have considered a certain act as not scandalous, a cleric should thereby so convince himself that his own superior's prohibition was unjust, he would not be bound in the internal forum by the suspension imposed as a sequence to the violation of the prohibition. However, even though in the forum of conscience the cleric would not be bound by the effects of the suspension, still, in the external forum where he is considered to have incurred the penalty by violating the prohibition, he would have to observe the suspension, not indeed because of the binding force of the suspension itself, but because of the demand of the natural law, for he is bound to avoid scandal and all contempt of authority. If there is a doubt at all on the part of the subject as to the justness of the superior's suspension, he must observe the penalty in both *fora*. The cleric, however, has a means of freeing himself temporarily of the effects of the suspension whenever the law permits the making of an appeal *in suspensivo.*[58]

Before a superior may inflict a suspension he must, as a general rule, issue some kind of admonition or threat. With regard to the *latae sententiae,* this threat or admonition is taken care of by the precept or law itself.[59] When this remains unheeded by the subject the way is prepared for imposing the penalty. But in exceptional cases canon 2222, § 1 empowers the superior to inflict a penalty even without this previous warning. Such cases occur when it is likely that scandal has been given or also when the delict is invested with a special degree of heinousness or malice. In the case

spectacula adeant, vel si talarem vestem deponant."—*AAS,* XVIII (1926), 312-313.

58 Canons 2219, § 2; 2243.

59 Canon 2242, § 2; Cfr. Pennacchi, *Commentaria In Constitutionem Apostolicae Sedis,* II, 335.

of grave scandal, the public welfare demands that the culprit be punished as soon as possible, rather than just corrected. In the case of a very serious offense, the private good of the individual necessitates immediate penal action, because thus alone the special gravity of the crime will be taken cognizance of and effectively punished. Such punitive action by the legitimate authority serves best as a guaranty for precluding the danger of scandal and averting the imminent disruption of the social order and peace. When he makes use of canon 2222, § 1, the superior is of course not limited to imposing a suspension by way of a censure; he may also employ it for the inflicting of a vindictive penalty when the delinquent cleric has already repented and nothing else remains to be achieved than the reparation of scandal, the restoration of the disturbed social order, or in the case of individuals, the restoration of their injured rights or moral interests. The terminology of canon 2222, § 1 is of a general nature and therefore allows the application of the censure or vindictive penalty alike in accordance with the circumstance of the case.

Besides the elements of a grave and external violation of a law or precept as well as the factor of grave imputability, there is another essential requisite which enters into the infliction of a suspension. It is the fulfillment, in every respect, of those conditions which the law sets down before a suspension can be imposed upon anyone.

First of all the crime must be complete in the sense of law.[60] No *latae sententiae* suspension can ever be incurred unless the crime, against which the law or precept was enacted, has been committed and consummated in such ways as to meet exactly the conditions established by the superior for the incurring of the penalty.[61] As regards the *ferendae sententiae* suspension, there is no thought of becoming liable to this penalty as long as this same condition is not fulfilled. This is true regardless of whether the sanction for the suspension arises from the preceptive mandate of the law or discretionary option of the superior. Furthermore, the same rule holds regardless of whether the nature and reservation of the imminent

60 Canon 2242, § 1.
61 Canon 2228.

suspension be determined in its ultimate species by the will of the legislator or the discretion of the superior.[62]

Before a *ferendae sententiae* suspension may be inflicted there are still other conditions which must be verified. The commission of the crime must be a certainty,[63] for no one is to be punished or condemned as long as his crime is not evident by proof or other equally reliable indications. As long as a doubt persists, the favor of the law will rest with the suspect. Hence if the fact of the crime be doubtful, or if it be doubtful with whom this fact is to be identified, then no one may be condemned specifically by name, for it is better to leave unpunished the misdeed of the guilty than to invoke a penalty upon the innocent.[64] But, if the crime is certain, though the perpetrator be unknown, a decree or sentence of suspension could be published[65] which would bind the guilty person at least in the forum of conscience. It is not equally certain that he would be bound to the external observance of the penalty, for the rule in canon 2232, § 1, though it deals directly with *latae sententiae* penalties only, yet seems to imply in a general way that the potential shielding of one's good name is sufficient reason for the non-observance of the suspension in public. Precisely because the guilty person is not known, therefore the opportunity of escaping infamy still remains for him despite the intervention of the decree or sentence. Thus he seems excused in the external forum until he can be identified as the perpetrator of the crime.

Not only must there be certainty about the commission of the crime, but there must also be assurance that legitimate prescription has not run its course, if a suspension *ferendae sententiae*, when inflicted, is to have any effect.[66] The time-periods beyond which the introduction of a criminal case in court is precluded by legal prescription are classified and enumerated in canon 1703. Prescription becomes operative the day the crime is committed,[67] but the

[62] Canons 2217, § 1, n. 1, n. 2; 2223, § 2, § 3.

[63] Canons 2233, § 1.

[64] Cocchi, *Commentarium*, V, (De Delictis et Poenis), n. 48.

[65] Canon 2242, § 1.

[66] Canon 2233, § 1.

[67] Canon 1705, § 1.

law determines this "day" differently according to the type of crime involved.

A crime may be considered as being either a *delictum continuatum*, or a *delictum permanens* (*successivum*), or a *delictum collectivum* (*habituale*). The *delictum continuatum* is a crime consisting of many acts which are only a means to carry out an intention previously made, as for example, concubinage, incest, sodomy and the fomenting of hatred against ecclesiastical authority. All acts pointing to the intended delict form one crime, unless they are rendered individually distinct by reason of a warning or a condemnatory sentence. Prescription in this case becomes operative only with the completion of the last act.[68] The *Delictum permanens* (*successivm*) is a state of crime. It takes its origin from the placing of a single act which is of itself a complete crime and whose effects are such, that without requiring a new act, they endure as long as the perpetrator continues in that state which the crime itself induced. Such crimes would be, for example, apostacy, heresy, concubinage, etc. This kind of *delictum* may be multiplied just as the previous one by admonitions and a condemnatory sentence issued during the period when the culprit refuses to depart from his criminal state. Prescription for this type of crime begins from the day the crime itself ceases.[69] The *delictum collectivum* (*habituale*) consists in the repetition by a definite person of individually criminal acts which positive law considers as constituting only one punishable misdemeanor. A crime of this kind would be, for example, usury, prostitution, etc. As regards prescription, it becomes applicable only upon the cessation of the last act. It may be said also, that this type of *delictum* may be interrupted by the pronouncement of condemnatory sentence, so that each act will then become a distinct crime.[70]

The advantage which prescription affords the delinquent cleric

[68] Canon 1705, § 3; Cfr. A Coronata, *Institutiones Iuris Canonici*, IV, n. 1704.

[69] Canon 1705, § 2; Cfr. A Coronata, *Institutiones Iuris Canonici*, IV, n. 1705.

[70] Canons 1705, § 3; 2208, § 1; A Coronata, *Institutiones Iuris Canonici*, IV, n. 1706.

will not bar the superior from using the rights accorded him in canon 2222. Should society demand a reparation of scandal the superior is not hindered from prohibiting the cleric temporarily from the exercise of his sacred functions. He has the right and even the duty of not promoting to orders a cleric for whose fitness he can not vouch.[71] These jurisdictional acts must not be overlooked, despite the fact that prescription has run its course, because the superior must maintain and further the interests of the common good.

Since it is a necessary condition for the application of penal sanctions that a crime be perfectly and completely consummated in accordance with the requirements of the law, a cleric who has merely attempted to commit a crime, or who has in some way been frustrated in executing it, or whose mutually essential or indispensable cooperation has not contributed to the perpetration of a consummated crime does not incur a *latae sententiae* suspension nor does he become liable to a *ferendae sententiae* suspension decreed by precept or instituted by law. Attempted or frustrated crimes can become the basis for a specific suspension only then when the law contemplates them separately as crimes to which specific sanctions are attached.[72] The same rule obtains in reference to any and all cooperators as long as the crime in which they had a part was not sufficiently executed to allow its identification with the category of crime contemplated in the sanction established by the superior. On the other hand, cooperators are liable, together with the agent executing the crime, if their participation is one which makes of the crime a mutual enterprise, or reveals it as a misdeed which of its very nature requires the intervention of an accomplice, or, finally, which would not have been perpetrated under the circumstances without the influence of their cooperation.[73] This is true even then when the persons with whom they cooperate escape all penal sanction because they lack the age required by law to subject them to such sanctions.[74]

71 Canon 973, § 3.
72 Canon 2235.
73 Canon 2231; Cfr. Canon 2209.
74 Canon 2230.

Although a fuller development will be given later in Chapter VI, still to complete the various conditions which must precede the infliction of a suspension, cursory mention should be made here of the warning or threat which the law directs the superior to employ under ordinary conditions.[75] Before any suspension can be inflicted the superior must ordinarily rebuke the cleric and threaten him with this particular penalty should he fail to amend his ways. It is only when scandal has been given or the heinousness of a previously committed crime is exceptionally grave, that the law permits the superior to depart from this ordinary procedure and to suspend the cleric immediately without at first issuing the customary warnings and threats.

Relative to the question of a crime's publicity, it is immaterial whether the delinquency be occult, public, or notorious. It may be penalized with a suspension, as long as it was sufficiently external, in the sense that it was seen or could have been seen.

It may be said in a general way that the best method of determining whether a crime is public or not, is by considering the number of people who witnessed the crime and the number of inhabitants of the place where the offense was committed. Many canonists are of the opinion that at least six persons in a small town must know of the crime before it can be considered public. One might reply to this that much would seem to depend on the character of the persons who witnessed the crime and the circumstances under which it was committed.[76] One or two garrulous persons would be sufficient to render a crime public. The Code in canon 2197, n. 1, calls a crime public either when it actually has been made known to a multitude of people or when circumstances are such that one can reasonably judge that the crime will easily or inevitably become known. The Code thus seems to have adopted the popular sense of the term *public*. It considers a crime public when it is generally known in the community. It also considers the crime public, when

[75] Canons 2233, § 2; 2222, § 1; Response of the Pontifical Commission for the Authentic Interpretation of the Canons of the Code—July 14, 1922—*AAS*, XIV (1922), 530.

[76] A Coronata, *Institutiones Iuris Canonici*, IV, n. 1648.

because of circumstances it has become practically impossible to keep the fact occult. According to the conclusion drawn from canon 2197, n. 4, a public crime is constituted, when not only the infraction of the law is known, but also when the delinquent to whom the crime is actually attributed is known.

A crime becomes notorious, when added circumstances increase its publicity. Thus, a crime can be notorious *notorietate iuris,* when the cleric has been condemned by a sentence of a competent court and the sentence has become absolutely final, likewise, if the cleric voluntarily makes a confession of his guilt in court either orally or in writing. Furthermore, the crime can be notorious *notorietate facti,* when the crime has become so definitely publicized that it can not be concealed by any artifice or any legitimate excuse.[77]

An occult crime, on the other hand, may be occult either materially or formally, that is, when the crime itself or the person to whom it is imputed is unknown. A crime, though materially public, may yet remain formally occult. This is the case, when the fact of the crime is public knowledge but its imputability to a definite individual remains a secret.[78]

This question of public, notorious and occult crimes plays an important part in the cessation of suspension and also in cases of judicial trials. According to canon 1933, § 1, public crimes alone are the object of a criminal trial.

THE SUBJECT OF SUSPENSION. Since the nature of suspension is concerned exclusively with acts proper to clerics, it is evident that they alone are amenable to the effects of this ecclesiastical punishment. All clerics, therefore, whether individually or collegiately, are the proper subjects of this sanction of suspension. The only exception is the Supreme Pontiff. He can not incur a suspension *latae sententiae* established by the common law of the Church, because he is the highest lawgiver and is not bound by his laws, since no one can be his own superior. Furthermore, no suspension can be inflicted upon him, because canon 1556 gives no one the right to judge him.

[77] Canon 2197, n. 2, n. 3.

[78] Canon 2197, n. 4.

In reference to suspension, the term *cleric* embraces all classes of ecclesiastics from the simple tonsured cleric to the consecrated bishop. Canon 108, § 1 declares that those who have dedicated themselves to the divine ministry at least by the first tonsure are called clerics. They alone have the legal capacity for the power of orders and jurisdiction and the right to pensions and ecclesiastical benefices, each of which may be affected in some way by a suspension.[79]

In ordinary circumstances, it is of vital importance for the infliction of a suspension that the cleric be the subject of the superior who is meting out the punishment. This rule admits of an exception in respect to transient clerics, for a superior not their own may inflict a suspension upon them whilst they are sojourning in his territory. A more detailed consideration will be accorded this principle in a later paragraph. There are also clerics whose immediate superior may lack the necessary jurisdiction to inflict a suspension upon them. To this class belong the clerics who are sons of the rulers of countries or sovereign states. It belongs to the pope alone to inflict or declare a suspension in cases in which these clerics are concerned.[80]

As a lay person becomes a subject of his Ordinary in virtue of his domicile or quasi-domicile,[81] so a diocesan cleric is subject to his Ordinary through incardination in the diocese.[82] With regard to a religious, the relationship of subject and superior is established by the vow of obedience.

When a cleric is incardinated in a diocese, this bespeaks his perpetual intention to serve that diocese, just as a domicile for a lay person connotes his intention of continued residence in a place,

[79] Canon 118.

[80] Canon 2227, § 1.

[81] Canons 92; 94; 1561.

[82] Canon 111; A private response of the Pontifical Commission for the Authentic Interpretation of the Canons of the Code—"Whether one who is ordained by his own Bishop for the service of another diocese, is incardinated in that other diocese according to c. 111, § 2, or in the diocese of his own Bishop according to c. 969, § 2.—Reply—In the affirmative to the first part; in the negative to the second."—Bouscaren, *Canon Law Digest*, p. 89.

whereby he subjects himself to his Ordinary. A cleric may also acquire those rights and duties which attach to the status of quasi-domicile. This is readily understood in the case of a religious who has sought and obtained an indult of secularization. Since he is not definitely released during the first process of this indult's execution, from his membership in the religious community, he can not during his probationary status form an absolute intention of perpetual service in the diocese. The extension of the time during which he may remain absent from his monastery or convent for service in the diocese rests with the discretionary will of the *episcopus benevolus receptor.* The bishop may extend the period of probation to three full years, upon the lapse of which he may prorogue this period for another three years. When this second period has elapsed and the bishop has not dismissed the religious, the latter becomes *ipso facto* incardinated in the diocese. The secularization of the religious then attains its ultimate effects and his new status becomes that of a diocesan cleric.

The bishop may also accept the religious without demanding from him a previous probationary service in the diocese. If he thus accepts him absolutely and unconditionally, only one execution of the indult is necessary. The religious immediately becomes incardinated in the diocese and thenceforth shares the rights of a diocesan cleric, represented in the indult which grants him permanent secularization.[83]

The indult of secularization given to a religious connotes the fact of his incardination in the diocese and thus subjects him to the

83 Canon 641, § 2; Cfr. Schäfer, *De Religiosis,* p. 574, f.:—"Hic, si rescriptum sub formula 1 [receptio pure et simpliciter] recipit, conficit decretum exsecutoriale, quo statim indultum saecularizationis conceditur oratori ideoque ipsa incardinatio in Diocesim; si autem rescriptum datum fuerit sub formula 2 [receptio pro experimento], Episcopus primum concedit indultum exclaustrationis, pro tempore scilicet experimenti; tempore autem hoc transacto vel etiam prius, si ipsi placeat, Episcopus concedit indultum saecularizationis. Quod si in casu obtentae formula 2 integrum sexennium transierit a die concessi indulti exclaustrationis, et quin Episcopus saecularizationem formaliter concesserit, Religiosus, nisi antea dimissus fuerit (ab ipso Episcopo), ipso facto Dioecesi incardinatus manet."

episcopal Ordinary as a lay person is subjected in virtue of a domicile. The indult of exclaustration granted to a religious implies the status of probationary service under the vigilance of the diocesan Ordinary, which renders him subject in his obedience *vi voti* to this Ordinary as a lay person would be subject in view of a quasi-domicile.[84] During this probationary period the religious may not be suspended by the Ordinary of his religious institute. His subjection to this Ordinary has been stayed in the interim, and he becomes the subject of the Ordinary of the diocese in which he now sojourns and in which he hopes to be eventually incardinated.

All clerics, whether bishops or cardinals, are amenable to the suspensions defined by the laws of the Code, unless these laws are held in abeyance temporarily in the place where they are residing. This fact, however, is noteworthy, namely, that no cardinal and no bishop, whether residential or titular, incurs a *latae sententiae* suspension, unless express mention is made of the cardinal or bishop in the sanction of the law.[85] With regard to the *ferendae sententiae* suspensions mentioned in the Code, it is the sole right of the pope himself to inflict these on cardinals and bishops.[86]

Transient clerics, who temporarily reside outside of their diocese,[87] are no longer subject to its laws, unless from the nature of the law, or the intention of the superior there arises a personal obligation.[88] Therefore, it may be said that under circumstances these clerics, although absent from their own proper diocese, may still be suspended by their Ordinary. They become subject to suspensions while outside of their diocese, if there is in their own diocese a penal law, whose violation beyond the diocesan limits would have a harmful effect on the diocese itself. They would also incur a suspension, if they violated a personal law to which such a penalty is

[84] Canon 639:—" . . . Ordinario territorii ubi commoratur, loco superiorum propriae religionis, subditur etiam ratione voti obedientiae."

[85] Canon 2227, § 2. Examples of an express mention of a cardinal or a bishop are found in canons 2330, 2370, 2373.

[86] Canons 2227, § 1; 1557, § 1, n. 2-3.

[87] Canon 91.

[88] Canon 8, § 2:—"Lex non praesumitur personalis, sed territorialis, nisi aliud constet."

attached.[89] A law is considered personal if it is enacted for a community essentially personal, as for instance, laws which refer to exempt religious, or if it concerns the juridical state or qualities of persons, as for example, if the bishop should prescribe the fulfillment of some condition before a cleric may be admitted to orders, or if the law imposes an essentially personal obligation, for example, if the bishop decrees that all the clerics of the diocese must confine themselves to the wearing of black clothes alone. Finally, a law is personal if the superior declares that all his cleric-subjects are bound by the law even while absent from his territory.[90]

Unlike a law, a general precept is not to be considered as territorial. The universality of its binding force within a determined and defined area suggests a territorial limitation. However, the intrinsic nature of the general precept indicates clearly that it engenders a personal obligation in each individual member of a certain community or class for which it was intended. It is merely one injunction; but in effect, it is as multiple as there are individuals embraced within its scope. Thus, it takes on the nature of a personal precept for each person; and consequently, according to canon 24, it binds each individual even when absent from the diocese.[91]

Transient clerics may also be bound by the particular penal laws of the diocese in which they sojourn or through which they are travelling at the time. They must obey these laws and are subject to the suspensions invoked by them, when the legislation is concerned with the maintenance of the public order or the requirements demanded for the recognition of legal solemnities and judicial acts.[92]

Among authors the greatest discrepancy will be found in their explanation of the nature of laws which concern the public order. The better opinion seems to be the one which claims that only those laws are to be considered as concerning the public order, which tend to avoid a common danger, such as public scandal and harm to

89 Canon 14, § 1, n. 1.

90 Michiels, *Normae Generales*, I, pp. 310-315.

91 Cocchi, *Commentarium*, I (Normae Generales), n. 85; Michiels, *Normae Generales*, I, 520.

92 Canon 14, § 1, n. 2.

the inhabitants. The question is not whether the observance of these laws will prove to be of some positive utility to the community, but rather, whether their non-observance will prove harmful or detrimental to the community, either in its government or in the measures of safety and security for the inhabitants. Laws concerning the good of the public order and the security of legal solemnities have for their purpose the avoidance of a common danger rather than the promotion of the common well-being. Since transients are not bound by law to work for the furtherance of the well-being of a strange diocese, their obligations in such a diocese will at most be negative in character. The existence and binding force of these negative obligations, however, is urged by the natural law itself; and the natural law binds a cleric at all times and in all contingencies to avoid scandal and abstain from the infliction of harm. If these negative duties have been violated by a positive transgression, then of course further duties of a positive character will arise whereby the scandal given will have to be removed or the harm done will have to be repaired.[93]

In view of these considerations, a transient cleric is bound by all the local laws whose violation would give scandal. For a fuller determination of the laws comprised in this category, one must explore the various contingencies and exigencies which furnished the occasion for the enactment of a certain law binding in a given territory or diocese.

A transient cleric is subject also to the diocesan laws or statutes which concern the moral life and conduct of the clergy, especially such laws as regulate the morality of clerics or set up certain authoritative norms in reference to what must be considered as foreign or unbecoming to the clerical state. Furthermore, he is subject to positive compliance with the diocesan statutes in all such matters as the alienation, acquisition, or mortgaging of ecclesiastical property.[94]

[93] Cappello, *De Censuris*, n. 19; Vermeersch-Creusen, *Epitome*, I, n. 83; Teodori, *Appollinaris*, IV, (1931), 139; Michiels, *Normae Generales*, I, 318-321.

[94] Canons 132; 133; 138; 139; 140.

It should not be urged as an objection that a positive compliance with local law or statute implies more than the merely negative obligation of avoiding scandal or of not occasioning harm. First of all, practically all of these positive observances of the law by a transient cleric in a strange diocese are linked with a *ius dispositivum* in his regard. The law which he observes is not of an absolute, but only of a conditional character in his case. He is not brought under the law unless he chooses by his own negotiations to use the law for effecting a bestowal, an exchange or a juridical confirmation of canonical rights and obligations. But, even if one would have to regard the local law as a *ius cogens,* that is a law which binds transients as absolutely as it binds residents, the need of positive compliance with this law on the part of transients would argue no more than the negative obligation of the latter to avoid the placing of any acts that would result in scandal or harm. The law that essentially binds the transient is *not* to give scandal, *not* to inflict harm. If it so happens that he can not fulfill this duty without the placing of positive acts in accordance with a law which demands the doing of things, the performance of conditions or the active discharge of peremptory acts, then his subjection to this law still retains the natural law as its primary source for the positive obligation. That which of necessity is done as a positive act is but the indirect postulate or accessory demand of the natural law itself, in as far as the unrestricted obligation of the avoidance of scandalous and harmful consequences must at all times be respected. It is an altogether incidental issue whether the achievement of this obligation implies the positive performance of duties or whether it rests in the refraining from prohibited acts. Thus a transient cleric will at times become subject to local positive legislation, not indeed in as much as the law contemplates the active promotion of the welfare of the public order, but in as far as the violation of the enactment would occasion scandal and harm, thereby disrupting the maintenance and continued conservation of that order.

Finally the transient cleric is bound by those particular laws which include mention of transients. A law so enacted establishes the very presumption that it is concerned with the maintenance of the public order. It is presumed the lawgiver included them under his law precisely for this public reason.

Sometimes, in making certain diocesan laws concerning his clerics, the bishop's purpose may be to further their sanctity and to instil in the minds and hearts of the faithful a greater reverence for them.[95] If such is his intention, then, certainly, transient clerics are not bound by these laws, which strictly speaking, can not be said to concern the public order. Nevertheless, they would be bound if the people of the place would be scandalized by the non-observance of these enactments.

Transient clerics who are subject to those laws which concern the maintenance of the public order are bound also by the suspensions attached to the violation of these laws.[96]

An additional bond of subjection to the local Ordinary in penal matters arises *ratione delicti.*[97] As a consequence transient clerics are liable not only to the incurring of *latae sententiae* suspensions, but they are amenable also to the infliction of *ferendae sententiae* suspensions.

Relative to exempt clerical religious the question of subjection to diocesan penal laws presents a number of interesting points. First of all, the Code mentions in canon 615 that all regulars along with their houses and churches are exempt from the jurisdiction of the local Ordinary, except in such cases wherein the law has made express mention to the contrary. Canon 618, § 1 extends this privilege of exemption to institutes of simple vows, if it has been specially conceded to them by a particular indult. Such a privilege is enjoyed by the Passionists and Redemptorists.

Since this privilege is a personal one, there can be no doubt that a regular or a religious cleric enjoying this privilege by particular grant or indult, is removed from the jurisdiction of the local Ordinary everywhere and in all matters, even penal, unless the law expressly limits this exemption in such matters over which the Ordinary is granted authority and jurisdiction. This exemption, how-

95 Van Hove, *Ephemerides Theologicae Lovanienses,* I, (1924), p. 161.

96 Canon 2226, § 1:—"Poenae adnexae legi aut praecepto obnoxius est qui lege aut praecepto tenetur, nisi expresse eximatur."

97 Canon 1566.

ever, does not favor the commission of crimes with impunity. The religious superior, as Ordinary, will uphold the penal sanctions of the law. Should he fail to fulfill this duty upon notification from the local Ordinary, then the latter is authorized to punish or suspend the religious cleric whose crime was committed outside of his religious house.[98] This is the provision of the law when a religious is legitimately absent from his house. On the other hand, should the religious leave his house illegitimately, for example as a fugitive or an apostate, he loses his personal exemption and the bishop may suspend him immediately, without notifying the religious superior.[99]

Even in those matters in which exempt clerical religious are subject to the local Ordinary, they are free from the suspensions attached to the violation thereof, if the Ordinary himself grants an exemption or if the religious enjoy this added privilege from the Holy See. Medicant Orders[100] are generally regarded as having a special apostolic privilege, whereby they are exempt from censures enacted by the local Ordinary, even in those matters in which they are subject to his law. It must be remarked, that this privilege applies solely to censures. It does not include vindictive penalties and penal remedies. There are three exceptions to this general rule, in which even regulars and all clerical exempt religious who enjoy the same privilege, as for example the Jesuits,[101] are subject to a diocesan censure of suspension. They, therefore, are liable to the censure of suspension, if they preach without the bishop's permission, if they hear confessions without the required jurisdiction from him, and finally, if they set up for public veneration images of an unwonted or offending character.[102]

[98] Canon 161, § 2.

[99] Canon 616, § 1.

[100] Compendium Privilegiorum Minorum, v. *Exemptio*, n. 9, 23, seq. St. Alphonsus, *Theologia Moralis*, VII, n. 26, Lyszczarczyk, *Compendium Privilegiorum Regularium*, art. IV, n. 5.

[101] Bull of Paul III, *Licet Debitum*, 18 oct. 1549—*Bullarium Diplomatum et Privilegiorum Sanctorum Romanorum Pontificum*, tom. VI (editio Taurinensis), Bulla LXV, 394.

[102] Gregorius XV, const. *Inscrutabili*, 5 febr. 1622—*Fontes*, n. 199.

In regard to the legal force of these privileges in the light of canon 613, § 1, there is no doubt that they retain their force, if the religious have obtained them from the Holy See by direct grant. But, if the privilege was obtained in the past by communication there is a divergence of opinion. Some authors[103] claim that the use of these privileges is restricted to those religious who have received them directly from the Holy See, to the exclusion of those who have received them through communication, because canon 613, § 1 as a particular law for religious, contains the revocation of communicated privileges required by the more general provisions of canon 4, since it evidently intends an exhaustive enumeration of the privileges which the religious possess under the new law, and definitely enumerates only those contained in the Code and those which may have been directly conceded. Other authors[104] maintain that religious still possess those privileges which are contained in the Code, those which they have in any way received in the past, and those which shall have been directly conceded by the Holy See in the future, which latter can not be communicated, because as they say, the subjunctive form *concessa fuerint* is to be taken as implying potentiality which *per se* prescinds from any question of time, but refers to the future. Canon 613, § 1 does not revoke these privileges, and therefore, they are still in force by virtue of canon 4.

In practice, however, in virtue of canon 209 and in deference to the authority of those canonists who uphold the milder view, all religious who received a privilege of specific exemption through communication may continue to make use of it, until the Holy See issues an authentic interpretation of canon 613, § 1.[105]

[103] Biederlack-Führich, *De Religiosis*, n. 145; Blat, *Commentarium*, II, n. 689; Chelodi, *Ius de Personis*, n. 280; Roelker, *Principles of Privilege According to the Code of Canon Law*, The Catholic University of America, Canon Law Studies, n. 35, Washington: The Catholic University of America, 1926, pp. 52-56.

[104] Vermeersch-Creusen, *Epitome*, I, nn. 615-713; Cocchi, *Commentarium*, II (De Personis), n. 111; Fanfani, *De Iure Religiosorum*, p. 362; *Commentarium pro Religiosis et Missionariis*, III (1922), p. 205; Augustine, *Commentary*, III, 333-334.

[105] Il *Monitore Ecclesiastico*, XXX (1918), p. 366:—"Sappiamo che l'ap-

Some of those matters over which the Ordinary has a right may be enumerated as follows: to pontificate in the churches of exempt religious;[106] to preach in the churches of regulars and other exempt religious;[107] to enlist the help of religious and of religious benefices for the support of the diocesan seminary; [108] to visit the schools, oratories, asylums, orphanages of exempt religious in matters pertaining to religious and moral instruction, not, however, the domestic schools of these religious;[109] to impose on benefices the obligation of temporary pensional payments coterminus with the life of the newly appointed beneficiary;[110] to visit the hospitals and orphanages of exempt religious for the sake of canonical inquiry about the teaching of religion, the probity of morals, the exercises of piety and the ministration of the sacraments and sacramentals;[111] to order the religious to abstain from the celebration of divine services, if, in the judgment of the local Ordinary, they prove a hindrance to the catechetical instruction and the preaching of the gospel in parochial churches;[112] to command the recitation of public prayers and the *oratio imperata;*[113] to force them to abide by the rules of the diocese in admitting outside or transient priests to the celebration of Mass;[114] to order them to conform to the established norm relative to the offering acceptable for manual stipends;[115] to command them to observe the diocesan rulings on the proper safeguards for divine worship and the integrity of faith and morals;[116] to order them to participate in the public proces-

plicazione di tale canone 613 è sospesa finchè la S.C. dei Religiosi non avra terminato il lavoro di revisione che sta compiendo sui privilegi delle varie Religioni e Instituti."

[106] Canon 337, § 1.

[107] Canon 1343, § 1.

[108] Canons 1355-1356.

[109] Canon 1382.

[110] Canon 1429.

[111] Canon 1491.

[112] Canon 609, § 3.

[113] Canon 612; S.R.C., n. 2613 ad 1 et 2; n. 3985.

[114] Canon 804, § 3.

[115] Canon 831, § 3.

[116] Canon 1261, § 2.

sions;[117] to order them, in accordance with his discretion, to assist in the work of religious and catechetical instructions;[118] to command them to give a short explanation of the gospel or some portion of Christian doctrine on all Sundays and feast-days of precept in their churches or public oratories;[119] finally, every five years, the local Ordinary must make a canonical visitation, either in person or through a delegate, of every house of clerical congregations of pontifical right, even those of religious enjoying exemption. This visitation, however, must extend only to the church, sacristy, public oratory and places where confessions are heard.[120]

According to a private response, which in this case has the force of a general interpretation from the general manner in which the questions were asked, a local Ordinary may not make a canonical visitation of the non-parochial churches of regulars and those enjoying the privileges of exemption, every five years, as he does of other non-exempt churches, merely to ensure the observance of the general laws of the Church. Furthermore, he is forbidden to visit habitually these churches every five years to see that his particular laws concerning the safeguards of divine worship and the integrity of faith and morals are carried out in virtue of the right accorded him by canon 1261. He may do this only when he has positive knowledge that these particular laws are not being observed in the churches of exempt religious and regulars.[121]

117 Canons 1291-1292.

118 Canon 1334.

119 Canon 1345.

120 Canon 512, § 2, n. 2.

121 Wernz-Vidal state the case which occasioned the response. They say, that in a certain city a delegate of the local Ordinary made a canonical visitation of a Jesuit non-parochial church. The superior of the house to which this church was attached placed no objection to the delegate's act. The Jesuit provincial, however, upon learning of this violation of exemption reminded the local Ordinary that the church in question enjoyed exemption and consequently was not subject to the quinquennial visitation of the Ordinary or his delegate. He claimed that the right of visitation as expressed in canon 1261, § 2 obtained only then when the bishop enacted special legislation in reference to the matters mentioned in canon 1261, § 1, and subsequently conducted his visitation for the purpose of certifying its observance or enforcing its fulfillment.

These are the principal cases in which the local Ordinary may issue penal mandates. Other instances are found in canons 454, § 5; 465, § 4, § 5; 471, § 3; 472, n. 1; 451, § 1; 476, § 4; 477, § 1; 631, § 1, § 2; 1291, § 1; 1349, § 2; 1406, n. 7; 1425, § 1, § 2, etc.

The practical conclusion to be drawn from the enumeration of these episcopal rights is, that where the bishop has a right to legislate and command, he also enjoys the right to inflict suspensions to ensure the observance of his laws and precepts.[122] Consequently, since religious are subject to the bishop in these matters, they are likewise bound by the suspensions attached to the violation of them.[123] Thus if a bishop makes a law in regard to divine worship for the removal of superstitious or unbecoming practices, all religious are bound by the law, according to canon 1261; and if the law contains an *ipso facto* suspension, all clerics alike without exception are liable to the vindictive sanctions written into the law. If the penal saction is of the nature of a censure, then such exempt religious as the Mendicants and the Jesuits and other religious en-

The local Ordinary repudiated the provincial's plea and denied the claim of exemption.—*Ius Canonicum,* III (De Religiosis), 429-430 in footnote. The litigated question was thereupon forwarded to the Holy See in the following queries:

"I. Utrum ordinarius loci templa Societatis Jesu in sua diocesi existentia modo praedicto quinto quoque anno visitare possit? Et quatenus negative:

"II. Utrum in casu, quo leges diocesanae non quidem novam materiam juxta canonem 1261 afferunt, sed solum leges ecclesiasticas urget ordinarius ad visitationem manum apponere possit? Et quatenus negative:

"III Utrum visitatio, de qua in canone 1261, § 2, eodem modo instituenda sit ac solita quinquennalis visitatio ecclesiarum non exemptarum? Et quatenus negative:

"IV. Utrum ad visitationem juxta canonem 1261, § 2, extendi possunt responsa S.C. Ep. et Reg. ante novum codicem data, ut nempe ordinarius visitationis jure in tantum solum generatim utitur, in quantum positivam habeat notitiam leges particulares a se latas in ecclesiis regularium exemptorum non observari? Responsum datum die 8 mensis Aprilis, 1924: ad Ium, IIum, et IIIum, negative; ad IVum affirmative."—*Commentarium pro Religiosis,* IX (1928), 243-247.

122 Canon 2220.

123 Canons 2226, § 1; 619:—"In omnibus in quibus religiosi subsunt Ordinario loci, possunt ab eodem etiam poenis coerceri."

joying the same exemption (as mentioned on p. 137) would of course escape this particular penal sanction, because of their specially privileged exemption.

Where the territory is exempt, as a prelature *nullius*, then any cleric, whether religious or secular, who violates a diocesan penal ordinance within the limits of this territory, does not incur an *ipso facto* suspension threatened by this particular law. The territory is considered extra-territorial, and therefore, beyond the jurisdictional powers of the local Ordinary. This extra-territorial immunity which is peculiar to the prelature *nullius*, when there is question of applying it to the houses of regulars and of religious enjoying the privileges of regulars, gives rise to a dispute.[124] Some authors[125] maintain that the exemption attaching to houses of regulars and other religious who enjoy the privileges of regulars rests fundamentally upon the personal exemption which each individual member of the religious community enjoys who is attached to these houses. The exemption is not because of the house itself but because of the religious dwelling therein. Other authors[126] claim that the houses of regulars enjoy extra-territorial immunity and therefore the principles regarding the incurring of penalties by transients must be applied to those who violate diocesan penal laws threatening *latae sententiae* punishments within these houses. Since there is a doubt, and since both views are considered probable, a secular cleric who violated a particular penal law of the diocese within the house of

[124] Oesterle, *Praelectiones Iuris Canonici*, I (Romae, 1931), 345.

[125] A Coronata, *Institutiones Iuris Canonici*, I, n. 623, note 1; Augustine, *Commentary*, III, 336; Vermeersch-Creusen, *Epitome*, 1, 717; Melo, *De Exemptione Regularium*, p. 21; Biederlack-Führich, *De Religiosis*, n. 35; Fanfani, *De Iure Religiosorum*, n. 356. Canons 337, § 1 and 804, § 3 are a strong argument against those who claim that monasteries enjoy extra-territorial immunity; for if this were true, then the situation would be, that, contrary to the prescripts of the above named canons, a local Ordinary would need permission to exercise pontificals within these monasteries, and further he would be powerless to oblige the resident religious to observe his special mandates regarding the "celebret".

[126] Capello, *De Censuris*, n. 20, 8o; Noldin, *Theologia Moralis*, I, n. 151; Genicot-Salsmans, *Institutiones Theologiae Moralis*, I, n. 97; St. Alphonsus, *Theologia Moralis*, VII, n. 24.

regulars and privileged religious, in virtue of canon 15, can not be held to a suspension threatened by the law.

Finally, all clerics, both regular and those exempt by privilege, may be bound by laws and penalties which the Holy See enacts in the place where they permanently reside or in places where they are simply transients. An example of a law to which these clerics are bound, though they be transients, is a decree of the *Vicariatus Urbis* issued on May 25, 1918. Here all clerics, both regular and secular, were forbidden to attend cinemas in the city of Rome. Should they violate this prohibition, so continues the decree, action will be taken against them even to the extent of a suspension *a divinis.*[127]

Not only a physical but also a moral person may be affected by the ecclesiastical punishment of suspension. According to canon 2285 this can be effected in a threefold way: either the individual members of the collegiate body suffer the suspension, or the community as such, or the community and the individual members simultaneously. If the suspension falls on the individual members, they become subject to all the effects, general or particular, total or partial, according to the tenor of the decree or sentence. If the suspension is inflicted on the community in its corporate capacity, the collegiate moral person is deprived of the exercise of those rights which belong to it as such. Such rights comprise, for example, the right of ecclesiastical suffrage accruing to the collegiate body, the holding of title to churches or benefices, the privilege of the *ius patronatus,* and the right of nominating candidates for ecclesiastical offices.[128] The suspension which is inflicted on the individual members and the moral person at the same time has a cumulative

[127] "Essendoci noto come non sempre nè da tutti gli ecclesiastici dell'uno e dell'altro clero siano osservate le savie disposizioni che in materia di pubblici spettacoli furono date da questo Vicariato con decreto del 15 luglio 1909, ricordiamo e rinnoviamo ora, per ordine ed autorità del Santo Padre, la proibizione assoluta al clero, così secolare come regolare, di assistere alle produzioni che si svolgono nei pubblici cinematografi di Roma, anche se fossero di soggetto sacro senza alcuna eccezione. Contro i trasgressori procederemo con le pene canoniche compresa la sospensione *a divinis."—AAS,* X (1918), 300.

[128] Canons 105; 471; 403; 1460.

effect. On the one hand, the individuals suffer the restriction of some of their personal prerogatives, and the community, on the other hand, is prohibited from the exercise of rights requiring corporate action.

The same separable effects come into play when there is question of a moral person, as those which obtain in reference to an individual cleric. Thus, there may be the suspension *a beneficio, ab officio, a iurisdictione,* etc. It must always be remembered that the infliction of a suspension upon a moral person as such contemplates the inhibition of the exercise of only such spiritual rights which the community of clerics enjoys in its character as a collegiate body or moral unit. Such a suspension does not affect the personal ecclesiastical rights of the individual members composing this corporate unit.

The foundation in law for the suspension of a moral person is the fact that such a corporate body, legitimately established as a juridical entity by a competent superior, possesses a collective will. Therefore, in this capacity it is capable of rights and obligations different from those inherent in its members as private individuals.[129] Wherefore, if the moral person alone is suspended, every member of the community must obey the punishment, no matter whether there is present any personal guilt or not. Such an action is not unjust, because in no way are personal rights curtailed. The individual clerics may continue to say Mass and exercise the other sacred functions of their state, even though the moral person had been suspended *ab officio.*

When the suspension has been inflicted, not only on the moral person as such but also on the individual members, the effects are understood to bind the guilty alone. The innocent are, therefore, free to exercise all their personal rights, unless natural law or the avoiding of scandal urges them otherwise, because no one can be suspended for the crime of another.[130]

THE NORMS FOR INCURRING AND THE NORMS FOR EXCUSING. With reference to what has been said thus far concerning the physi-

[129] Wernz, *Ius Decretalium,* VI, n. 18.

[130] St. Alphonsus, *Theologia Moralis,* VII, n. 317.

cal and moral subject, relative to the infliction of a suspension, these points must be borne in mind. The subject, whether known or unknown, present or absent,[131] must be, first of all, legally capable of a suspension. Then, there must be present a grave crime in the sense of law, namely, a grave, external, morally imputable violation of a law or a precept, to which has been attached a suspension.[132] This crime must be certain and not yet legitimately prescribed.[133] Furthermore, there must precede every infliction a threat, and in the case of censure a warning. The only exception to this general rule is, when there is present grave scandal or the crime is of an exceptionally serious character. Then the superior, in virtue of canon 2222, § 1, may inflict a suspension immediately without giving a previous threat or warning.

As to the incurring of a *latae sententiae* suspension, the crime must be complete and must correspond to the category and conditions as defined in the law.[134] Then again, to incur a suspension of this kind, the delinquent cleric must know that the law or precept forbids something under penalty.[135] It is not necessary, however, that he be fully cognizant of the nature of the penalty, namely, whether it is an excommunication, a suspension, or an interdict, or even whether or not it is reserved.[136] As long as the cleric knows the crime is punishable and nevertheless violates the law, he incurs the penalty attached to it. No previous admonition is necessary, in the case of a censure, because the law itself is a warning.

In general, it may be said that whatever excuses from a mortal sin also excuses from a *latae sententiae* suspension. Therefore, if the matter is not sufficiently grave the cleric will not incur the suspension. If it is impossible to fulfill a law threatening a suspension, or also if there is a defect of advertence, or a lack of deliberation, or a want of sufficient or readily acquirable knowledge, then likewise

[131] Canon 2242, § 1.
[132] Canon 2195, § 1.
[133] Canon 2233, § 1.
[134] Canon 2228.
[135] Canon 2202.
[136] Vermeersch-Creusen, *Epitome*, III, n. 422; Cocchi, *Commentarium*, V. (De Delictis et Poenis), n. 223.

no suspension is incurred. This, it is evident, concerns the forum of conscience. If there is *de facto* an external violation of the law or precept, the presumption is that all the conditions demanded by the law for the incurring of a *latae sententiae* suspension are present, and hence the offender in good faith would be bound by the suspension in the external forum, until the contrary is proven.

The general principle is that affected ignorance, namely, the deliberate will to be ignorant, does not excuse a cleric from incurring a suspension, no matter whether the ignorance concerns the law itself or merely the penalty. This would equally apply even if the law contained phrases, such as, *praesumpserit, ausus fuerit, scienter, studiose, temerarie, consulto egerit* or other similar expressions. Outside of the case of affected ignorance, whenever these words or their equivalent are used, any diminution of imputability, whether on the part of the will or on the part of the intellect, excuses from every type of suspension, because these words demand full cognition and deliberation. Should the law be wanting in phrases of this kind but merely mentions the suspension to be incurred on the occasion of its violation, then an ignorance that is crass or supine will not excuse from the *latae sententiae* suspension, no matter whether it is medicinal or vindictive. By crass or supine ignorance is meant that want of knowledge which arises from a seriously grave culpability, because little or no trouble was taken to become acquainted with the truth. On the other hand, if the ignorance is not crass or supine but simply grave, namely, an ignorance which arises from the fact that the cleric has made at least some effort to know,—even though it was culpably insufficient to attain its end—then he would be excused from all medicinal suspensions but not from those which are vindictive in character. However, in this case, the superior is free to punish this cleric with some other appropriate penalty or penance, if circumstances warrant such an action.[137]

Then, if the above mentioned expressions like *praesumpserit,* etc., are not used, drunkenness, the omission of due diligence, mental debility and the impetus of passion do not excuse from a

[137] Canon 2229, § 1, § 2, § 3, n. 1, § 4.

latae sententiae suspension, as long as the act remains gravely culpable.[138] Nor does grave fear excuse from such a suspension, if the threats occasioning the fear are made directly for the purpose of contemning faith or all ecclesiastical authority or the crime, if committed under such fear, would be detrimental to souls. The cleric thus coerced is bound to resist the pressure brought to bear upon him, and that, under pain of incurring the suspension attached to the law.[139]

The question might be asked whether *metus levis* frees a cleric from a *latae sententiae* suspension when such words as *praesumpserit, ausus fuerit, scienter,* etc., are found in the law? One's first impression is that *metus levis* excuses a cleric from a penalty of this kind, because the text of canon 2229, § 2 expressly decrees that any diminution of imputability either on the part of the intellect or on the part of the will frees the delinquent from the penal effects of the law.[140] But, throughout the Code, each law which makes mention of a diminution of imputability clearly directs that *metus gravis* removes that required responsibility which a law demands as a requisite for the incurring of a penalty.[141] No where is there any statement to the effect that *metus levis* influences an act to the extent that it takes away or affects the culprit's liability, and thereby frees him from the penal sanction.

The general principle of law must be kept in mind, namely, whatever excuses from grave imputability excuses likewise from the incurring of the penal sanction attached to the violation of a law.[142] *Metus levis*, as seen from its definition, lacks that strong impelling force which is the essential characteristic of *metus gravis*. It may be defined as a fear which does not influence a resolute man and only slightly affects one who is less firm. Since the amount of moral

138 Canon 2229, § 3, n. 2; 2201, § 3.

139 Canon 2229, § 3, n. 3; 2205, § 3.

140 Canon 2229, § 2:—" . . . quaelibet imputabilitatis imminutio sive ex parte intellectus sive ex parte voluntatis eximit a poenis latae sententiae."

141 Canons 2205, § 2; 2218, § 1, § 2; 2229, § 3, n. 3.

142 Canon 2218, § 2:—"Non solum quae ab omni imputabilitate excusant, sed etiam quae a gravi, excusant pariter a qualibet poena tum latae tum ferendae sententiae . . . etc."

duress which a person suffers from *metus levis* is so slight, it is evident, there is absent a motivating force sufficiently powerful enough to induce the serious diminution of real freedom which the Code demands to excuse one from incurring a penal sanction. In fact, it may be said, that a cleric who because of *metus levis* violates a grave penal law renders himself seriously contumacious and thus becomes a fit subject for the incurring of a *latae sententiae* suspension, since he allows himself to be motivated in his transgression by some trivial cause.

The phrase *quaelibet imputabilitatis imminutio* must be interpreted in harmony with canonical norms. Since *metus gravis* alone is recognized by the Code as excusing one from grave imputability and as a result, likewise from the incurring of penalties, no other fear is sufficient to take away the delinquent's amenability to these penalties. *Metus levis* diminishes the culprit's imputability so slightly that the rule may be applied: *parum pro nihilo reputatur*. The conclusion, therefore, is that any cleric who transgresses a law while laboring under *metus levis*, when this law has written in its text such expressions as *praesumpserit, ausus fuerit, scienter*, etc., renders himself liable to the incurring of *latae sententiae* suspensions threatened by this law.[143]

Canon 2202,§ 3 declares, that what concerns ignorance applies also to inadvertence and error. It is clear that when a cleric violates a penal law of the Church through inadvertence or error, he does not act wilfully, unless there is present some culpability. Complete inadvertence and error are, therefore, placed on the same plane with invincible ignorance, and consequently, follow the same norms as given above. Gravely culpable inadvertence or error, in like manner, is placed on an equal basis with vincible ignorance. It must further be remarked, that in this whole question of ignorance, inadvertence and error, no ignorance, inadvertence or error concerning the law or its penalty is generally presumed.[144] This pre-

143 Cfr. Bouuaert, "De Metus Influxu Quoad Valorem Actuum et Quoad Delicta et Poenas Secundum Codicem Juris Canonici,"—*Monographiae Juridicae Ex Ephemeride Ius Pontificium Excerptae Eiusve Cura Editae*, Series I, Fascic. XIII (1926), nn. 1-15.

144 Canon 16, § 2.

sumption, however, is a mere supposition of the law. When direct arguments or proofs to the contrary can be established, this presumption must give place to the demonstrated truth, for a presumption is at most an improper test of proof, the probable conjecture concerning a thing still uncertain in itself. When the truth is known, the presumption yields to it.

CHAPTER VI

THE JUDICIAL TRIAL

Besides the exceptional course for which provision is made in canon 2222, § 1, there are two methods of inflicting a suspension. The one is by judicial sentence; the other is by a precept administered in writing or intimated in the presence of two witnesses.[1] This latter is known as the extrajudicial method. The present consideration will be concerned exclusively with the formal trial which always precedes a judicial sentence. Later on, in chapter VII, the rules governing the extrajudicial method will be discussed.

When a law or a precept has been violated, in which a *latae* or *ferendae sententiae* suspension has been threatened for transgressors, the juridical elements inherent in the case give rise to two kinds of suits. The one, known as the criminal suit, contemplates not only the declaration or infliction of penalties but also, whenever there is need, the procurement and discharge of the satisfaction and expiation necessitated by the crime. The other suit, called a contentious suit (*actio contentiosa*), has for its objective the reparation and compensation of damages caused by the commission of the crime.[2] Since any further explanation of this kind of trial or suit is irrelevant to the purpose of this chapter, it suffices to state the fact of the possibility of such a suit arising in connection with criminal proceedings.

Before any criminal action at court can be undertaken, the essential and fundamental object demanded by law, that is, the existence of a public crime,[3] must actually be verified. The law further requires that the crime be certain and not prescribed by the legal statute of temporal limitation.[4]

Canon 1703 directs that crimes which are not reserved to the

[1] Canon 2225.
[2] Canon 2210, § 1.
[3] Canon 1933, § 1.
[4] Canon 2233, § 1.

Holy Office for a judgment must be prosecuted within an available period of three years after the commission of the crime. For questions of injury to personal honor or repute, the crime must be prosecuted within one year. If there is question of qualified crimes which violate the sixth and seventh commandments, then the available time for prosecution is extended to five years. If the matter to be prosecuted is a crime of simony or homicide then prescription runs its full course only after the lapse of ten years usable for the act of prosecution.

The crime, besides being certain and non-prescribed, must possess the elements of publicity, both material and formal, namely, not only must the crime be known, but also the fact that the act is imputable as a crime must also be known.[5] Then again, the crime must be such that its existence can be proved in the external forum. For this proof, truly demonstrative arguments must be available, or at least such indications which establish a sufficiently probable incrimination of the suspect, before a formal accusation may be lodged against him in court.[6]

Consequently, no occult crime falls within the jurisdiction of the court. Were a cleric summoned to court for such a crime, he would have a right to object to the prosecution. The court, however, will rule on this point. If the defendant's objection is nevertheless overruled and the court proceeds to take action, the cleric has redress in an appeal to a court of higher instance.

It is not, however, necessary to institute a criminal trial, when the crime is certain and notorious because then there are present

[5] The real meaning of material and formal publicity may be better understood from an explanation given by Michiels of the *delictum materialiter* and the *delictum formaliter occultum*:—"Delictum *est occultum materialiter, si lateat delictum ipsum,* idest ipsum factum criminosum, qua factum, puta si Titius occiderit clericum, sed vulgo credatur mortem fuisse naturaliter ortam; *formaliter, si lateat delicti imputabilitas,* idest quando factum ipsum est publicum, sed ignoratur dolus vel culpa delinquentis, puta si publice sciatur Titium fuisse a Petro occisum, sed vulgo creditur Petrum mortem intulisse ex mero casu fortuito vel justae defensionis causa."—*De Delictis et Poenis,* I, 120.

[6] Canon 1946, § 2, n. 3; Vermeersch-Creusen, *Epitome,* III, n. 258; Noval, *De Processibus,* n. 751.

sufficiently convincing documentary proofs to establish the certitude which the court itself would seek to substantiate.[7] In such an event, the superior may proceed extrajudicially and inflict or declare the suspension immediately without any judicial investigation. Nor is it necessary to administer any canonical rebukes, nor is it necessary to institute formal accusations, not even to cite the culprit. Although the Code takes no cognizance of a procedure of this kind, yet it is not wanting in legal value, since in pre-Code times notorious crimes could be penalized without the ordinary judicial formality.[8] This fact alone suffices to render this legal practice legitimate, especially in view of canon 6.

Similarly it becomes unnecessary to institute a criminal trial whenever a cleric has admitted or confessed the guilt of which he is suspected.[9] Upon the confession the Ordinary will generally administer a judicial rebuke.[10] There are, however, cases in which a judicial rebuke is inapplicable. These cases are the following: 1) Delinquencies which imply excommunication the absolution from which is most specially (*specialissimo modo*) or even in a special manner (*speciali modo*) reserved to the Holy See; also the crimes which entail infamy, deposition, degradation or the deprivation of benefice;

2) Cases in which there is need of the authoritative declaration of the vindictive or medicinal penalty incurred by the delinquent;

3) Situations in which the Ordinary deems the use of a judicial rebuke insufficient for the reparation of scandal and the rehabilitation of justice. In such cases no option remains. The Ordinary must either proceed to a declaration of the penalty already incurred

7 Canon 1747, n. 1; Wernz-Vidal, *Ius Canonicum,* VI (De Processibus), n. 720.

8 Cfr. C. 21, C. II, q. 1; Barbosa in Comment. super Part. II Decret., C. II, q. 1, c. 21, p. 204; Joannes Andreae in Comment. super Decret., *de verborum significatione,* c. XXIIII; c. 3, X, *de testibus cogendis,* II, 21; c. 9, X, *de accusationibus,* V, 1; *S. Romanae Rotae Decisiones seu Sententiae,* V (1919), Dec. X, nn. 6-7.

9 Canons 1747, n. 3; 1947.

10 Wernz-Vidal, *Ius Canonicum,* VI (De Processibus), n. 728 in fine.

or invoke the stronger sanction of a condemnatory sentence whenever his rebuke would fail of its desired effect.[11]

In all cases wherein the crime is not yet fully certified or in which an admission or confession of guilt has not intervened to make possible the administration of a judicial rebuke or the official declaration of the penalty already incurred, a previous special investigation must be made to prepare the way for a formal accusation in court, which eventually will be followed by the court's judicial sentence. The possibility of initiating such an investigation in order to determine whether and in how far the incrimination is justified, may arise from a number of considerations or circumstances such as the knowledge which is had of the case through rumors, gossip or public hearsay, through acts of denunciation or reports of guilt, through charges or complaints of the harm and damages sustained, through informal investigations or general inquiries made by the Ordinary, and the like. Such a special formal investigation is needed regardless of whether the vindictive or medicinal canonical penalty is to be inflicted or whether it is to be declared as already existent.[12]

It is to be noted that in criminal proceedings there may be two successive stages in the judicial procedure, namely, the procedure by inquisition and the procedure upon accusation.

In the inquisitorial procedure the Ordinary or his delegate collects material relative to the case, and when he has gathered a sufficient amount, or it is impossible to find more, he passes judgment in the form of an opinion. The defense in this procedure seems to proceed from the Ordinary or his delegate just as much as the charge. The Ordinary or the delegate must inquire into everything that might prove the accused to be not guilty; and although the accused may assist and help the one making the inquiry, yet he certainly retains the status of one to be examined rather than the position of one defending himself.

The accusatorial procedure, on the other hand, is consequent upon the findings of the inquisition. Here there is question of a

[11] Canons 1947; 1948.

[12] Canon 1939, § 1, § 2.

real plaintiff and defendant. The plaintiff who will urge or demand the declaration or the infliction of a suspension upon the accused cleric is the promoter of justice.[13] This type of process demands that the accusation be laid before the accused and an opportunity given him for immediate defense. Whether or not he will avail himself of this defense is completely left to himself. He is free to engage in a defense or to pass it by. He may plead guilty or challenge the promoter of justice to prove his charge.

The investigation preparatory to the trial must have as its purpose solely the accumulation of data to be used in the formal accusation of the cleric under suspicion. And, while it is in progress, the utmost secrecy and circumspection must be rigorously observed, lest the rumor of the crime be spread thereby, and the good repute of some innocent party be endangered. The honor of the clerical state and the delicate esteem of the priesthood, which are so indispensible for any beneficial ministrations among souls, demand such secrecy.[14]

The Ordinary has the independent right to make this investigation. As a general rule, however, he should commit the handling of the case to one of the synodal judges. And when a special reason urges, he may even select someone else to make the investigations.[15]

The Vicar General does not by reason of his office enjoy this right. He needs a special mandate, since the making of the investigations is an exercise of judicial power. Nor can it be said that the *Officialis* has the right to make the investigations, because the law expressly mentions the Ordinary.

The delegate judge who is making the investigation is limited to the matter of the investigation exclusively. It is his duty to collect all possible evidence bearing on the case, not only that which may convict the accused, but also that by which he may be exonerated from the charge. He should be especially solicitous to obtain evidence of the latter kind when it is of such a nature that, if not pro-

[13] Canon 1934.
[14] Canons 1943; 1623.
[15] Canons 1940; 1941, § 1; 1573.

cured at once, it may become unavailable by delay. He should not fail to keep in mind the accompanying circumstances, as these will play a great part in the formation of his opinion.

Once the material has been gathered, the office of the investigator terminates. He may not exercise the office of judge later when the case is brought to trial. This provision, however, is not for the validity of the act.[16] He is at liberty to summon any one, of whom he thinks information concerning the crime in question could be obtained. To assure himself of the veracity of their statements, he may administer an oath to obtain the truth and also to ensure secrecy regarding the affair.[17] It must not be forgotten that before the delegated judge begins the investigation, he himself must take an oath to observe secrecy, to fulfill his office conscientiously and to abstain from bribes.[18]

At the completion of the investigation, all *data* must be referred to the Ordinary together with the unbiased opinion of the one who made the inquiries, concerning the certainty of the crime and the fact that the act is imputable as a crime.[19] The Ordinary, or at his special command the *Officialis,* shall then by decree order, that if the denunciation appears to lack a solid foundation, a declaration to that effect be issued and appended to the acts of the investigation. All the documents shall be placed in the secret archives. If, on the other hand, the indications really point to a crime, but are not sufficiently cogent to justify an accusatorial procedure, these acts, too, shall be deposited in the same archives. The conduct of the cleric shall thereafter be watched. If the Ordinary deem it advisable he shall also give the cleric a hearing in the matter or even resort to cautions and warnings according to canon 2307, if the case would warrant such action. Finally, should the case appear certain or at least probable, then, with sufficient reasons militating for the open-

[16] Cfr. Canon 1941, § 3; De Meester, *Compendium,* III, pars 2a, n. 1629; Noval, *De Processibus,* n. 774.

[17] Canons 1941, § 3; 1944.

[18] Canons 1621-1624.

[19] Canon 1946, § 1.

ing of a criminal trial, he shall order the accused to be summoned.[20]

In accordance with circumstances, the Ordinary can reestablish the disturbed harmony of the social order in a twofold way: he will administer either a judicial rebuke or enforce the holding of a criminal trial. The purpose of the rebuke is to preclude the criminal trial and to reclaim the culprit from his delinquency. Hence it intervenes not as a threat against a crime which is likely to happen, but as a reproof for the crime which has taken place.[21] In this it differs from the extrajudicial admonition whose purpose is to fortify a still corrigible person against committing a crime. The judicial rebuke must, as a rule, contain not only salutary admonitions, but also some appropriate remedies or prescriptions of penances or good works, which serve to make public reparation for the violation of the law through the restoration of wounded justice and the extirpation of the scandal given.[22]

Since the judicial rebuke is to take the place of the penalty,[23] it can not be inflicted by the Vicar General without a special mandate. Nor has the *Officialis* this right, because the canon expressly speaks of the Ordinary.

In the matter of suspensions no judicial rebuke is permitted, if there is question of passing a declaratory sentence relative to the penalty which has been already incurred in the commission of the crime. It is also forbidden when the rebuke will not suffice to repair the scandal.[24] On the other hand, the law permits the rebuke, when the delinquent has confessed his crime or as was stated before, when the Ordinary wishes to avoid a criminal trial.[25] As to the number of times it may be granted, canon 1949 clearly prescribes that it may be employed once or twice, but not a third time against the same offender for the same offense. Wherefore, if the de-

[20] Canon 1946, § 2, n. 1, 2, 3.

[21] Wernz-Vidal, *Ius Canonicum*, VI (De Processibus), n. 728; Vermeersch-Creusen, *Epitome*, III, n. 267.

[22] Canons 1947; 1952.

[23] Canon 2309, § 4.

[24] Canon 1948, nn. 2, 3.

[25] Canon 1947.

linquent after the second rebuke commits the same crime, criminal procedure must be instituted, or, if begun, continued according to the form outlined in canons 1954-1959.

It must be remembered that no cleric is bound to confess his crime in court. If he should be asked by a judge whether or not he is guilty of the crime, he is not bound to incriminate himself. The reason is because the Code does not impose this obligation. In fact the Code expressly states in canon 1743, § 1, that if the parties are questioned by the judge, they must respond and disclose the truth, except when questioned about the crime committed by them. Even in his day, St. Alphonsus claimed strong probability for the view which held that a delinquent need not make himself known.[26] In uttering his denial the accused is looked upon as making a mental restriction; he denies the crime in as much as it need not be confessed by him.[27]

Confession of the crime will not necessarily preclude a judicial sentence. Sometimes the judicial rebuke, when employed, will remain inefficacious in its intended effect. The common good may demand that the truth relative to the commission of the crime and its responsible author be established judicially. In these instances, the Ordinary would be bound to pass sentence in a public trial.[28]

If the rebuke has proved fruitless and ineffective in restraining the cleric from his criminal ways and if all means of avoiding a criminal prosecution have been exhausted, then the Ordinary, or the *Officialis* by special mandate, shall order the acts of the investigation to be submitted to the promoter of justice.[29] He, in turn, will frame the formal libellus of judicial accusation or indictment and present it to the judge. Thus, the formal trial opens, with the promoter of justice taking the part of the plaintiff.

Since the Ordinary has made a previous examination of the content of the libellus, the *Officialis* must admit the bill of accusation

[26] *Theologia Moralis*, IV, n. 274.

[27] Aertnys-Damen, *Theologia Moralis*, I, n. 1227; Marc-Gestermann, *Institutiones Morales Alphonsianae*, II, n. 2309.

[28] Wernz-Vidal, *Ius Canonicum*, VI (De Processibus), n. 729.

[29] Canon 1954.

and confine his investigation to the bill. He may not eject what the Ordinary has already admitted and accepted. If it should happen that there is some defect in the libellus, the *Officialis* should for prudence sake notify the Ordinary. Then the Ordinary and the promoter of justice can reconsider these defects and rectify them.[30]

When the libellus has been accepted, the court constituting a collegiate tribunal of three judges,[31] will cite the delinquent and demand an answer to the charges and accusations preferred against him. Should the defendant, when duly summoned, fail to appear in court on the day and at the hour named in the citation, he may be declared in contempt of court.[32] After repeated threats he may be punished according to the provisions of the law.[33] The defendant is then presumed to have renounced his rights of defense and to have thrown himself upon the justice and mercy of the court for an equitable settlement. The court accomplishes this through the agency of an advocate who takes the place of the defaulter.[34]

The contumacious defendant is not totally excluded from a voice in the trial. He is even permitted to appear to give an account of his defense before a sentence is pronounced. After the sentence, however, he no longer enjoys this right; and, the only redress for him is the *restitutio in integrum,* which he must request within three months from the date of the notification of the sentence.[35]

If the accused appears, when summoned, he shall be granted a hearing according to the norms set down in canons 1742 to 1746. The oath, however, can not be demanded of him.

Sometimes scandal might arise, when it is learned that a cleric who has been brought to trial, continues to exercise his sacred ministry. Consequently, the law permits the judge to make use of an administrative measure, to forbid the exercise of the sacred ministry or the public celebration of Holy Mass. This, it must be remarked,

[30] Roberti, *De Processibus,* I, n. 251.

[31] Canon 1576, § 1, n. 1.

[32] Canon 1711 seq.

[33] Canons 1842-1851.

[34] Canon 1655, § 1; Wernz-Vidal, *Ius Canonicum,* VI (De Processibus), n. 507.

[35] Canons 1846; 1847.

is a prohibition which is administrative rather than penal, precisely because of the parity of this case with canon 2222, § 2. No irregularity would follow its violation, since the prohibition must arise *mediante poena canonica.*[36] It must further be noted that it is the *public* exercise of sacred functions and the *public* celebration of Mass which is to be forbidden and not the *private.*[37]

When the time arrives for the issuance of the sentence, the judge must consider the number of offenses committed. As a general rule, each crime demands a separate punishment.[38] If, however, the number of crimes should call for too great a number of suspensions, the judge is at liberty in his discretion to inflict the severest suspension, and, if circumstances warrant such an action, he may add some further penances or remedial punishments. He is also at liberty to mitigate the suspensions in accordance with equity.[39] He must judge whether the crime was consummated or not and regulate the infliction accordingly. If both the consummated crime and the attempted crime have suspensions attached to them, the law directs that use is to be made of that penalty alone which is enacted for the consummated crime.[40]

Moreover, the judge must never forget that, before he can undertake to issue a condemnatory or a declaratory sentence, he must have moral certitude concerning the crime in question.[41] When this is had the sentence is to be drawn up by the *ponens.*[42] It shall be subscribed by all the judges considering the case and also by a notary.[43] The Pontifical Commission for the Authentic Interpretation of the Code declared on July 14, 1922 that the signatures of all the judges of a collegiate tribunal are necessary for validity.[44]

Unless there is an urgent reason for repairing a scandal, it is left

[36] Canon 985, n. 7.
[37] Canon 1956.
[38] Canon 2224, § 1.
[39] Canon 2223, § 3, n. 3.
[40] Canon 2224, § 2, § 3.
[41] Canon 1869, § 1.
[42] Canons 1584; 1872.
[43] Canon 1874.
[44] *AAS*, XIV (1922), 528.

to the discretion of the judges to suspend the execution of a vindictive penalty of suspension attached to a law or a precept *ferendae sententiae* and inflicted by a condemnatory sentence, if the crime is the first one which the offender of hitherto good repute has committed. But this leniency is not without its condition. If the cleric within the next three years commits another offense either of the same or of a different kind, he shall be liable to the penalty of both offenses.[45]

It is evident, that this legal provision applies only to the vindictive penalty of suspension, because of the contradiction that would arise if in the case of a censure equal leniency were granted. The censure's purpose is to break the contumacious will of the delinquent. To suspend the sentence in this case would be to defeat this purpose. It is also evident, that the law applies solely to the penalty of suspension *ferendae sententiae*, because the judge has no option once the penalty of suspension *latae sententiae* has been incurred. It is impossible for him to suspend the effects. The law, however, leaves it indeed to the discretion of the judge whether or not to issue a declaratory sentence, as long as an interested party or the public welfare does not demand otherwise. But at the instance of either, the judge can not but proceed to a declaration.[46] When this is issued, the effect of the suspension, concerning which the declaration has been made, is acknowledged as operative from the moment when the penalty was actually incurred.[47]

The condemnatory and declaratory sentences, as pronounced by a tribunal of judges, bring with them those invalidating effects which the Code so often refers to in connection with the censure of suspension.[48] They differ, therefore, from the extrajudicial infliction of the penalty, whether vindictive or medicinal, or the mere declaration consequent upon the violation of a law or precept, to which a suspension had been annexed *latae sententiae*. The princi-

[45] Canon 2288.

[46] Canon 2223, § 4.

[47] Canon 2232, § 2:—"Sententia declaratoria poenam ad momentum commissi delicti retrotrahit."

[48] Cfr. canons 2283; 2284.

pal factor to be always borne in mind is that these invalidating effects have their force only when the suspension is the outcome of a trial and judicial sentence, condemnatory or declaratory.

Finally, after the sentence has been passed and the guilty party informed, whether or not the sentence should be declared publicly is left to the prudence of the judge. He should, however, undertake to publish the sentence when the enormity of the crime, the scandal given, the danger of others becoming corrupted, or the continued obstinacy of the cleric render this step useful and necessary.[49] This is, indeed, a very efficient way for constraining an offending cleric to return more speedily to his path of duty, because such a publication will bring added disgrace and confusion to his delayed amendment. The seriousness of the suspension will all the more clearly and drastically be impressed upon the offender, when he finds himself shunned by the faithful in all those things to which the Church has attached her ominous prohibitions.

How and in what manner this publication will be effected, remains with the decision of the Ordinary or the judge, who may determine whether the sentence of suspension is to be made known in the whole diocese or simply in the parish of the guilty cleric. It can be made either by public announcement in the church during divine services or by having it posted on the doors of the church or in other public places or even by giving it publicity in the newspapers.[50]

[49] Kober, *Die Suspension,* p. 65.

[50] Cfr. S. B. Smith, *Elements of Ecclesiastical Law,* III, 212.

CHAPTER VII

EXTRAJUDICIAL PROCEDURE

The Church has deemed it necessary, both for the spiritual good of the common weal and particularly for the welfare of the individual cleric, to depart, in certain instances, from the procedure customary in formal trials and to establish an extrajudicial method which finds no counterpart in the civil law, where the infliction of penalties outside of the court-room is unknown. Sometimes the immediate infliction of a suspension is imperative, both for the chastening of the offending cleric and also for the reparation of the crime and its disastrous effects upon the social order. Then again, there are times when a judicial formal trial is not necessary. The crime may have been notorious, or there may be at hand convincing documentary evidence which removes all doubt as to the certainty of the crime, the identity of the criminal and the grave imputability attaching to his misdeed. In such cases the principles of the natural law necessitate no investigation for the infliction or declaration of suspensions in accordance with the demand for the one or the other of these penalties. Then, too, a formal trial may be impossible, even though a real public crime is in question. This might happen when the civil authorities interfere, or where the cleric himself makes use of means to prohibit any attempt at a trial. The superior may then employ the extrajudicial procedure and inflict or declare a suspension. Finally, there are times when the formal trial is absolutely forbidden. This is true especially when the affair at hand involves an occult crime. The Code clearly directs, in canon 1933, § 1, that only public crimes may be prosecuted before an ecclesiastical tribunal.

If a cleric is guilty of a certain and notorious crime, it suffices for the Ordinary to inflict or declare the suspension immediately, as was stated in Chapter VI. The pre-Code law is accepted as the directive norm in the absence of any pertinent legislation. There is no need for a formal process in this case, since the object of this process has already been attained. Its object simply is to gather evidence which is sufficient either to condemn the culprit or to exonerate him. The notoriety of the crime is evidence enough of the presence of a delictual act. Posited that a threat of suspension is expressed in the law or precept, the cleric guilty of this notorious crime may be suspended immediately without further ado. But, even if there were no previous threat of suspension and the crime was notorious or simply public, the fact of the particular gravity of this crime as well as the grave scandal consequent upon its commission would warrant the superior's use of canon 2222, § 1, in virtue of which he may instantly inflict a suspension, when conditions there expressed have been verified.

Outside of these cases a superior may not suspend a cleric without exhausting every means at his disposal to ensure himself of the cleric's incorrigibility. He enjoys a twofold approach for securing and certifying his knowledge of the cleric's delinquency and incorrigibility whilst at the same time safeguarding all the dictates of social justice and Christian charity. These two methods may be designated the *preparatory* and *constitutive* processes.

Before discussing anything relative to the preparatory or constitutive methods or precesses, it is of importance to find and trace the source of the present law governing the extrajudicial procedure. For the special procedure regulating the infliction of the suspension *ex informata conscientia,* the Code offers a set of rules in canons 2186 to 2194. But is primarily contemplates merely the cases of occult crimes. Cases of public crimes are considered only in extraordinary circumstances, namely, when for some reason or situation beyond his control or adjustment, the Ordinary can not resort to the customary method of a judicial criminal trial. But, for the ordinary cases of public crimes, as well as for cases in which there lurks a strong suspicion of guilt, one must seek elsewhere for the indication of a procedural norm. Such a norm seems supplied by the Code in the manner of its procedure against concubinary clerics. No other norm seems available which would apply to situations in which a superior wishes to bring his clerical subject to task before proceeding to the extreme measure of suspension. As a consequence the rule of canon 20 would seem to favor the adoption of this extrajudicial method or process. It would not appear to be a groundless contention to insist that such a norm must be followed, since, first of all, the natural law itself demands some kind of summary process when the guilt of a cleric remains to be certified and determined, and secondly, because throughout the section on penal remedies in the Code, the mind of the legislator manifestly stresses the utility of the less stringent antidotes of canonical cautions, rebukes, reproofs, penances and authoritative surveillance, before inclining to and favoring the drastic method of inflicting canonical penalties.[1] Thus the ultimate sanction of a canonical penalty, such as suspension for clerics, will result only after the application of the intermediate successive steps of penal remedies has proved futile. And so, each of these steps is but a link in the chain of procedure which can be ultimately used as legal fetters to secure the certainty of guilt against all possible elusion. This method is carried out in the procedure against concubinary clerics. Since the Code proposes no separate or different norm for the infliction of a suspension extrajudicially, one may fairly and rightly conclude that the same norm is thus made available for the latter contingency.

THE PREPARATORY PROCESS. In using the preparatory method or process the Ordinary must first of all have recourse to canonical admonitions and cautions, if he judges them useful and promising of success. By means of these acts, he will call upon the cleric to amend and correct his conduct, if the latter be in the proximate occasion of committing a criminal deed or if he be already under the grave suspicion of guilt.[2]

Before undertaking any admonition the Ordinary should hear the delinquent in regard to the offense. He should tell him of the charge pending against him and acquaint him with some of the evidence. That the accused be allowed to defend himself is evident, because then the Ordinary will be able better to see the peculiar circumstances under which the cleric did the act. If the accused or the suspect can not fully clear himself, then canonical admonitions and cautions should be employed.

The first is the informal or paternal admonition which is always

[1] Canons 2214, § 2; 2233, § 2; 2223, § 3, n. 3; 2222, § 1; 2307; 2308; 2310.
[2] Canon 2307.

secret. It is merely a fatherly talk with the cleric entreating him to conduct himself in a becoming manner, not only for his own good but the good also of the clerical state which he is bound in conscience to respect. It may be communicated either personally or through another agent or in writing. When the paternal admonition is secret, the account of it is to be placed in the secret archives.[3] The Ordinary must make a private note of the fact or if made by another, he must retain the certification, in order to justify himself in the event of a legal recourse against him.

The formal or strictly canonical warnings and rebukes may be given either at once, before any paternal admonition, if the Ordinary thinks it necessary, or after the cleric makes light of the paternal admonition or even refuses to accept it. This type of warning and rebuke is undertaken in a legal fashion, before a notary or two witnesses or by registered mail.[4] They are ordained, first of all, for the correction of the cleric by calling his attention to his reprehensible conduct, and secondly, to furnish a definite foundation for a conviction consequent upon proof of his eventual contumacy.[5] No matter how severe and strong the warning or rebuke is there should be no threat of suspension contained therein. This should be reserved for the canonical precept or injunction. The formalities observed in the warning and rebuke are for the purpose of providing ready proof of the cleric's obstinacy, should he refuse to amend. By these formalities it may afterwards be shown that the warning and rebuke were formally addressed to the delinquent. In order, however, not to injure unnecessarily the reputation of the warned or rebuked cleric, the witnesses may be sworn to observe secrecy. A record stating the number of times these warnings and rebukes were administered must be made and preserved in the diocesan archives. The Code leaves it to the discretion of the Ordinary to make use of the warnings or cautions, the rebukes or reproofs merely once or repeatedly.[6] De Meester implies that one warning

[3] Canon 2309, § 1, § 5.

[4] Canons 2308; 2309, § 2.

[5] *S. Romanae Rotae Decisiones seu Sententiae,* I, Dec. V, n. 10.

[6] Canon 2309, § 6.

is sufficient in all cases in which the law does not expressly call for repeated admonitions.[7]

The formal canonical warning just spoken of is the one which must ordinarily precede the infliction of the censure of suspension. It is not prerequired for the infliction of the vindictive penalty. A mere threat is necessary in this case to warn the culprit. But, since the censure's purpose is the breaking up of contumacy, there must be some means of determining this fact. The canonical warning lends itself as a ready means.

Whether or not the canonical warning is necessary for the valid infliction of a censure seems to be disputed. Cappello[8] and Salucci[9] are of the opinion that the censure would be invalid. Augustine, on the other hand, claims that the censure would be valid, but unjust.[10] Some way of determining whether contumacy is present or not is demanded. It need not be by a warning. It could be by precept or a so-called *monitorium,* which corresponds to a mandatory writ of a court or an episcopal edict commanding something under threat of suspension. The Code does require a warning before a censure is to be imposed as a *ferendae sententiae* penalty. No such requisite is demanded for the incurring of a *latae sententiae* censure. The law is sufficient warning. But when the Code makes mention of the warning to be given prior to the infliction of a censure in canon 2233, § 2, it offers no evidence to show that the warning is necessary for validity. Consequently, in view of canon 11 which demands the specific inclusion of an invalidating clause in the law in order to connote the corresponding effect of invalidity, it appears to be a safe conclusion to maintain that this warning need not be regarded as a condition necessary for validity. As a result the infliction of a censure without such a previous warning can not be seriously questioned relative to its validity. If laws which have invalidating clauses written into them do not bind and lack all com-

[7] *Compendium,* III, pars 2a, n. 1724. For instances where the law calls for repeated warnings cfr. canons 649, 660, 662

[8] *De Censuris,* n. 34.

[9] *Il diritto penale secondo il codice di diritto canonico,* I, 160.

[10] *Commentary,* VIII, 117.

pelling force as long as their legal interpretation remains in doubt,[11] then there is still more reason for questioning the binding force of a law concerning which there is not merely a doubt in its meaning, but a doubt about its very existence. Doubtfully existent laws surely exert no more compelling force than doubtfully applicable laws. Since, then, one can rightfully doubt the very existence of an invalidating clause in canons 2233, § 2 and 2242, § 2 relative to the need of a warning prior to the infliction of a censure, a censure inflicted contrary to this provision of law would nevertheless be validly inflicted, and therefore necessitate its observance, unless its infliction were manifestly unjust. As long as the injustice of the inflicted censure remains within the pale of doubt, the censure must be observed both as a private as well as a public duty. The law favors the probability of the competent superior's just procedure rather than the likelihood of the subject's unjust oppression.[12]

If the previous warnings and rebukes have brought no results or if no favorable results can be anticipated, then the Ordinary has a full right to impose a precept, wherein he clearly states what the cleric must do or avoid in order to escape a threatened suspension.[13] Although the law in giving this right makes no mention of the Ordinary expressly, still from a comparison with the previous canons, which place in the hands of the Ordinary alone the right to impart canonical warnings and rebukes, it is evident that, if his authority is required by law for the administration of the lesser penal remedies, then the law must require at least an equal authority for the application of the severer sanctions, such as the enjoining of a canonical precept or the threat of a suspension. Such authority the Ordinary possesses.[14] It remains for him and him alone to exercise the powers implied by canon 2310. The Vicar General, though an Ordinary in the sense of canon 198, is barred in virtue of canon 2220, § 2. Since he has no power of inflicting penalties, he is also without the power to handle the issues which lead directly to their infliction. The *Officialis* or judge is also lacking

[11] Canon 15.

[12] Canon 2219, § 2.

[13] Canon 2310.

[14] Canon 335.

in the power and authority relative to these matters. First of all he is not an Ordinary in the sense of canon 198. Then again, since he has only judicial power, he can only apply the penalties already enacted or specified by law or precept,[15] although he is given some discretional option in their application.[16]

In issuing the canonical precept, the Ordinary should first of all cite the offender to appear before him. If he appears, then the Ordinary will undertake to impose the precept before two witnesses. Should the cleric, on the contrary, disobey the summons, then the precept with the accompanying penal threat should be sent by registered mail.[17] If he should refuse the letter, and of course tender no receipt, it seems that then the same norm would apply as for the refusal of a citation,[18] namely, the threat of suspension would be considered as operative. Consequently, should he violate either the mandatory or prohibitory provision of the precept, criminal action can be taken against him. The same norm would apply, because this is the only adaptable rule in the Code which would meet the requirements of the situation in question. Using the principles of canon 20, therefore, the rule governing the refusal of a citation serve as a norm in the case where the cleric refuses to receive or to acknowledge the registered letter.

After the precept has been issued, the next step in the preparatory process is for the Ordinary to subject the cleric to surveillance, in order to determine whether the precept has been violated and if so, when, where, how and before whom. This action of the Ordinary, however, should be in secret, if public surveillance would compromise the good repute which the cleric may still enjoy. It should not be employed in every instance, but only when the gravity of the case requires it, or when there is danger of the cleric relapsing into the same crime.[19]

THE CONSTITUTIVE PROCESS. When it becomes evident that the

[15] Canon 2220, § 1.

[16] Canon 2223, § 2, § 3.

[17] Canon 2225.

[18] Canon 1718:—"Reus qui citatoriam schedam recipere recuset, legitime citatus habeatur."

[19] Canon 2311.

precept has been violated, then the Ordinary must make use of the constitutive process. This is concerned with the accumulation of evidence sufficient to take penal action. The Ordinary must, therefore, establish the fact of the violation, and then, either declare the *latae sententiae* suspension which has been incurred, or inflict a *ferendae sententiae* suspension provided of course, that in the case of a censure, the cleric has given no sign of repentence after the violation. There is not required any further threat or any new warning before the suspension is inflicted. Upon sufficient proof of the violation of the precept, the penalty can be inflicted immediately. This was the principle voiced by the Pontifical Commission for the Authentic Interpretation of the Canons of the Code in response to the question, whether according to canon 2233, § 2, for the violation of a particular precept which has a sanction of a censure *ferendae sententiae*, the censure can be inflicted immediately upon proof of the offense; or whether a new warning must precede the infliction of the censure.[20]

This completes the extrajudicial procedure in cases in which the affair deals with a public crime. But, when there is question of an occult crime or even a public crime in difficult exceptional cases, the Code has instituted another extrajudicial procedure which applies solely to the extraordinary means of punishment called the suspension *ex informata conscientia.*

THE SUSPENSION *Ex Informata Conscientia.* It is not the purpose of this dissertation to treat at length the suspension *ex informata conscientia.* Its mere summary outline here is given to complete the present discussion of the extrajudicial procedure.[21]

In order to use the suspension *ex informata conscientia* the Ordinary must again be certain that a grave crime has been committed. To determine the gravity, it is necessary that a summary process of investigation be instituted.[22]

[20] July 14, 1922—*AAS*, XIV (1922), 529.

[21] For a detailed treatise of this type of suspension cfr. Murphy, *Suspension Ex Informata Conscientia,* The Catholic University of America, Canon Law Studies, n. 76, Washington: The Catholic University of America, 1932.

[22] Canons 1939, § 1; 2190; Wernz-Vidal, *Ius Canonicum,* VI (De Processibus), n. 804.

The crimes for which a suspension *ex informata conscientia* may be inflicted are usually divided into two classes, namely, occult and public crimes. The ordinary case deals with the crime that is either materially or formally occult. While the Code primarily limits the use of this suspension to occult crimes, it admits its use for public crimes only under well defined circumstances. These crimes constitute the extraordinary cases in which recourse can be had to the suspension of *ex informata conscientia.* The first exceptional case of these public crimes is had when conscientious and trustworthy witnesses have made known the offense to the Ordinary, but will not in any way be induced to testify in court to the crime, so that there are no other proofs available by which the offense can be proved in a judicial trial. The second case occurs when the guilty cleric impedes the judicial process either by threats or other means. The third exceptional case embraces two circumstances, namely, adverse civil laws and the fear of grave scandal.[23]

In the infliction of the suspension *ex informata conscientia,* either as a censure or as a vindictive penalty, the Ordinary does not make use of a sentence but of a decree. He issues his statement without any of the customary formalities. Canon 2187 explains that neither judicial formalities nor canonical warnings are required. The law, however, is clear in stating that the decree is to be given in writing, unless circumstances demand otherwise, thereby implying that at times it may be given even orally. If this is the case, then it would seem that the suspension should be pronounced before at least two witnesses, so that it may be sustained in the external forum.

When the suspension is inflicted by a written decree, care should be taken to post the date, month and year. These annotations play an important part for the computation of the penalty's duration, for the law suggests that the suspension be temporary rather than perpetual.[24] Whilst this remains true, yet the possiblity of inflicting this suspension as a censure is not excluded from the Ordinary's power. The very next sentence of the canon con-

[23] Canon 2191, § 1, § 2, § 3, nn. 1-2.
[24] Canon 2188, nn. 1-2.

firms this.[25] It grants an optional right to the Ordinary to choose between the double character of the suspension. But, if he decides upon the censure, he must notify the cleric of the reason for which the censure was inflicted; otherwise his decree remains invalid.[26]

To declare the cause of the suspension is indeed a departure from the general rule. In this process it is ordinarily left to the discretion of the Ordinary to make known to or to conceal from the cleric the reason for the suspension. It is only when he thinks it advisable to reveal the cause that he may do so. He shall undertake to do this with paternal solicitude and charity, so that the suspension accompanied with paternal admonitions may serve not only for the expiation of the crime but may lead also to the amendment of the individual and avoidance of the occasions of sin.[27]

In the decree mention should also be made of the fact that the suspension is *ex informata conscientia.* If these words are not used, then phrases of a similar significance should be employed. This is necessary as a condition for the validity of the decree.[28] With the exception of the infliction of the suspension *ex informata conscientia* ordinarily canonical warnings and threats must precede the infliction of a suspension. In cases of special gravity or of grave scandal they are not required.[29] Since, however, the suspension *ex informata conscientia* is inflicted without any warnings or threats, it is necessary that there be present some way for the cleric to determine the validity of the decree and his consequent duty to accept the suspension. This certification is offered by the use of a special terminology such as *ex informata conscientia, for reasons well known to the Ordinary, on account of intimate and unmistakable knowledge in the case,* or other equivalent expressions.[30] If the decree lacked this legal formality, its validity would not be certi-

[25] Canon 2188, n. 2:—"Potest vero infligi etiam tanquam censura . . . etc."

[26] Canon 2188, n. 2:—". . . *dummodo* hoc in casu clerico patefiat causa propter quam suspensio irrogatur."

[27] Canon 2193.

[28] Bouix, *De Iudiciis,* II, 340.

[29] Canon 2222, § 1.

[30] Canon 2188, n. 1.

fied. Therefore, the use of one or the other of the above phrases appears as a condition for the decree's validity.

Finally, the decree must indicate in how far the Ordinary intends to extend the limits of the suspension, namely, whether the penalty is to be total or partial. If no qualification is made, then the penalty is always to be considered as the total suspension *ab officio.*[31] Whenever the suspension is qualified with a view to indicating only a partial limitation of clerical rights, then the specific canonical terms as enumerated and defined by the Code in canon 2279, § 2 should be used to attain this purpose.[32] Too great confidence, say Vermeersch-Creusen, should not be placed in the knowledge of the cleric. Therefore the Ordinary should clearly indicate just what acts are included in the one or several prohibitions engendered by the suspension.[33]

[31] Canons 2186; 2279.
[32] Canon 2188, n. 3.
[33] *Epitome*, III, n. 375.

CHAPTER VIII

REMEDIES AT LAW

In ordinary judicial matters a cleric who feels that justice has not been rendered to him by the judge or tribunal can appeal to a court of higher instance, and further, even to the Holy See.[1] In ordinary administrative matters a cleric who feels similarly aggrieved at a decision given by his immediate superior can have recourse to the next higher superior, and also to the Holy See.[2] This is the fundamental right of lay persons and clerics alike. Its basis is derived from the very nature of the hierarchical constitution of the Church, in which the exercise of subordinate jurisdiction by a lower superior is always subject to review by the authority of a higher superior.

APPEAL AND RECOURSE. For redress against a miscarriage of justice, the cleric has at hand a twofold legal remedy. In the first place, he may appeal his cause by bringing the injustice of the sentence pronounced against him to the attention of the superior. In the second place, he has the right of recourse when there is question of an unjust decree or precept.[3] The distinction between these two kinds of remedies is this. The appeal can be used only against a sentence and the recourse only against a decree or precept. Furthermore, an appeal is exclusively judicial in the sense that it is concerned with a judicial sentence. The recourse, on the other hand, is a plain informal extrajudicial act, since its object is a decree or a precept. Then again, the appeal follows the stages from a lower to a higher court, whilst the recourse is usually carried directly to the Holy See. There may be times, however, when a religious, by virtue of his constitutions, is given the right to have recourse to his Supreme Moderator against a decree or precept of his Provincial. In case the constitutions do not specify this, then the law of canon

[1] Canons 1594; 1569, § 1.
[2] Canon 1601; 1569, § 2.
[3] Canons 1879-1891; 1601.

1601 must be followed, which ordains, that against the decrees of Ordinaries, recourse must be had to the various Congregations of the Roman Curia.

The Code sets down no special norms for recourse. Consequently, by invoking canon 20 the operative norms to be adopted must be borrowed from the specific provisions that are made for the administration of analogous laws. Such analogous laws with their accompanying provisions are contained in the legislation of the Code which pertains to the making of appeals.[4] Just as an appeal seeks redress from a higher court against a lower, so a recourse strives to obtain from a higher superior a reversal of the regulation decreed by a subordinate authority. The necessity of carrying the recourse immediately to the Holy See instead of to an intermediate higher superior, arises not from any essential discrepancy between the operation of recourse and appeal, but from the specific direction of the law as contained in canon 1601.

As a general rule every appeal begets a suspensive effect in the sentence of the court against which it is made. This it enjoys always unless the law makes an expressly contrary provision.[5] On the other hand, a recourse to a higher authority does not ordinarily suspend the execution of the decree, mandate or precept of the lower superior.[6] A stay of execution is granted only then when the law has, by way of specific concession to the contrary, deviated from its normal course to make it operative.

When redress is sought, whether by appeal or recourse, and such redress at the same time arrests the execution of the judicial sentence or extrajudicial decree, then it is designated as an appeal or recourse made *in suspensivo*. When the seeking of redress, whether by appeal or recourse, does not delay the execution of the sentence or decree, or in other words, when it devolves upon the higher court to grant a stay of execution, then the appeal or recourse is made *in devolutivo*.[7]

4 Canons 1879-1891.
5 Canon 1889, § 2.
6 Canon 1569, § 2.
7 Canon 1889, § 1.

The rules regulating the nature of the juridical effects consequent upon appeal and recourse are not absolute. In either of these two situations the law specifies certain exceptions to the general rules.[8] With regard to the *censure* of suspension, it is important to note that regardless of the manner in which this censure is inflicted, the law indeed admits an appeal or recourse in accordance with the nature of redress made available, but in both instances the operation of the law will be *in devolutivo tantum.*[9] As is evident from the wording of canon 2243, § 1, *latae sententiae* censures of suspension are not included in its consideration. Against these there is simply no possibility of appeal or recourse. Such a possibility would be tantamount to the potential defiance of law.[10] Then, too, the very basis for an appeal or recourse is lacking, because no question can be raised concerning the justice of the suspension or the formalities with which it was imposed. These factors alone can open the way for a rehearing or reviewing of the case.[11] The *latae sententiae* censure of suspension is executed *ipso facto* and binds in the internal and external forums as soon as the crime, forbidden under threat of censure, is committed.[12] The cleric, however, is not devoid of all redress. If he can not observe the censure without infamy or loss of reputation he is not bound in the external forum by the effects of the suspension, until a declaratory sentence has been pronounced, or unless the crime is notorious.[13]

If a declaratory sentence is passed, then the appeal is only *in devolutivo*, because of the fact that a censure must be observed in the external forum once a declaration has intervened. The non-observance of the censure presupposes a danger to one's repute. After the public declaration the non-observance itself would become

[8] Relative to appeal a provision contrary to the general rules appears in canons 1610, § 3, 2243, § 1. Relative to recourse such exceptional rulings may be noted, for instance, in canon 647, § 2, n. 4, 2243, § 2, 2287.

[9] Canon 2243, § 1.

[10] Ayrinhac, *Penal Legislation in the New Code of Canon Law*, n. 80.

[11] Vermeersch-Creusen, *Epitome*, III, n. 439.

[12] Canon 2217, § 1, n. 2; 2232, § 1.

[13] Canon 2232, § 1; Cappello, *De Censuris*, n. 74; Chelodi, *Ius Poenale*, n. 28.

a scandalous issue. Canon 2232, § 1 intimates by implication rather than by direct statement that a censure must be observed after a declaratory sentence. If the observance can under circumstances be omitted *ante sententiam declaratoriam,* one will conclude that such freedom is not granted after the declaration. Without forwarding any reasons, Ayrinhac merely states that there might be an appeal against a declaratory sentence *in suspensivo.*[14] Noval holds for an appeal *in suspensivo,* because every appeal is of this kind unless the law expressly provides for the contrary.[15] Since, however, the censure must be observed in the external forum after a declaratory sentence has been issued, there can be no doubt that any appeal in this case will be solely *in devolutivo.* Then again, the declaration makes the effects of the already incurred censure operative from the moment of the committed crime. If then, no appeal is granted in the case of such an incurred censure, would it be reasonable in the case of the declared censure to grant not only an appeal, but one *etiam cum effectu suspensivo?* Concerning the internal forum there is no difficulty, for if there is any injustice, the cleric would not be bound by the effects of the censure.

A recourse or appeal *in devolutivo* signifies the placing of a disputed issue before a higher superior or in a court of higher instance. In this it is like the recourse or appeal *in suspensivo.* But, it further implies that while the cause is pending the execution of the decree or sentence may not be neglected. In this it is unlike an appeal or recourse *in suspensivo,* which does not necessitate compliance with the tenor of the sentence or decree, until it is confirmed by a higher court or sealed by the decision of a higher superior.[16]

When a judicial sentence or extrajudicial precept threatens either a *latae* or *ferendae sententiae* censure of suspension, the law permits an appeal or recourse. In this instance, however, a distinction must be made.

First, if the matter is such as not to admit of an appeal or recourse *in suspensivo,* then should an appeal or recourse be lodged,

14 *Penal Legislation in the New Code of Canon Law,* n. 80.

15 *De Processibus,* p. 541.

16 Canon 1889, § 1; Bouix, *De Judiciis,* II, 254.

the injunction attaching to the sentence or precept which threatens the suspension would continue in force, even though the threatened suspension be a *latae sententiae* censure.[17] Cases falling under this class would be, for example, if a bishop should issue a decree or precept threatening suspension on the occasion of a canonical visitation of a diocese, a monastery or any other religious house according to the provision of canon 512;[18] or if the bishop commanded under penalty of suspension the uniting, transferring and division of a benefice, or ordered under threat of the same penalty the pastor to leave his benefice;[19] or if the Ordinary, by a decree threatening the censure of suspension, forbade the reading of a forbidden book, or by the same kind of a decree revoked a cleric's faculty to preach.[20]

Secondly, if the matter of the sentence, decree or precept threatening the suspension admits of recourse or appeal *in suspensivo*, then again a distinction must be made. Should the cleric appeal or make recourse from the censure of suspension alone, the obligation to observe the prescriptions of the superior still continues, but the cleric will not be subject to the censure in the interim. When, on the other hand, the appeal or recourse is made not only against the censure but also against the very sentence, decree or precept, the effect is then suspensive and, consquently, the cleric is freed not only from observing the censure but also from complying with the injunctions contained in the sentence, decree or precept.[21]

As to the vindictive penalty of suspension *ferendae sententiae*, any appeal or recourse from a sentence or decree has suspensive

[17] Canon 2243, § 2.

[18] Canons 345; 513, § 2; by analogy with canon 345 also canon 274, n. 5. What the bishop is empowered to do, the Metropolitan may also accomplish when he supplants the negligent suffragan in the act of canonical visitation. Canon 274, n. 5 must also be included here, since the term *canonica visitatio* of the canon embraces the act of canonical visitation at monasteries as well as elsewhere in the diocese.

[19] Canons 1428, § 3; 2146, § 1, § 3. The decree binds, but the Ordinary may not immediately appoint a new pastor. A substitute is to be designated.

[20] Canons 1395, § 2; 1340, § 3.

[21] Canon 2243, § 2.

effect, unless the law expressly declares otherwise.[22] A *latae sententiae* suspension which is vindictive in character, does not permit of an appeal or recourse. The reason is the same as that alleged for the *latae sententiae* censure: the penalty takes effect immediately upon the violation of the law or precept.

THE *Fatalia Legis.* The *fatalia legis* play an important part in questions of appeal and recourse.[23] They are the delays or limits of time conceded by law to a person for the purpose of performing some particular act, with the result that, if this right is not exercised within the interval of time granted, then the right to perform the action is extinguished forever as far as this particular case is concerned. Because of the very effective sanctions employed to enforce the use of rights and concessions which are granted for a limited time only, these *fatalia legis* must be acknowledged as peremptory in their nature. Accordingly, canon 1881 ordains that the appeal or recourse be presented to the superior, against whose sentence or precept, the appeal or recourse is taken, within ten days of usable time from the notice of the publication of the sentence or decree. Canon 1883 further declares that the case must be taken to the higher superior within a month from the placing of the appeal or recourse before the lower superior. Should the cleric fail to act within the time specified for the appeal or recourse, the case becomes irrevocably adjudged.[24]

In the case of a censure, where the matter of the sentence or the precept admits of an appeal or recourse *in devolutivo tantum,* no time limit need be defined. The censure inflicted upon the cleric takes effect immediately and needs no execution. Since the appeal or recourse is not suspensive in effect, there is no necessity of setting a time limit. The affair may be brought to the attention of the higher superior at any time during the continuance of the censure.

When, however, the appeal or recourse is *in suspensivo,* then

22 Canon 2287.

23 Cfr. canon 1634, § 1.

24 Canons 1886; 1902, n. 2. Cfr. also the resolution given by the Sacred Congregation of the Council, in which ten days of usable time is set down as a norm.—14 Jan. 1924—*AAS,* XVI (1924), 164-165.

the effects of the sentence or decree do not operate pending the appeal or recourse. The need of the *fatalia* is evident in this circumstance. If a cleric would wait a long time to make this recourse, the ends of justice would be frustrated and the one having jurisdiction over the suspension would be powerless to put it into effect. Consequently, the legislator has set limits beyond which there is no hope of appeal or recourse, in order to obviate any interference with the progress of justice.

WHERE APPEAL AND RECOURSE ARE TO BE LODGED. The highest superior who is competent for any appeal or recourse is the Holy Father himself.[25] As to the competence of the various Sacred Congregations, the following facts must be borne in mind. When an appeal is made to the Holy See, it is received by the Tribunal of the Rota. Such, however, is not the case with regard to recourse. The right to receive a recourse from the decrees or precepts of Ordinaries rests within the exclusive province of the Sacred Congregations.[26] Of course, it must be remembered that the constitutions of religious institutes may not be overlooked in this regard. The provisions determining the superior to whom appeal and recourse must be made must be the guide in this matter. Generally speaking, therefore, recourse must be made to one or the other of the following Congregations, depending upon the nature of the particular case.

a) The Sacred Congregation of the Council is competent in recourse for secular clerics against the decrees or precepts of their Ordinaries.[27]

b) The Sacred Congregation of Religious is competent if recourse is had by a religious against the local Ordinary or against any of his superiors if the constitutions do not determine otherwise.[28]

c) The Sacred Congregation of the Propagation of the Faith is

[25] Canon 1569.

[26] Canon 1601.

[27] Canon 250.

[28] Canon 251.

competent to receive the recourse of clerics living in places which are subject to it.[29]

d) The Sacred Congregation for the Oriental Church is competent in questions dealing with the Orientals.[30]

e) The Holy Office is competent if the recourse is concerned with affairs in which it has sole jurisdiction.[31]

As a practical suggestion, it may be stated that should a doubt arise as to which Congregation is competent in a certain case, the recourse may be sent to the Cardinal Secretary of State. He, then, will forward it to the proper Congregation.

Superiors lower in rank than the Apostolic See are by the law of the Code incompetent to receive or accept a recourse, with the exception of those religious superiors, however, whose constitutions empower them to receive a recourse. For the handling of appeals, the Code has provided a gradation of instances which ultimately culminate in the person of the Roman Pontiff as the last possible court of appeal. The appeal from the tribunal of a suffragan will be lodged in the court of his Metropolitan. The appeal from the Metropolitan's court will be carried to the tribunal of that local Ordinary, suffragan or otherwise, whom the Metropolitan has once for all selected with the approval of the Holy See. The appeal from the court of a Metropolitan who is without suffragans or from the court of a local Ordinary who is subject immediately to the Holy See will be borne to the judicial forum of some neighboring Metropolitan. This Metropolitan will be he whom the two above mentioned Ordinaries have selected with the approval of the Holy See as the one at whose provincial council they will attend and the ordinances and statutes of which they will recognize as binding in their territories.[32]

Amongst clerical exempt religious the appeal from the court over which the provincial superior presides will be brought to the tribunal of the Supreme Moderator of the Order or Congregation. The

[29] Canon 252.

[30] Canon 257.

[31] Canon 247.

[32] Canons 1594, § 1, § 2, § 3; 285.

appeal from the court of an abbot or other superior of an independent monastery will be to that of the Supreme Moderator of that monastic congregation.[33]

Appeal and recourse are considered as ordinary remedies of law for defense against an injustice. Such means are conceded to all, unless the law specifically provides otherwise and expressly excludes the use of these modes of redress.

No Appeal or Recourse Admissible. Canon 1880 enumerates the instances when appeals are prohibited. To act contrary to the provisions stated therein would not only be unlawful but also invalid. The reason for this is that the cause which has been adjudged has moreover become a *res judicata.* Consequently the sentence or judicial decree brooks no delay of execution, which ordinarily the intervention of an appeal would occasion.[34]

1) There is no appeal allowed from a sentence issued personally by the Supreme Pontiff. Since an appeal is an approach to a court of higher instance calling upon it to pass judgment on the sentence of a lower tribunal, this factor has no longer any foundation when sentence has been passed by the Holy Father. In his august person he constitutes a court than which no higher exists on earth.[35] This follows from the primacy of jurisdiction inherent in his sovereign pontificate. Consequently, there is excluded every appeal to a General Council.[36]

Mention is also made in canon 1880, n. 1 of the related fact that a sentence issued by the Sacred Apostolic Signatura likewise precludes all further appeal. This ruling naturally follows upon the premise that this court constitutes the Church's supreme ordinary tribunal.[37]

2) There is no appeal admissible from a sentence or judicial decree of a judge delegated by the Holy See to consider a particular case, if the special mandate of this judge contains the clause *appellatione remota.* This does not mean that all legal remedies are ex-

[33] Canon 1594, § 4.

[34] Cfr. Bouix, *De Judiciis,* p. 247-266.

[35] Canon 1556.

[36] Canon 228, § 2.

[37] Canon 1602.

cluded. The cleric has the privilege of using others for the purpose of having an unjust sentence rectified, as for example, the *restitutio in integrum.*

3) There can be no appeal from a sentence that is invalid. The law always presupposes a valid sentence when it grants an appeal. Relative to the question of suspension, a sentence must be considered invalid if it has been passed by a tribunal that lacked the required number of judges as prescribed by law.[38] It must not be thought that this is the only way in which a sentence becomes invalid. Besides the general principles regulating the valid exercise of jurisdiction,[39] there are other factors, conditions and formalities which the IV Book of the Code mentions as prerequisites for a valid sentence.[40]

4) There can be no appeal if the sentence has become a *res judicata.* A sentence is considered as becoming an adjudged matter, when two uniform sentences have been pronounced,[41] when the sentence has not been appealed within the time specified by law, or if appealed, it has not been prosecuted before the appellate judge within the required time,[42] or when no appeal is admissible against a single sentence, due to the legal restrictions spoken of in 1880.[43] Again it must be recalled that, although an appeal is inadmissible, still the cleric is free to avail himself of the extraordinary remedy of seeking for a *restitutio in integrum,* provided the verdict of the judge is manifestly unjust.[44]

5) An appeal is not admitted from a definitive sentence that has been pronounced in virtue of reliance upon an oath administered for the sake of deciding the litigation. An example of this in regard to suspension is had when a cleric has confessed his crime under

[38] Canon 1576, § 1, n. 1.

[39] Canons 199-201; 1556-1568; 1892, n. 1.

[40] Canons 1646 and 1654 with canon 1892, n. 2; canons 1655-1666 with canon 1892, n. 3; canon 1711, § 2 with canon 1894; canons 1871, § 2, and 1874, § 4 with canon 1894, § 2; canon 1874, § 5 with canon 1894, n. 3, n. 4.

[41] Canons 1902, n. 1; 1571.

[42] Canon 1902, n. 2.

[43] Canon 1902, n. 3.

[44] Canons 1905; 1906.

oath and as a consequence the tribunal has issued a sentence of condemnation. Against such a sentence no appeal is sustained.

6) An appeal is not admitted from a judicial decree or from an interlocutory sentence which has not the force of a definitive judgment or verdict. An appeal in these cases would become possible only if the decree of the judge or his interlocutory sentence could be acknowledged as incidental to or connected with the primary issue in which an appeal has been lodged against the final definitive sentence. Thus the appeal could be lodged not against the judicial decree or interlocutory sentence as such, but indirectly because of their inclusion in the primary cause. Of themselves judicial decrees and interlocutory sentences are generally matters of minor import which admit of revision or even recall by the judge before the closing of the principal issue of the trial.[45]

7) An appeal is not allowed in all cases for which the law has determined a speedy and instant settlement. These cases as intimated in a number of canons in the Code[46] are happenings or situations which involve the more atrocious crimes which demand a quick and ready application of criminal justice, lest great and irretrievable harm result for Christian society, through shameful example which goes even temporarily unpunished, through baneful scandal which needs prompt reparation, through odious damages which demand almost immediate compensation, through outrage and insult upon the clerical state which compel timely and drastic intervention on the part of authority. If for some reason of prudence these cases call for settlement judicially rather than administratively, then the verdict which seals the judgment of the case takes on a special degree of finality, one which bars completely the ordinary legal remedy of an appeal.

8) An appeal is also rejected by law in the case of a sentence adverse to one who has acted in contempt of court. The culprit continues to suffer his disbarment as long as he has not cleared himself of this contempt. If he has manifested such contempt during the course of the trial, the judge nevertheless upon warning

[45] Canon 1841.

[46] Canons 1956-1958; 2223, § 1; 2243, § 1, § 2; 2401.

him[47] proceeds with the trial even to the pronouncement of the final sentence. But, in so acting the judge is not to omit any of the legal formalities required.[48] If, on the other hand, the cleric appears in court before the final sentence, his claims and proofs must be recognized. However, he is denied all those privileges which other defendants enjoy. He may not offer dilatory exceptions; nor may he reject witnesses.[49] The case continues without interruption.

All this implies of course that the suspected culprit was really contumacious. If it can be proven that his contempt was merely apparent because of circumstances which prevented him from making his appearance, then he may petition a *restitutio in integrum*.[50] If the final sentence has been passed before the cleric decides to abandon his contumacy, he is allowed three months from the notification of the sentence, within which to seek from the judge who pronounced the sentence, a *restitutio in integrum* for the purpose of lodging an appeal against the sentence.[51] This he must do within three months from the time he was notified of the sentence.[52] The appellate court will then pass on the justice or injustice of the sentence.

9) Finally, an appeal is precluded if the cleric against whom sentence has been passed has expressly declared in writing that he renounced his right to appeal. This he may do before or after the sentence. If it precedes the sentence, the right of the cleric to make an appeal is not precluded if evident injustice has been done him, because it is generally admitted that the renunciation is made contingent upon the fact that the sentence be consonant with justice.

These nine cases mentioned in canon 1880 constitute an exhaustive enumeration. There are no other excepted cases in which appeal is denied. Consequently, there is open to every cleric the widest opportunity for legal defense against any gross miscarriage

[47] Canon 1729, § 1.
[48] Canon 1844, § 1.
[49] Canons 1628, § 1; 1764, § 4.
[50] Canons 1687, § 1; 1846.
[51] Canons 1847; 1906.
[52] Canons 1847; 1906.

of justice in cases where a suspension has been inflicted upon him. It is only when one of these nine restrictions against an appeal is present, that an ordinary means of defense is denied him. The reason is because the sentence is considered as having become a *res judicata*, thereby creating a *praesumptio iuris et de iure*, which precludes all possibility of direct proof by means of which an attack could be made or an objection sustained against the equity and justice of the verdict.[53]

It was stated before that laws regarding appeals may by virtue of canon 20 apply equally to questions of recourse. But this fact must always be understood in this sense, that there is present an adaptable parity between these two methods of legal redress. In invoking as a norm any of the foregoing nine ways in which all appeal is disallowed, care must be taken to ascertain with certainty whether the case of recourse meets exactly the prerequisites demanded by the Code to bar one from any legal redress to a higher superior. Not all of these nine cases as enumerated by canon 1880 are applicable to questions of recourse. Those alone may be invoked whose adaptability to cases of recourse is really possible.

[53] Canons 1902, n. 3; 1903; 1904, § 1, § 2; 1825-1828.

CHAPTER IX.

THE VIOLATION OF SUSPENSION

THE IRREGULARITY—WHEN IT IS INCURRED—THE EXCUSING CAUSES. For the safeguarding of her laws the Church has by virtue of her coercive power instituted the canonical sanction of suspension, whose purpose is either to repair the scandal given by the delinquent cleric or to bring about his amendment and to deter others from following his example. But, the suspension thus established did not always prove effective enough to prevent a cleric laboring under it from exercising those sacred functions which the penalty forbade. Thus the sacred ministry was very often degraded and profaned by unworthy clerics. Consequently, to impress upon all clerics the seriousness of a suspension and to protect the honor of the sacred ministry and to secure respect for her sacred ministers and the dignity of divine worship, the Church threatened and continues to threaten an irregularity on all clerics who deliberately violate the suspension they have incurred.[1]

In effect the irregularity forbids the reception of orders and their exercise. This, however, is not to be considered strictly a penalty, even though it has been incurred for the violation of a suspension, because the penal element of the irregularity is not primarily intended by the Church but only secondarily and concomitantly.[2] The primary intent, as stated above, is to safeguard the sacred ministry from profanation.

To contract an irregularity the violation of the suspension must constitute a gravely sinful and external act, either public or occult, in the sense that, although no one witnesses the violation of the sus-

[1] Canon 985, n. 7:—"Sunt irregulares ex delicto . . . qui actum ordinis, clericis in ordine sacro constitutis reservatum, ponunt, vel eo ordine carentes, vel ab eius exercitio poena canonica sive personali, medicinali aut vindicativa, sive locali prohibiti."

[2] Wernz, *Ius Decretalium,* II, n. 96; St. Alphonsus, *Theologia Moralis,* VII, n. 350 seq.

pension, still it could have been seen. The fact of its perceptivity is sufficient to bring about the impediment.[3] It is the common opinion of eminent theologians that clerics in sacred orders who violate a suspension commit a sin *ex genere suo mortale,* because they contemn a grave precept of the Church.[4] The phrase *ex genere suo mortale* connotes the possibility of *parvitas materiae.* But, the principal factor must always be remembered, namely, that the irregularity is incurred only when the suspension is violated intentionally and maliciously.

A cleric suspended *a divinis* would sin venially and hence would not incur an irregularity *ex delicto* if he exercised merely a minor order. Likewise the deacon would be excused from an irregularity, who would sing the *Dominus Vobiscum* in choir.[5]

Furthermore, when canon 988 declares that ignorance of the irregularity *ex delicto* does not excuse from its effects, this refers to ignorance of the irregularity itself as resulting from the violation of the suspension, and not to the ignorance of the effects of a certain suspension. Thus if a cleric exercises the functions of his suspended orders, knowing that he thereby violates his suspension in a serious matter, but is ignorant of the fact that this violation entails irregularity, he nevertheless becomes subject to it. If, on the other hand, a cleric is ignorant of the effects of the suspension, as for example, when he is ignorant of the fact that the ministrations which he performs really constitute a solemn act of orders and thus violates the prohibition of the suspension, then he would be excused from the irregularity, because whatever culpability may have attached to his exercise of legally prohibited acts, it was not of sufficient gravity to make him guilty of a mortal sin.

If one is physically forced to violate his suspension, he would not be guilty of a crime,[6] and consequently, would not incur an irregularity. The one who forces another to violate the suspension would, however, become subject to the irregularity, provided that he

[3] Canon 986:—"Haec delicta irregularitatem non pariunt, nisi fuerint gravia peccata . . . itemque externa, sive publica sive occulta."

[4] Cfr. Aertnys-Damen, *Theologia Moralis,* II, n. 1028.

[5] Gasparri, *De Sacra Ordinatione,* I, n. 371.

himself is a cleric,[7] unless circumstances were such that he too was not responsible for his deed. The one forced in this manner, even though he inwardly consents to the act, is nevertheless excused from the irregularity, because for the external forum no crime is acknowledged. Should any one have witnessed the violation of the suspension by the person subjected to the violence, he could only have gathered that the culprit had no other choice than to yield to the force against his will.[8]

The cleric who violates his suspension in the face of grave fear, though it be only relatively grave, incurs no irregularity. Nor is the cleric subject to it if the violation is occasioned by some necessity or grave inconvenience. The reason is because the obligation of not exercising certain sacred functions follows from a purely ecclesiastical penalty. Their exercise is not interdicted by the natural law. Thus, when the prohibition of a purely ecclesiastical law clashes with what the natural law not only allows as something licit, but even approves as something commendable, then the positive ecclesiastical precept will always yield to the more absolute disposition of the natural law, when circumstances render compliance with the ecclesiastical precept intensely burdensome or gravely detrimental. Canon 2205, § 2 confirms this conclusion when it declares that such factors or circumstances generally exclude the presence of crime completely. Hence should a cleric assay the solemn exercise of orders forbidden him by the suspension, intending thereby to avoid scandal or loss of reputation, he would not contract the irregularity.

In a case in which a suspension is evidently invalid, the utter disregard of this penalty would not bring about an irregularity. The presumption is on the side of validity, at least in the external forum, reason is clear, because the basis for the irregularity is a crime. But, a crime would not be present as long as there was no suspension whose prohibitions could be violated. It must be remembered of course, that the suspension must be evidently invalid before a

[6] Canon 2205, § 1.

[7] Canons 2209, § 1; 2231.

[8] Gasparri, *De Sacra Ordinatione*, I, n. 208.

cleric may undertake to ignore it. If there is any doubt, then the and consequently, the cleric must observe the suspension in order to escape the effective threat of supervenient irregularity in case of violation.

A norm which is of practical import in the question of this irregularity is the following. The intention of the cleric when disregarding the suspension may not comprise any deliberate intent of violating the penalty.[9] His sole intent must be to strive for the use of such means as the law puts at one's disposal for removing the obligation of observing the penalty. Besides the above mentioned instances, where there is a diminution of imputability or a total absence thereof, there are circumstances in which the Code permits the cleric to disregard his suspension temporarily. In these cases the cleric is not looked upon as violating his suspension but as availing himself of opportunities given him by law to safeguard his good name and to be of spiritual assistance to his neighbor. Thus a cleric would not be considered as violating his suspension which he incurred *latae sententiae*, if he laid aside its observance in the external forum because of danger of scandal or the loss of his good name.[10] Similarly, there would be no violation and consequently no irregularity, if the suspended cleric were legitimately asked by the faithful to administer the sacraments.[11]

Contrary to the old law which made no distinction between the prohibited exercise of acts belonging to major and minor orders in the question of incurring an irregularity,[12] the present law in canon 985, n. 7 refers only to the penally interdicted exercise of acts reserved to clerics in sacred orders. From the classification and definition of various terminologies employed by canons 949 and 950 in reference to the sacrament of orders, it is perfectly clear that the phrase *ordo sacer* must be understood as exclusively designating some major order. Consequently, whenever there is a violation of a suspension, there must be an illegitimate exercise of acts attaching

[9] Kober, *Die Suspension*, p. 97.

[10] Canon 2232, § 1.

[11] Canon 2284 with reference to canon 2261.

[12] Kober, *Die Suspension*, p. 96; Gasparri, *De Sacra Ordinatione*, I, n. 361.

to major orders before the irregularity mentioned in canon 985, n. 7 will be incurred.

To incur the irregularity, the acts proper to major orders must be performed in a solemn manner.[13] The ceremonies must be so carried out that those who witness them will realize that objectively they are not feigned, but in keeping with the external rite. Hence, should a priest who is suspended *a divinis* withhold his intention while celebrating Mass or administering Baptism, he would nevertheless become irregular, despite the nullity of the Mass or the ineffective administration of Baptism. His external acts betray no sense-perceptible defect or objective lack of reality which could induce spectators to regard his acts as a mere nugatory performance or, at least as being devoid of the sacred meaning and object which their external rite normally implies. On the contrary, he would incur the irregularity precisely because his acts are in all seeming reality the active performance of a sacred sacrificial function and the fulfillment of a sacred sacramental rite. In a word, his acts are the solemn acts of sacred orders from whose exercise he is barred by the suspension *a divinis.*

Furthermore, before an irregularity can ensue upon the violation of a suspension, the prohibited act which is exercised must be properly an act of sacred orders. It is immaterial whether that act is exercised as the ordinary act of the power of orders or as an act whose performance is made possible by a special papal indult.

Relative to the suspension *a pontificalibus* a doubt might arise whether or not the violation of this suspension would give rise to an irregularity, since there is no direct exercise of orders. While the suspension directly forbids the exercise of those functions which according to the rubrics require the use of pontifical insignia, it indirectly forbids the exercise of those orders from which the use of the pontifical insignia can not be dissociated at the moment. The facts are so connected that the placing of the latter inevitably implies the accompaniment of the former. Consequently, the exercise of these orders becomes interdicted because of the factor of insepar-

[13] Kober, *Die Suspension,* p. 101; Gasparri, *De Sacra Ordinatione,* I, n. 368; Augustine, *Commentary,* IV, 495.

able association. Hence any violation of the suspension on the part of a bishop would bring about the irregularity. This would occur even though the bishop exercised these functions without pontificals, for the suspension *a pontificalibus* prohibits not only the performance of such sacred functions in which pontificals are actually used, but it forbids also the exercise of all sacred functions which by liturgical law require pontifical insignia in their *normal* administration.[14]

It must be noted that, before a cleric becomes irregular, he must be guilty of the violation of a suspension which is already operative in his regard. Consequently, though a cleric who knowingly receives orders from a bishop who is suspended by a declaratory or condemnatory sentence thereby *ipso facto* incurs a suspension *a divinis,*[15] yet, he does not incur an irregularity through the act of con-celebration. The suspension incurred by the cleric is altogether consequent upon the completed reception of orders, for, as Suarez claims, the act of reception of orders is not looked upon as complete until the Mass of con-celebration is ended.[16] The rubrics required for the rite of ordination begin and end with the Mass. But, until they are consummated, the rite of ordination has not been completed. And, until the rite of ordination has been completed, the juridical reception of orders has not taken place. If, then, the rite of ordination coincides in its consummation with the end of the Mass, then, too, the suspension, which under the circumstances is incurred only upon the completed reception of orders, could not be operative before the end of Mass. Thus, the recipient of the orders was not under suspension during the Mass. Therefore, being as yet free from suspension, he does not become irregular for any act of sacred orders he may have exercised during the ceremony of ordination.

Formerly, canonists were not in agreement on the question whether it was the *censure* of suspension alone which brought about the irregularity or whether the violation of the vindictive penalty

[14] Canons 2279, § 2, n. 9 and 337, § 2. Cfr. Gasparri, *De Sacra Ordinatione,* I, n. 367.

[15] Canon 2372.

[16] Cfr. *De Censuris,* Disp. XXXI, sec. I, n. 71.

also which produced the same effect. Ballerini-Palmieri,[17] Genicot[18] and D'Annibale[19] restricted the incurring of the irregularity to the violation of the censure. Suarez,[20] Kober[21] and also Benedict XIV[22] maintained that the irregularity was incurred no matter whether there was a violation of the censure or of the vindictive penalty. The latter opinion was considered the more common one before the issuance of the present law.

Today the Code favors the same opinion. Hence the irregularity *ex delicto* is incurred by the violation of either the censure or the vindictive penalty of suspension which prohibits the exercise of an act of sacred orders.[23]

Another factor to be remembered is that the medicinal suspension, when inflicted as a *ferendae sententiae* penalty by a judicial sentence, allows an appeal *in devolutivo tantum.*[24] *A fortiori,* a like suspension, when inflicted by an extrajudicial decree or precept allows recourse *in devolutivo tantum.*[25] But, the vindictive penalty of suspension inflicted as a *ferendae sententiae* penal sanction allows a recourse as well as an appeal *in suspensivo,* in accordance with the method employed in its infliction.[26] Consequently, the exercise of all acts of sacred orders, from which a cleric is suspended, would not induce an irregularity, while the recourse or appeal from the vindictive suspension is pending. In the case of the censure of suspension, the inflicted penalty must be observed, since both the appeal and recourse are *in devolutivo tantum.* A transgression against the prohibition imposed by the censure would beget a status of irregularity in the offending cleric.

17 *Opus Theologicum Morale,* VII, n. 632 and n. 492.

18 *Theologia Moralis,* II, n. 633, note 3.

19 *Summula,* I, n. 386.

20 *De Censuris,* Disp. XXVI, sec. II, n. 4.

21 *Die Suspension,* p. 95.

22 *De Synodo Dioecesana,* lib. XII, c. VII, n. 5.

23 Canon 985, n. 7:—"Qui actum ordinis, clericis in ordine sacro constitutis reservatum, ponunt, vel eo ordine carentes, vel ab eius exercitio poena canonica sive personali, medicinali aut vindicativa, sive locali prohibiti."

24 Canon 2243, § 1.

25 Canons 1601; 1569, § 2.

26 Canon 2287.

When a cleric under suspension repeatedly exercises a forbidden act of orders, how many irregularities would he incur? To answer this question, it is necessary to distinguish in regard to the *causa materialis* of the irregularity. In canon, 989, the Code adopts the ruling that, with the exception of deliberately committed homicide, no irregularity is multiplied by repeated acts of the same species. It may be said, therefore, that a priest who is suspended *a divinis* would incur only one irregularity, if he repeatedly violates his suspension by the frequent offering of holy Mass. On the other hand, the same canon 989 directs that, when the prohibited acts are specifically distinct, then there are accordingly as many irregularities incurred as there are transgressions for which the law has threatened an irregularity. In view of this fact, therefore, a priest who is suspended *a divinis* would incur a separate and distinct irregularity for each exercise of his prohibited sacred orders which constitutes a specifically distinct act. He would become irregular if he says Mass; he would incur also an irregularity if he baptizes, because to say Mass and to administer the sacrament of Baptism necessitates the placing of two specifically different acts.

CHAPTER X.

THE CESSATION OF THE CENSURE OF SUSPENSION

CONDITIONS NECESSARY FOR THE GRANTOR AND GRANTEE RELATIVE TO THE ACT OF ABSOLUTION. The general principle of law governing the cessation of the censure of suspension is § 1 of canon 2248. It is clearly stated in this canon that a censure, once it is contracted, can be remitted only by absolution. This is the only way in which the cessation of the censure is brought about. Although a cleric becomes contrite and thus merits to be absolved, he is nevertheless bound by the effects of the suspension until the censure has been removed by absolution. To maintain the contrary opinion would be to contradict a decision of the Holy Office, which condemned the proposition: "*Quoad forum conscientiae reo correcto ejusque contumacia cessante, cessant censurae.*"[1]

A distinction must be drawn between a threatened censure and a censure already contracted. In the former case the threatened censure ceases with the cessation of the authority of the superior who issued the ordinance to which the censure is attached, unless the superior's command has been formulated in some document or expressed before two witnesses.[2] A censure of this kind needs no absolution. Absolution is necessary only when the censure has been incurred.

By absolution from a censure of suspension is meant a specific and determined act of external administration, founded on the virtue of justice, by which rights and their exercise are restored to the contrite and repentant delinquent. It is essentially necessary, according to canon 2242, § 3 that the culprit have all those dispositions which are demanded for the tribunal of Penance, namely, sorrow, purpose of amendment and a firm resolution to make satisfaction and to repair scandal. When these dispositions are present, the superior is bound in justice to grant absolution. However, it is left to his judgment to inflict a vindictive penalty or some canonical

[1] Denzinger-Bannwart, *Enchiridion Symbolorum*, n. 1144.

[2] Canon 24.

penance, in order to secure the reparation of the scandal given and the restoration of the social order.[3] Should the penitent refuse to accept the vindictive penalty or a determined canonical penance imposed upon him, there might be doubt as to the sincerity of his dispositions. It is then left to the judgment of the superior whether or not absolution may or should be granted. If he should decide not to grant absolution because of the refusal on the part of the penitent, then he should take care that the penance imposed is not beyond the reasonable endurance of the penitent nor out of proportion to the gravity of the crime. Should the penance be too severe or out of proportion to the crime, the superior would indeed be acting unjustly in refusing absolution because the penitent refused to accept the additional penance. He would be guilty of a grave sin.

Ordinarily in absolving from censures, there is demanded a serious promise to repair the scandal and to make satisfaction. Before the Code an oath was demanded to confirm the promise.[4] The oath was not however required for validity, but merely served as a measure of prudence and could be omitted if circumstances showed that the penitent was sincere.[5] Today there can be no doubt that the promise must be made, but there is no law which expressly requires the taking of an oath in confirmation of the promise. Whether or not the promise is to be substantiated by an oath is left to the prudent decision of the one granting the absolution.

Suppose a cleric laboring under a censure of suspension feigned sincerity of repentance, in the sense that outwardly he promises amendment and satisfaction, whereas inwardly his will is to the contrary. St. Alphonsus says that if the principal cause for which the absolution is given is wanting, then the absolution is invalid.[6]

The concession of absolution from a censure before the penitent ceases to be contumacious is valid or invalid depending on the person who is absolving. If the superior absolves from a censure

[3] Canon 2248, § 2.

[4] C. 10, X, *de sententia excommunicationis,* V, 39; c. 51, X *de sententia excommunicationis,* V, 39.

[5] C. 52, X, *de sententia excommunicationis,* V, 39.

[6] *Theologia Moralis,* VII, n. 132.

which he or a subject of his had inflicted either by law or precept, the absolution is illicit but valid. If, on the other hand, absolution from the censure is given by a confessor or by any inferior, this absolution is not only not licit, but even invalid, because the superior does not grant the faculty to absolve, except under the express condition that contumacy be no longer present.[7] Should a judge absolve from censures which have been legitimately established and which he has applied in accordance with the norms of law, his act would be invalid, unless he himself is the superior, or there is question of his own law or precept or law or precept of his subject.[8]

Once absolution has been validly conceded, it can not be revoked. Nor can it be said that the suspension once absolved revives, except in those cases where such an effect is specified as a penalty for the violation of some legal condition.[9]

Since one censure of suspension is specifically distinct from another and since suspension is in no way an impediment to sanctifying grace, a cleric laboring under several suspensions may be absolved from one to the exclusion of the others, even though he were properly disposed to receive absolution from all of them.[10] Should a cleric forget to mention a suspension in his petition for absolution, the censure will only cease if the absolution was given in a general way. Ordinarily every suspension must be mentioned specially, otherwise the absolution will remove only those censures which have been expressly indicated.[11] The case might happen where a suspended cleric, in confessing his sins, lacks contrition for one of his many mortal sins. In such a circumstance, every mortal sin would remain untouched by the absolution, even the one which occasioned the suspension and of which he is truly repentant. The suspension, however, would be remitted by virtue of the absolution, because while the cleric was wanting in the requisite dispositions for the absolution from his sins, he nevertheless possessed that contri-

[7] Canons 2241, § 1; 2242, §§ 1, 3; 2248.

[8] Cfr. Cappello, *De Censuris*, n. 91.

[9] Canons 2248, § 3; 2252; 2254.

[10] Canon 2249, § 1.

[11] Canon 2249, § 2.

tion and that repentance which the Code demands as a prerequisite for the absolution from censures.

Would an *ab homine* censure of suspension be included in a general absolution? There seems to be a doubt from canon 2249, § 2 as to what really is the legislator's intention. In this canon he makes no mention of this type of censure as being excluded from the possibility of absolution when the form is general. It is evident from other sections of the Code,[12] when the legislator wishes to include the *ab homine* censure in any provision of law, he clearly indicates this fact. In view of the nature of the *ab homine* censure it seems probable that the lawgiver thought it superfluous to mention specifically this form of penalty in canon 2249, since it is difficult to imagine how one who is in good faith could be so oblivious of the existence of such a penalty that he would forget to make mention of it in his petition for absolution. The very most that seems possible of concession in the case is to grant that decisive proof can not indeed be gathered from the wording of the law, in order to maintain beyond all doubt the contention that a penitent must perforce be in bad faith whenever he omits mention of an *ab homine* censure. With that the law is not directly concerned. It constitutes a question which the law leaves for its determination to the moral order in its own right. But, a query of direct concern in canon 2249, § 2 is the following. Granted the possibility of good faith in a penitent who has omitted mention of the *ab homine* censure, does the cleric receive absolution from it when a general absolution is granted by one who has the necessary faculties to impart it? The question is immediately limited in this way, since canon 2247, § 3 clarifies the issue with reference to the confessor who has no power over the reserved censure if it be *ab homine*. Because of the fact that the Code in canon 2249, § 2 remains silent in reference to the *ab homine* censure, whereas in other canons it never fails to make ample provision to include or exclude this type of penalty, the practical solution of the question is, that, in virtue of canon 19, the law must be interpreted as it is expressed in the canon. Consequently, since the censure *specialissimo modo* reserved is the only one excepted by

[12] Canons 2247, § 3; 2252.

the law, it is this type of penalty alone that suffers exclusion. To exclude the *ab homine* censure from the general absolution would be far from giving the canon a benign interpretation as canon 2219, § 1 directs, and it would be far from favoring the penitent. In practice, therefore, every *ab homine* censure may be looked upon as remitted by a general absolution, if in his confession the penitent concealed it in good faith.[13]

The Church supplies jurisdiction and renders the absolution valid which a confessor grants, who is ignorant of the reservation of the censure of suspension. The only exception is the suspension *ab homine*. The latter may be said to be the only exception, because suspension is never classified as *specialissimo modo* reserved to the Holy See, which canon 2247, § 3 also excepts from the power of the confessor.[14] Whenever there is reason to doubt about a reservation, namely, whether the censure which is now being considered is reserved, or whether the censure agrees in every detail with the legal conditions which may induce a reservation, any confessor may absolve from the censure.[15] A doubtful reservation is always looked upon as no reservation.

The confessor's power to absolve from censures is reserved to the internal sacramental forum. Occasionally, however, he may obtain faculties from a legitimate superior to absolve from censure in the external forum. In this case, care must be taken in reading the document of delegation to determine how far his powers extend. If the superior makes no express restriction to the internal forum, his faculties are considered as pertaining to both the internal and external forum.[16]

After a review of the various important elements entering into the conditions which must be fulfilled by the grantor and the grantee relative to the act of absolution, the next consideration will re-

[13] Cfr. A Coronata, *Institutionis Iuris Canonici,* IV, n. 1755.

[14] Canon 2247, § 3:—"Si confessarius, ignorans reservationem, poenitentem a censura ac peccato absolvat, absolutio censurae valet, dummodo ne sit censura ab homine aut censura specialissimo modo Sedi Apostolicae reservata."

[15] Canon 2245, § 4.

[16] Canons 202; 1044; 1045, § 3.

gard the legal specifications which limit or extend, lessen or augment the jurisdiction of the one imparting absolution.

I. Absolution from Suspension in Ordinary Circumstances.

a) *Non-reserved Suspension.*

It was the opinion of some pre-Code authors that a confessor could absolve from all censures which were not reserved, so that the effects of the absolution would prevail even in the external forum. Such, for instance, was the opinion of Wernz. He claimed that pastors and all approved confessors enjoyed this faculty.[17] The opinion of Kober[18] and Suarez[19] restricted the power of the pastor and confessor. Both asserted that the absolution from censures pertained solely to excommunication. Any lack of power to absolve from this ecclesiastical penalty would possibly endanger the salvation of the culprit. With the penalty of suspension it was different, because its effects did not sever the cleric from the Church. All absolutions were to be obtained from the bishop alone.

The present law limits the faculty of any approved confessor[20] to the granting of absolution in the sacramental forum only.[21] There is absolutely no restriction whatsoever placed on his power to absolve from non-reserved censures of suspension in that forum.

Outside of the tribunal of Penance, any one who has either ordinary or delegated jurisdiction in the external forum over the culprit, may absolve him from his non-reserved censure of suspension.[22] Canons 198, § 1 and 488, n. 8 enumerate those who enjoy jurisdiction in the external forum, as Ordinaries. These are the Roman Pontiff for the whole Church; and for their respective teritories, residential bishops, abbots and prelates *nullius* and their Vicars General, administrators, vicars and prefects apostolic, the abbot primate, abbots superior of monastic congregations, abbots of inde-

17 *Ius Decretalium*, VI, n. 175.

18 *Die Suspension*, p. 139.

19 *De Censuris*, V. Disp. XXIII, sec. II, n. 3.

20 Canons 875, § 1; 876, § 1; 881.

21 Canons 2253, n. 1; 202, § 2.

22 Canon 2253, n. 1.

pendent monasteries, supreme moderators of religious institutes, provincials and the vicars of these who have the equivalent of provincial power. With regard to pastors and local superiors of exempt clerical institutes, these have indeed jurisdiction in the external forum. Local superiors, however, may receive special faculties from their constitutions.[23]

b) *Reserved Suspension.*

In general, it may be stated that he alone has the right and power to absolve from a reserved censure who possesses that faculty by express concession of the Code or specific act of delegation from a qualified superior.[24] In particular, however, the following prescriptions of the law must be noted.

All *ab homine* censures are reserved to him who inflicted the censure or to him who passed the sentence or to his competent superior, successor or delegate.[25] It is not in his mere capacity as judge, but rather in his status as an Ordinary, that a superior enjoys the right of absolving from a censure which is reserved to the one who has imposed it by the use of a judicial sentence. In accordance with law, a judge can only apply the penalties which have been legitimately established or constituted.[26] If he has *ex officio* applied a penalty constituted or designated by the superior who is an Ordinary, he has no power to remit the penalty which he applied.[27] In virtue of his office no judge is an Ordinary. He fulfills his judicial function in the name and with the power of the Ordinary whose authority he vicariously exercises. If as judge he is excluded from granting absolution in the external forum from a non-reserved censure, then all the more must he remain excluded from granting absolution in the external forum from censures which

23 Vermeersch-Creusen, *Epitome*, III, n. 453; Cocchi, *Commentarium*, V, (De Delictis et Poenis), n. 77, b; Blat, *Commentarium*, V, n. 77; Fanfani, *De Iure Parochorum*, nn. 200-202; *Commentarium pro Religiosis et Missionariis*, IV (1923), pp. 75-341.

24 Canon 2235, § 1.

25 Canons 2245, § 2; 2253, n. 2.

26 Canon 2220, § 1.

27 Canon 2226, § 3.

are reserved. A judge who is at the same time an Ordinary may not only enact and constitute censures, but he may also absolve from them when they are incurred and remit them after being inflicted and applied by his authority. A judge who is not an Ordinary may neither enact nor constitute censures, nor may he remit the censures which he has applied. He can only impose the censures which by law are to be inflicted (*ferendae sententiae*) and apply the penalties to which a delinquent has become subject by condemnation of the Ordinary (*ab homine*). But, the Ordinary who has the right and power to absolve from an *ab homine* censure, may use this faculty in behalf of the delinquent, even if the latter has changed his domicile or quasi-domicile and has thus ceased to be that Ordinary's subject.[28]

If a cleric under an *ab homine* censure of suspension should have become incardinated in a new diocese, does his new Ordinary constitute the "successor" who may absolve him from that censure, or would the cleric have to turn to his former Ordinary for absolution? It is true a change of subjection gives the cleric a new superior who may in turn be termed a successor, because he succeeds the cleric's former Ordinary in authority over him. This idea, however, is not what the Code contemplates. A successor, according to the Code, is not one in whom there resides an authority distinct from that enjoyed by the subject's former superior, rather it is he who succeeds to the same power and authority which his predecessor relinquished, so that legally he is considered the same person.[29] It is hard to believe that the meaning of the term "successor" used by the Code is a departure from its pre-Code legal signification. In the old law, it was the successor to the one in office who remitted all penalties inflicted by the former incumbent.[30] Since this is the

[28] Canons 1572, § 1; 2253, n. 2.

[29] Reg. 46, R. J., in VIo:—"Is, qui in ius succedit alterius, eo iure, quo ille, uti debebit."

[30] C. un, *de maioritate et obedientia*, I, 17, in VIo:—"Episcopali sede vacante potest capitulum, seu is, ad quem episcopalis iurisdictio tunc temporis noscitur pertinere, iis, quibus posset episcopus, si viveret, ab excommunicationis sententia, sive iuris sive hominis fuerit, absolutionis beneficium imperti-iri, nisi, ei fuerit a sede apostolica specialiter interdicta potestas."

meaning accorded by the old law to the word "successor",[31] then by virtue of canon 6, n. 4, the word is to receive the same interpretation today. Therefore, it is not the new Ordinary who is constituted the "successor" in the sense of law. Consequently, he is powerless to absolve from an *ab homine* censure of suspension inflicted by another.

Censures of suspension reserved *a iure* may be remitted by him who instituted the censure, or by him to whom it is reserved, and by their successors or competent superiors, or their delegates. Wherefore, every Ordinary has the faculty to absolve his subjects from a censure of suspension reserved to the Ordinary, and a local Ordinary has the power also to absolve transients. The absolution from a censure which is reserved to the Apostolic See must be received from the same Holy See or from others who have obtained a faculty from the Holy See to absolve.[32]

When, therefore, a suspension is reserved, a simple confessor can not, in ordinary circumstances, absolve from the censure. Since suspension is a penalty which does not impede the reception of the sacraments, the simple confessor can absolve the penitent from his sins but not from the censure,[33] for such a censure does not import the reservation of the sin.

Certain confessors receive faculties from the Code itself to absolve from reserved censures. This is the case of those confessors chosen by Cardinals and bishops according to the provisions of canons 239, § 1, n. 2 and 349, § 1, n. 1. Cardinals and bishops have the right to select any priest as a confessor for themselves and the members of their household. The priest thus selected *ipso iure* receives jurisdiction to absolve from censures of suspension no matter how they are reserved.

Then there are those confessors who enjoy the faculty to absolve from certain reserved censures in virtue of certain privileges granted by the Holy See. All Regulars and members of some clerical exempt institutes which participate in the privileges of Regulars have

[31] Kober, *Die Suspension*, p. 136.
[32] Canon 2253, n. 3.
[33] Canon 2250, § 1.

the unique faculty which empowers them to absolve from censures reserved to the Ordinary by common law or by the Holy See.[34] This fact is stated absolutely because there is a doubt whether those religious may still use past privileges in which they merely participate by comunication, and because of this doubt their legal effectiveness must be sustained. A further reason why these privileges still retain their legal force for those who merely communicated in them may be learned from canon 874, § 1. Although it appears clear from this canon that religious no longer possess jurisdiction over the laity in virtue of their former privileges,[35] yet because of the fact that the canon contains no clause abrogating former privileges and customs, by virtue of canon 4 and canon 209 the use of doubtful privileges can not be denied the religious confessor until the Holy See definitely determines the matter.

With regard to the confessor and the hearing of the confessions of religious, the following must be noted. A confessor who has received his jurisdiction from the local Ordinary, or one who has received it in virtue of an office which he exercises under the supervision of the local Ordinary, as for example, a pastor, is restricted by the reservation in force in the territory in which he exercises his office. But, such a confessor *ipso iure* receives the power of absolving from any, reserved suspension instituted by a religious superior.[36] Those confessors who have been legitimately approved for the houses of exempt clerical institutes may absolve from censures of suspension reserved in these institutes.[37]

Only those suspensions which are *latae sententiae* censures and which are reserved by an Ordinary inferior to the Holy See are affected by the territorial limits of this Ordinary's jurisdiction. When the censure of suspension is an *ab homine* or a *ferendae sententiae* penalty, it is reserved everywhere to him who inflicted it, or to him who passed the sentence, or to his competent superior, successor, or

[34] Lyszczarczyk, *Compendium Privilegiorum Regularium,* art. III, n. 12.

[35] Vermeersch, *Theologia Moralis,* III, n. 447; Melo, *De Exemptione Regularium,* p. 100.

[36] Canon 519.

[37] Canon 518, § 1.

delegate.[38] If a *latae sententiae* censure of suspension is reserved to the Holy See by the common law, the jurisdiction of every simple confessor is affected everywhere, because the common law in this matter is universal and binds in the whole Church.

The reservation of a *latae sententiae* censure of suspension, when established by an Ordinary, has no legal force outside of the jurisdiction of this Ordinary.[39]

The restriction of the confessor's power of jurisdiction—and this is the essence of reservation—is limited to the territory of the Ordinary who reserved the suspension, so that only those confessors who are within the jurisdiction of the Ordinary will lack the power to absolve from the reserved suspension. Any simple confessor outside of this territory may absolve the cleric, even though the latter has incurred the suspension in his own territory, and thereupon went to another's territory for the express purpose of obtaining absolution.[40]

Should the suspension be likewise reserved in the other territory to which the penitent goes for absolution, then a difficulty of interpretation of law seems to arise, by reason of the fact that reservation restricts the jurisdiction of the confessor. The censure of suspension reserved in the first diocese loses its reservation once the cleric leaves this diocese, despite the incidental fact of the coexistence of a similar reservation in the second diocese.[41] Reservation of censures implies a positive withdrawal of jurisdiction for a particular case. This withdrawal of jurisdiction, however, is limited solely to that censure which the Ordinary has threatened for the violation of his particular penal law. Consequently, its effects can only be felt by the subjects of this Ordinary and by transients who violated this law within this Ordinary's territory. It can in no way extend to a censure which has a similar reservation in another diocese, because first of all, reservation ceases once the culprit leaves the territory, and secondly, the common law concedes to the confessor of the

38 Canons 2245, § 2; 2247, § 2.

39 Canon 2247, § 2.

40 Canon 2247, § 2.

41 Canon 2247, § 2:—"Reservatio censurae in particulari territorio vim suam extra illius territorii fines non exserit . . . etc."

second diocese ample power to absolve, in the sacramental forum, from non-reserved censures,[42] a power no Ordinary can curtail by any positive restriction relative to his own penal sanctions. Therefore, when the cleric seeks absolution from the confessor in the second diocese, he requests the remission of a non-reserved censure, from which the confessor can absolve since there is no longer any question of reservation.

The consideration of reservation and non-reservation outside of a diocese raises the question of maritime faculties given by law in canon 883, § 1, § 2. In relation to suspension, the jurisdiction granted by this canon to the confessor gives him the faculty to absolve from the censure of suspension reserved by the local Ordinary of the port at which the ship stops. It does not include those censures reserved to the Ordinary by common law, because this law binds the culprit and the confessor everywhere, even at sea; and since the law in canon 883, § 1 does not empower the confessor to absolve from these reserved censures while at sea where the faculty appears to be even of greater necessity than on land, it hardly seems probable that the law would make a concession and grant this faculty to be exercised in port. Then again, it can hardly be expected that a priest know what is reserved and what is not reserved in every port at which thė boat stops, and therefore, to remove all scruples regarding the possibility of an error in judgment or to obviate any difficulty or inconvenience that might arise in making a careful investigation concerning this matter, the law in canon 883, § 2 gives the confessor the general faculty to be used in any port in handling cases which might possibly entail a reservation by a local Ordinary. Furthermore, the phrase *casibus reservatis* from its general character includes not only the reservation of sins but also the reservation of censures. It likewise implies a reservation not by law but by a superior, as is evident from its frequent use in this connection in the Code. The context of § 2 also appears to exclude those censures which are reserved by comomn law to the Ordinary, because it is concerned exclusively with the absolution of those who come

[42] Canon 2253, n. 1:—"A censura non reservata, in foro sacramentali quilibet confessarius [potest absolvere]."

aboard the ship during its stay at a particular port, and the absolution of those people, who on land go the confessor during his absence from the boat. The presumption is, that possibly they might be under a sin or a censure that is reserved by the local Ordinary. The Pontifical Commission for the Authentic Interpretation of the Canons of the Code, in a response dated May 20, 1923, made it clear that the confessor may exercise his faculty while ashore for three days, but no longer if the Ordinary of the place can be easily approached.[43]

The faculty of canon 2253, n. 3 to absolve transients is restricted to local Ordinaries.[44] Major superiors of exempt clerical institutes are permitted to absolve merely their subjects from a censure of suspension reserved to the Ordinary. These subjects are not only those connected with the institute, that is, the professed, the novices and postulants, but also any others who dwell night and day in the religious house, as servants, students, patients or guests.[45]

Before considering the special faculties for absolving from the censure of suspension in urgent circumstances, it would be well to remark that, if absolution is restricted to the internal sacramental forum, then the one to be absolved must be present in order to benefit by it, for the nature of the forum here demands this.[46] On the other hand, those who enjoy the power in the external forum and even in the internal non-sacramental forum may absolve an absent cleric, either by letter, by telegraph, telephone, or through a procurator.[47] A distinction must be made if the absolution is granted by letter. In cases where an executor is demanded, the absolution becomes effective only at the time of the execution of the letter; on

43 *AAS*, XVI (1924), 114.

44 Canon 2253, n. 3:—"Quare a censura reservata Episcopo vel Ordinario, quilibet Ordinarius absolvere potest suos subditos, loci vero Ordinarius etiam peregrinos."

45 Canon 514, § 1.

46 Cocchi, *Commentarium*, V (De Delictis et Poenis), n. 58; Augustine, *Commentary*, VIII, 111.

47 Canons 2253, n. 2; 2239, § 1; Augustine, *Commentary*, VIII, 107.

the other hand, when no executor is required, the absolution becomes effective at the moment the letter is issued.[48]

Furthermore, religious Ordinaries as well as local Ordinaries may absolve in public cases from *latae sententiae* censures of suspension enacted by the common law. There are, however, a few exceptions. The cases excepted are: 1) Those which have been brought before a tribunal. For this it suffices, according to some canonists, that there should have been a judicial denunciation against them; according to others, the trial must have been begun, or if there has been only a denunciation the offender must have received notification of it.[49] 2) Censures reserved to the Holy See. 3) Penalties entailing inability to hold benefices, offices, dignities in the Church, penalties referring to the active and passive voice; or the privation from them, perpetual suspension, legal infamy, privation of the right of patronage, and of any privilege or favor granted by the Holy See.[50]

It is different with regard to occult cases. Every *latae sententiae* censure of suspension instituted by the common law, even those reserved to the Holy See may be absolved by any Ordinary or by one delegated *ad casum* or habitually. This same faculty may be used in cases in which the suspension was formerly public, but because of a lapse of time has become occult.[51]

II. Absolution from Suspension in Urgent Circumstances.

a) *In Danger of Death.*

When dealing with the faculties granted by law to any and all priests to absolve from censures those penitents who are in danger of death,[52] the Code reveals the solicitous care of the Church for the souls committed to her charge. Prior to the Code the faculties which the priest now enjoys in behalf of a penitent who is *in peri-*

[48] Canon 38.

[49] Cfr. A. Coronata, *Institutiones Iuris Canonici,* IV, n. 1737; Ayrinhac, *Penal Legislation,* n. 70.

[50] Canon 2237, § 1, nn. 1, 2, 3.

[51] Canon 2237, § 2.

[52] Canon 882.

culo mortis, were granted for the rarer cases when the penitent was *in articulo mortis.*[53] Whilst the phrase *in articulo mortis* included only such cases in which the danger of death was immediate or proximately imminent, the phrase *in periculo mortis*, now used in canon 882 and 2252, includes cases in which it is prudently estimated that danger is present, though it be admitted that the danger is not immediate or imminent. As long as one may prudently fear that death may result from the condition encountered in the penitent, the priest may use his special faculties. Even as long as the circumstances do not offer stronger probabilities for recovery than of eventual death, a priest may securely proceed in the use of his extraordinary powers and faculties.[54] Relative to this probable danger, it is immaterial whether it arises from some intrinsic cause, such as sickness, a lethal wound or old age, or whether it is consequent upon some extrinsic circumstance, such as war, a dangerous sea voyage, flood, earthquake and the like.[55] All are sufficient to place a cleric in danger of death and thus render him a fit subject for the use of canon 2252 by a priest called on to minister to him.

Should a priest doubt whether or not danger of death is present, he may nevertheless validly and licitly absolve from the censure of suspension, as long as he can judge, at the present moment, that the danger of death is really probable, for the Church will supply jurisdiction in virtue of canon 209. Similarly, if *post factum*, the priest realizes that he erred in judgment, by thinking danger of death present when it was not, he need have no fear, for by virtue of the same canon 209 jurisdiction was supplied.

The priest empowered to absolve in danger of death may be any one possessing the sacramental character of the priesthood, because canon 882, which treats of the same circumstance and also refers to canon 2252, uses the generic terminology *omnes sacerdotes*. Hence,

[53] The following responses use the phrase *in articulo mortis* S.C.S. Off., 9 May 1821—*Fontes*, n. 860; 13 Sept. 1859 ad 1—*Fontes*, n. 955; 17 June 1891 ad 3—*Fontes*, n. 1137; 29 July 1891—*Fontes*, n. 1141; 19 Aug. 1891 in Proemium—*Fontes*, n. 1143; 13 Jan. 1892 ad 6—*Fontes*, n. 1147.

[54] A Coronata, *Institutiones Iuris Canonici*, IV, n. 1760.

[55] Cappello, *De Censuris*, n. 114; Cocchi, *Commentarium*, V (De Delictis et Poenis), n. 78.

regardless of whether the priest be an apostate, a heretic, schismatic, degraded or reduced to the lay state, laboring under an irregularity, excommunication, suspension or personal interdict, or merely one who has no jurisdiction to hear confessions, or no jurisdiction in the place where he is to exercise his priestly powers, he grants a valid absolution to any cleric who is in danger of death, even if this is done in the presence of an approved priest.

Such a circumstance will not very likely take place, where an apostate, schismatic or heretical priest or any of the above mentioned priests will absolve in the presence of an approved priest. Should such a priest nevertheless undertake to absolve from a suspension, in the presence of an approved priest without being requested, his act would be a serious transgression. His ministration in this case would first of all be not improbably done in the state of mortal sin. Then again, ordinarily there would be question not merely of an absolution from a censure which does not require the state of grace in the act of its conferring, but of sacramental absolution as well, where most likely the both absolutions will coalesce in the one sacramental formula. If, however, his absolution concerned the censure alone, then the act would be venially wrong, because there would be a violation of an order of preference which naturally equity demands.

If the strict terminology of canons 882 and 2252 be considered closely, this general conclusion may be deduced, namely, that every censure of suspension may be remitted in danger of death, no matter how the penalty is reserved, whether to the Holy See or *ab homine.* The only obligation, with which the cleric in danger of death is burdened, is in connection with the suspension *ab homine.* There is no question of recourse after the absolution from a suspension reserved to the Holy See, for there are no suspensions reserved *specialissimo modo.* The canon speaks of making recourse after the absolution of a censure *specialissimo modo* reserved. The only suspension, therefore, which demands recourse is the suspension *ab homine.* Recourse must be made to the one who inflicted it within a month after the cleric's convalescence. If it is not made, the penitent pays bitterly for his neglect by falling back into the very same kind of penalty from which he was absolved. The nature of the newly incurred suspension will be similarly reserved as the earlier one. In making this recourse the cleric must accept the ordinances of the superior who imposes some suitable canonical penance and directs the means to be used in making whatever satisfaction may be required or in obviating whatever scandal needs to be undone.[56]

Since canon 2252 directly places the obligation of making recourse on the penitent, the priest *per se* is not bound to inform the penitent of this obligation. If the legislator wished to obligate the priest who absolved from the censure, he would have certainly made mention of this fact, as he did in canon 2254, § 1.[57] Nor can it be said, that the priest is bound *per accidens* to inform his penitent, because, since suspension only pertains to clerics, the presumption is always that the cleric knows his obligations, and therefore, the priest who absolves from a suspension *ab homine* in danger of death, need not remind the penitent of his obligation to make recourse.

If the recourse is had, but the penitent fails to perform the mandate enjoined, it seems that he would not fall back into the same censure. This appears clear from the grammatical construction of the sentence. The phrase *sub poena reincidentiae* is connected only with the phrase *tenentur obligatione recurrendi* which connotes the obligation of making recourse, without being necessarily applicable as a condition to the further duty or obligation *eorumque mandatis parendi.* Furthermore, the punctuation may also serve as a guide for the interpretation. A semi-colon is used to differentiate the two duties, the one the obligation of recourse *sub poena reincidentiae,* the other the obligation of observing the mandate of the superior, as a separate duty. In the one clause the *poena reincidentiae* is urged as a sanction for compliance with the obligation. In the other clause this sanction or penalty is not invoked.

Considering the discipline of the old law, where the Holy See re-

56 The Pontifical Commission for the Authentic Interpretation of the Canons of the Code declared, that this recourse can be made only to a bishop or superior who has faculties over such censures, and not to any bishop whatsoever. The words *facultate praeditum* qualify the word *Episcopum* as well as *aliumve.*—12 Nov. 1922 ad VIII—*AAS,* XIV (1922), 663.

57 Vermeersch-Creusen, *Epitome,* III, n. 452.

peatedly declared that disobedience to the mandate brought about a reincurrence of the same censure,[58] one would be inclined to hold the opposite opinion, namely, that disobedience to the mandate brings as a penalty the reincurrence of the same suspension. However, since there is question of the interpretation of a penal law, a strict interpretation, as directed by canon 19 is indicated for the law as it stands in the Code. One must admit that the interpretation is not free from doubtful issues in either of the two explanations advanced. But, precisely because of the duty of compliance with the ordinance of the superior remains a doubtful requirement for reincurring the censure when and after the obligation of making recourse has already been fulfilled, it can not be effectively urged as an obligation which binds *sub poena reincidentiae.* Canon 15 unequivocally insists that laws are devoid of all binding force when and as long as such laws remain in a state of doubt. Thus, the general principles of exactitude in the interpretation of penal laws, as expressed in canons 19, 2219, § 1, § 3, 2228, 2245, § 4 and 2246, § 2, as well as the general norm of canon 15 which insists on unequivocal certainty, furnish full guaranty for the admissibility of the less stringent interpretation, which is that disobedience to the mandate brings about no reincurrence of the censure.

Although there is no direct provision in canon 2252 for the use of § 3 of canon 2254, still it seems probable, that a priest absolving a cleric in danger of death from a suspension *ab homine* may excuse the penitent from the obligation of having recourse to the competent superior, if he prudently thinks that this recourse will be morally impossible for the penitent when he recuperates. Recourse becomes obligatory only after the convalescence of the penitent. This fact points to the certainty that no obligation is intended as long as a moral impossibility, such as the lack of complete convalescence persists. Furthermore, there may be other reasons which might prevent the penitent from making recourse even after he convalesces,

[58] "An obligatio standi mandatis Ecclesiae, a Bulla *Apostolicae Sedis* imposita, sit sub poena reincidentiae vel non? R. Affirmative."—S.C.S. Off., 19 aug. 1891—*Fontes*, n. 1143. "An obligatio standi mandatis Ecclesiae sit sub poena reincidentiae? R. Affirmative."—S.C.S. Off., 30 mart 1892—*Fontes*, n. 1151.

such as the interception of the letters or the danger of scandal. Consequently, invoking canon 20, there seems to be a legal foundation for the use of canon 2254, § 3 in connection with canon 2252. The priest in using this faculty must impose a proportionate penance and satisfaction for the suspension, over and above the ordinary penance for the absolution of the sins, which the penitent must perform within a specified time, under penalty of reincurring the same kind of censure.[59]

Some theologians, like Konings[60] and Genicot-Salsmans[61] exclude the absolution from the censure of suspension from the faculties granted by common law to confessors when handling cases of clerics who are in danger of death. They maintain that suspension does not impede the reception of the sacraments, and that in no way does it affect the salvation of the cleric. Despite the opinion of these authors, there does not seem to be any reason for excluding the power of absolving from the censure of suspension, because both canon 882 and canon 2252 make no distinction whatsoever. If the general principle of canon 2248, § 2 is borne in mind, it is hard to see how a priest can hesitate to absolve a penitent from a censure of suspension in danger of death, because the canon decrees that absolution can not be denied if the penitent has ceased to be contumacious.[62] Hence, it may safely be stated that if a cleric is repentent —and for this there is great likelihood since he is in danger of death —he must then be absolved. The absolution from the suspension, however, has its effect limited to the internal forum. The effect of the absolution does not extend to the external forum.[63] If the penitent dies and is known to have been absolved in danger of death, it may be presumed that the suspension was removed, and in the external forum he may be regarded as having departed this life in good standing. If the cleric lives, however, provided no scandal

[59] Canon 2254, § 3.

[60] *Theologia Moralis,* II, n. 1690, quaes. 5.

[61] *Institutiones,* II, n. 332.

[62] Canon 2248, § 2:—"Absolutio denegari nequit cum primum delinquens a contumacia recesserit ad normam can. 2242, § 3 . . . etc."

[63] The Pontifical Commission for the Authentic Interpretation of the Canons of the Code of Canon Law—28 dec. 1927—*AAS,* XX (1928), 61.

will result, he may deport himself as absolved from the suspension, unless his superiors demand that he remain under the suspension in the external forum, until he is absolved in that forum, or unless the suspension was such that it is necessary for him to make recourse to a competent superior.[64]

b) *Outside of the Danger of Death.*

When any reserved censure of suspension, which has been incurred *ipso facto*, can not be observed in the external forum without danger of giving scandal to others, or without danger of destroying the reputation of the cleric laboring under this suspension, then any confessor, whether Latin or Oriental,[65] may grant absolution in the tribunal of Penance alone. The only exception is for a priest of the Latin rite in the United States or Canada to absolve a Greek-Ruthenian or vice versa, from a censure of suspension reserved by the Ordinary of either rite, unless special faculties have been obtained.[66] In granting absolution, the confessor is seriously obligated to impose the burden on the penitent of having recourse, if the latter is not gravely inconvenienced by it. This recourse must be made to the Sacred Penitentiary, withholding however the real name of the cleric, or it is to be made to be the bishop or other superior having faculties, within one month from the day on which absolution has been granted.[67]

The Pontifical Commission for the Authentic Interpretation of the Canons of the Code issued a response in connection with canon 2252 which has a bearing on canon 2254, § 1. The Pontifical Commission declared that the phrase *facultate praeditum* qualifies the word *Episcopum* as well as the phrase *aliumve superiorem*. Consequently, recourse could not be had to, nor could the mandate be

[64] Canons 2251; 2252; cfr. Roberti, "De Absolutione in Periculo Mortis", *Apollinaris*, I (1928), 103; *AAS*, XX (1928), 61.

[65] Canon 905.

[66] S.C. Orient., Decretum 1 mart. 1929, Caput III, art. 31—*AAS*, XXI (1929), 157.

[67] Canon 2254, § 1.

issued by a bishop who had no faculties in the matter in which recourse was instituted.[68]

There is another factor in canon 2254, § 1 which seems to have no application to the censure of suspension, and that is the case where the penitent feels it a hardship to remain in sin during the time necessary to obtain the faculty from the superior for absolution. Ordinarily, when this condition is present, the confessor may make use of the faculties granted by the canon, because the other censures, such as excommunication and the personal interdict, which impede the reception of the sacraments, can not be absolved before the sin is remitted.[69] Suspension, on the contrary, does not impede the reception of the sacraments, and hence, the sin which occasioned the incurring of the censure may be taken away without removing this censure.[70] The hardship, therefore, brought about by the presence of an excommunication or a personal interdict is not verified in the case of a suspension, because of the fact that the sin may be remitted without at the same time absolving from the censure. It may be said, then, that only when there is danger of scandal or danger of losing one's good name, may a reserved suspension be remitted by the use of faculties granted by canon 2254.

It must further be noted that no *ab homine* suspension falls within the scope of canon 2254. The canon speaks exclusively of the *latae sententiae* suspensions, which are incurred *ipso iure.* The reader will recall that the statement was made in the III chapter of this dissertation, that no *latae sententiae* suspension may be looked upon as *ab homine,* even though the suspension came about in virtue of the violation of a particular precept. This opinion will find application here relative to canon 2254. A suspension established *per praeceptum ad instar legis* is not *ab homine,* and therefore, as a *latae sententiae* censure is included in the list of censures from which absolution may be granted in virtue of the faculties extended by canon 2254, § 1.

Amongst the provisions of this canon the law obliges the con-

68 12 nov. 1922—*AAS,* XIV (1922), 663.

69 Canon 2250, § 2.

70 Canon 2250, § 1.

fessor who absolves from the reserved censure of suspension to command the penitent to have recourse within a month to a superior properly qualified for issuing the needed instructions and to remind him that he will fall back into the same censure in the event of inexcusable neglect. The fulfillment of this obligation by the confessor which seriously binds him can not, however, be regarded as a prerequisite condition for the validity of the absolution he imparts. The canon makes no such statement, either expressly or equivalently, as canon 11 demands for acknowledging a law as invalidating. So, if a confessor would have neglected this duty, he would none the less retain the jurisdiction which the Code has granted him in these urgent circumstances. In thus using his faculties he is indeed acting in contravention of a serious law, but his act of absolution does not become invalid. The mere fact of neglect on the part of the confessor will not, however, excuse the penitent from making recourse,[71] since in the case the penitent is a cleric, it is not to be presumed that he is ignorant of his personal obligation of making recourse. If that were impossible for him, but the confessor could act in his stead, then the recourse would have to be undertaken in this alternate manner. Canon 2254, § 1 has *saltem per epistolam et per confessarium* to indicate alternate modes in instituting the recourse. It is not when one *or* the other of these methods proves impossible, it is when one *and* the other prove unavailable for making the recourse that the penitent becomes excused from this obligation.[72]

The canon furthermore rules that a penitent will reincur his censure, and therefore, if he be a cleric the suspension, if he has failed to make recourse *within a month.* In computing the month's time only those days are counted which lent him the opportunity

[71] Chelodi, *Ius Poenale,* n. 35; Cappello, *De Censuris,* n. 12.

[72] Various responses of the Holy Office substantiate this fact: S.C.S. Off., 23 June 1886 ad 2:—"per epistolam et per medium confessarii"—*Fontes,* n. 1102; 19 Aug. 1891 ad 2:—"onus sive per se sive per confessarium, recurrendi . . . etc."—*Fontes,* n. 1143; 13 Jan. 1892 ad 6:—"onus sive per se sive per confessarium ad S. Pontificem recurrendi"—*Fontes,* n. 1147; 30 March 1892 ad 1:—"onus sive per se, sive per confessarium ad S. Pontificem recurrendi" —*Fontes,* n. 1151.

for making recourse. The time-limit of a month must not be taken absolutely, that is, as a *tempus continuum*; it must be reckoned in a relative sense, that is, as a *tempus utile.*[73] If the cleric's opportunities for making recourse continue uninterruptedly, and he has failed to avail himself of them, at what precise time will he fall back into his suspension? The canon simply regulates that it will be after a month from the time when the obligation arose. But, some may ask further, just how many days does a legal month comprise? Is there a fixed number of days which may or must be accepted as constituting a month, or must the days be computed in accordance with the duration of a calendar month? Canon 34, § 3, nn. 2, 3, 4, furnishes a definite answer, because in the case under consideration, there is present a *terminus a quo,* namely the time when the penitent received absolution. The beginning and the ending of the time's computation will depend, therefore, on whether this act of absolution coincided with the beginning of the day or not. This factor, however, must always be borne in mind, that if there be days on which compliance with the obligation of recourse can not be carried out, then these days may not be counted as part of the month. The month will actually be made up of two or more intermittent periods of time. These must accrue to an accumulation of 30 usable days before the duration of the month will be completed.[74] From these specific rules it becomes evident just how much time is granted a penitent for making his recourse and at what time the reincurring of the censure of suspension will take place.

The censure of suspension which is reincurred is identical with the earlier censure in its specific nature and in the effect of its character as a reserved censure. It is not the same numerically. The earlier censure was absolved. A new, but specifically similar censure is incurred upon neglect to make recourse within the time allotted for executing this obligation.

If the confessor should take it upon himself to make this recourse for his penitent, and either intentionally or unintentionally fail to make the recourse, the penitent would of course not be under

[73] Canon 35.

[74] Canons 32, § 2; 35.

any obligation in the meantime, as long as he remains unaware of the confessor's neglect. He has used his right in accepting the confessor's offer to make the recourse for him. But, when he becomes aware of this neglect, and opportunity is once more presented to him for carrying out the obligation, then he must either assume the obligation personally or commit it to the performance of some other confessor. It is all the more important to insist on this rule when the penitent is himself a cleric.

Cappello[75] holds a contrary opinion, but in the light of considering the phrase *saltem per epistolam et confessarium* in the sense of alternate modes of procedure rather than simple alternatives, in which the ineffective use of one excludes the need of trying the other, the view just expressed appears to be more tenable. The two methods, of course, need not be invoked conjointly. But, it would surely seem reasonable to insist upon the use of a second method if the first has proved faulty. Likewise, it would seem unfair to grant a choice of either irrespective of its effectiveness.

If the penitent knows that the confessor is intentionally neglecting to make recourse and yet would be free from all obligation, why could he not chance a careless confessor for making the recourse and thus escape all further obligation? The penitent is not penalized when he finds out about the neglect of the confessor, whether this was intentional or unintentional. There was no lapse of a *tempus utile* in the meantime. It begins anew for him as well as for the new confessor who now is willing to assist him.[76]

The recourse demanded by § 1 of canon 2254 can not be made to another confessor even though he has the faculty of absolving from the suspension, for the law requires that recourse be made to the Sacred Penitentiary or to a bishop or to a superior who possesses the faculty.[77] However, according to § 2 of this same canon a penitent may, after he has made recourse to a properly qualified superior, approach a confessor who enjoys the needed faculties and,

[75] *De Censuris*, n. 128.

[76] Canons of the Code in which the particle *et* is used in a disjunctive sense: Cfr. canons 367 § 1 in connection with canon 331, § 1, n. 5.

[77] S.C.S.R.U. Inquis., 19 Dec. 1900 ad 3—*ASS*, XXXIII (1900-1901) 419.

upon confessing at least the crime along with the censure, receive absolution from him. In so doing, he may then accept the confessor's ordinances and instructions without being under obligation later on of abiding by the directions and injunctions received from the superior.

There is a peculiar provision in § 2 which directs that even after receiving direct and absolute remission of the crime and censure, the cleric may receive absolution a second time from the confessor. The apparent difficulty which this provision engenders is based on the fact that, although canon 2248, § 3 regulates that a censure once absolved never revives, yet canon 2254, § 2 rules that the cleric must repeat at least the crime and the censure annexed thereto and receive absolution.

To enjoy the right granted in § 2 of canon 2254, it is necessary that the penitent become a subject of the confessor before the latter may make use of his own faculties and of those privileges conceded by the canon. The cleric can do this in no other way than by an act of sacramental confession. The absolution (*consequatur absolutionem*) of which the canon speaks, is necessarily connected with the confession and is sacramental in character. Its purpose is not to again remit the censure, because this penalty had been previously absolved in virtue of § 1; its sole object is rather to produce sacramental effects when the cleric again submits, as sufficient matter for the valid reception of the Sacrament of Penance, the crime which had already been directly remitted by the power of the keys. Mention of the adjoining censure is prescribed merely to acquaint the confessor of the peculiar circumstance. Thus, the confessor's right to put into effect the concessions of the canon, which are reserved solely to the sacramental forum, becomes operative. He may, therefore, free the cleric from the obligation of observing whatever mandate the superior may issue, to whom the latter had previously made his recourse.

The need of recourse by the penitent is completely waived in such extraordinary cases where the fulfillment of this obligation remains morally impossible, that is to say, whenever the recourse can not be undertaken within a month. The canon uses the term *hic recursus*, as if to point unmistakably to the recourse as mentioned in the earlier parts of the canon. But, the obligation of recourse there designated is not set up as an absolute or perpetual obligation, but as a duty which can no longer be fulfilled after the lapse of a months' time, during which the official instructions must be sought. If not sought by the end of that time, the penitent indeed incurs the censure anew, but his obligation to make recourse ceases thenceforth, until he applies for absolution again.[78] Thus, it seems to follow that § 3 of the canon contemplates the same time-limitation with regard to the duty of making recourse. If the moral impossibility continues beyond a month, the obligation of recourse for instructions from a properly qualified superior ceases entirely.

Moral impossibility may arise for the penitent, if he can not write, or for the confessor, if he can not meet the penitent, as may easily happen in the case of missionaries or other transient priests, or if there is danger that the letters will be intercepted or if the recourse can not be undertaken, except amid circumstances frought with grave difficulties and serious inconveniences, as for example, the probable violation of the seal of confession, or the likelihood of scandal to the people.[79] As long as recourse is morally impossible, no matter in what way, the confessor may use the privilege given by law. He may also avail himself of the use of the canon even though a near-by confessor possessed the required faculties, because the Code speaks of an initial recourse to a superior and seems at least indirectly to exclude the superior's delegate from admitting a recourse, unless it follows upon a previous recourse to a superior.[80]

Then again, should the superior be close by, even in the very place where confessions are being heard, if there is danger of scandal or the loss of one's good name, recourse is considered morally impossible and the confessor may then absolve and impart also the necessary instructions and injunctions. In administering them, the confessor must enjoin upon the penitent those things demanded by § 3 of canon 2254. He must impose a suitable penance, as satis-

[78] Cfr. Cappello, *De Sacramentis,* II, n. 592; Chelodi, *Ius Poenale,* n. 35.

[79] Cfr. *Il Monitore Ecclesiastico,* XXX (1918), 218; XXXI (1919), 201; XXXII (1920), 239.

[80] Canon 2254, § 2; Cfr. Vermeersch-Creusen, *Epitome,* III, n. 454.

faction for the censure, over and above the ordinary sacramental penance, and inform the penitent, that unless he performs the specific penance within the time he, the confessor, allots for its fulfillment, the censure will be incurred anew.

THE PENALTY FOR THOSE WHO PERSEVERE IN THE CENSURE OF SUSPENSION. If a cleric perseveres in a censure of suspension for six calendar months, he is to be seriously admonished. If he will not heed this admonitory act and continues in his contumacy for a period of another month, he is to be deprived of his benefices or offices which he holds in the Church.[81]

The canon uses the word *censura*. Hence, anyone continuing in a vindictive suspension is not subject to this penalty as defined by the canon. Furthermore, the canon does not qualify the word *suspensio*. This is an indication that the general suspension is meant.[82] First of all, there is question here of an interpretation of a penal law. Since canon 19 rules that such laws should receive a strict interpretation, it seems only right to consider this censure as pertaining solely to the general suspension. Then again, this same canon devotes a paragraph to the consideration of those who persevere in their excommunication for a year. In view of the fact the censure of suspension is given joint consideration with the Church's severest penalty, excommunication, it seems reasonable to choose the severest of all suspensions, namely, the general suspension, as the one alone which will induce the penalties enumerated in the canon. Furthermore, this strict interpretation seems to be in harmony with the basic pre-Code law, in which similar punishments are meted out to those who should persevere in their suspension.[83] It must

[81] Canon 2340, § 2:—"Si clericus in censura suspensionis per semestre perseveraverit, graviter moneatur; et si, exacto a monitione mense, a contumacia non recesserit, privetur beneficiis aut officiis, si qua in Ecclesia forte habeat."

[82] For cantrast see canon 2278, § 2; Cfr. Pistocchi, *I canoni penali del Codice ecclesiastico esposti e commentati*, p. 124; Augustine, *Commentary*, VIII, 363; Eichmann, *Das Strafrecht des Codex Iuris Canonici*, p. 160; A Coronata, *Institutiones Iuris Canonici*, IV, n. 1971.

[83] C. 8, X, *de aetate et qualitate et ordine praeficiendorum*, I, 14;—"Quum bonae memoriae Clemens Papa praedecessor noster I. Buccarum, *Melearum*,

be remarked that in this law there was no qualification given to the suspension. Hence, it appears that in virtue of canon 19, the only suspension which would be subject to the provisions of this canon would be the general suspension. At least, it can be said that there is a doubt, and where such exists a mild interpretation must be assumed. In view of this fact the provisions of canon 2340, § 2 must follow from the general suspension alone.

Does this infer that a bishop could not deprive a cleric of his benefice, if the latter continued for six months in, for example, a censure of suspension a *divinis*? Canon 2299 § 1 sets down a norm which gives a practical solution to this question. It regulates that a cleric who possesses a benefice which in law is designated as irremovable (inamovible), can not be removed from that benefice except in those cases which are expressly mentioned in law. Consequently, following the provision of canon 2340, § 2, since there is express mention of a removal from a benefice as a punishment, such a cleric could be deprived of his irremovable benefice only then when he continues contumacious for six months in a general suspension. On the other hand, canon 2299, § 1 also rules that if a cleric possesses a benefice which is considered in law as movable (amovible), then for any just cause the superior could deprive him of this benefice. In this case the bishop could take action against a cleric who persevered for six months in any kind of suspension, no matter whether the censure was qualified or not, for certainly continued contumacy over a period of six months would be considered as a reasonable cause for depriving the cleric of his benefice.

PAPAL RESCRIPTS IN RELATION TO THE ABSOLUTION FROM THE CENSURE OF SUSPENSION. According to Michiels, an absolution *ad cautelam* is not required for the valid and licit enjoyment of privi-

Maium Raofacam et quosdam alios Baranenses clericos vocavisset, ut ad praesentiam ipsius accederent, H. archidiacono suo, quem graviter laeserent, responsuri, quia venire iuxta mandatum apostolicum contempserunt, in eos fecit *per Vigiliensem episcopum* sententiam suspensionis promulgari, in qua, *sicut dicitur*, triennio permanentes, quidam ex ipsis suspensi aliud beneficium ecclesiasticum sunt adepti . . . respondemus, quod non licet eis *nec* illa, quae habuerunt beneficia, vel quae postmodum sunt adepti aliquatenus retinere . . . etc."

leges granted by a papal rescript.[84] It is not required before a declaratory or condemnatory sentence of suspension, because canon 36, § 2 allows a suspended cleric to receive a papal rescript validly and licitly. Nor can it be said to be demanded after a declaratory or condemnatory sentence, because canon 2283 provides that a mere mention of the suspension in the rescript gives the cleric legal capacity to enjoy the favor. There is no positive legal prescription to prove the necessity of an absolution *ad cautelam*. Canon 66, § 3 can not be invoked, because the law there does not refer to the executing of rescripts granted directly by the Holy See but rather to the executing of rescripts granted indirectly through an inferior who enjoys special faculties. It was necessary for the Holy See to provide special power for its substitute, in these circumstances, to remove any censure that might impede the enjoyment of the favor.

The better opinion is that no absolution is required for the enjoyment of a papal rescript, if mention is made in the rescript of a suspension, which would ordinarily deprive one of the right to obtain such a favor. It must not be forgotten that, when mention is made of the suspension, this does not imply an absolution from all the effects but merely from the intervention of those effects which would interfere with the enjoyment of the papal favor.

Formulae for the Absolution of a Censure of Suspension. In general, it may be said that no set formula is necessary for the absolution of a censure of suspension. It is sufficient that there be used certain evident external signs which clearly indicate the imparting of absolution. The mere intention of absolving will not suffice.[85]

For the internal forum the ordinary form used for the absolution of sins suffices for the absolution of the censure of suspension.[86] In reference to the external forum, any form may be used for validity. The following formulae are suggested as helpful forms

[84] *Normae Generales,* II, 190.

[85] Kober, *Die Suspension,* p. 141; St. Alphonsus, *Theologia Moralis,* VII, n. 116.

[86] Kober, *Die Suspension,* p. 140; Cappello, *De Censuris,* n. 99.

for those who undertake the absolution from the censure of suspension.

(1) Ego te absolvo a vinculo suspensionis, in quam incurristi, et restituo te ad exsequutionem muneris tui vel ordinis aut ad beneficum tuum.[87]

(2) Quia de tali negotio, propter quod suspensionis sententiam incurreras, emendationem plenam, et poenitentiam condignam egisti; ideo sententiam suspensionis huiusmodi misericorditer relaxamus.[88]

According to the rubrics of the Roman Ritual, it is prescribed that the penitent say the *Confiteor;* after which the priest says the *Misreatur tui* and *Indulgentiam;* finally he pronounces the following formula:

> Auctoritate mihi ab N. tradita, ego absolvo te a vinculo suspensionis, quam propter tale factum (vel talem causam, etc.) incurristi (seu incurrisse declaratus es), in nomine Patris, et Filii ✠ et Spiritus Sancti. Amen.

There is also a formula for restoring the beneficial title and granting a condonation of all the beneficial fruits and revenues which were received in bad faith.

> Ego restituo tibi titulum (titulos) Beneficii (Beneficiorum), et condono tibi fructus male perceptos, in nomine Patris, et Filii ✠ et Spiritus Sancti. Amen.[89]

87 Kober, *Die Suspension,* p. 141.

88 Pontificale Romanum, *Ordo Suspensionis* . . . etc., III, 178.

89 *Rituale Romanum,* tit. III, c. 5.

CHAPTER XI

THE CESSATION OF THE VINDICTIVE PENALTY

THE MANNER OF CESSATION. The vindictive suspension may cease in various ways. It ceases with the expiration of the time designated at the moment of its infliction. It ceases by dispensation which may be given by him who inflicted it, or by his superior, or his successor, or by one to whom this power had been properly delegated. If the suspension has been inflicted *ad beneplacitum nostrum,* it terminates *ipso facto* with the cessation of the authority of the person who inflicted the penalty. It is immaterial how this power is lost, whether by express or tacit resignation, by administrative removal, by punitive deprivation, by transfer to another office, by the lapse of time predetermined for the possession of power, by expiration of the specially granted faculties, or by death.[1] The vindictive penalty also comes to an end by the grant of a dispensation. And lastly, it ceases at the death of the delinquent, or

[1] Canons 183-195. In the case of one who holds his authority by way of delegated faculties, the communicated powers cease when his mandate has been executed, when the duration of his delegated powers has expired, when he has acted in the full number of cases entrusted to him, when the final cause or motive for the grant of power committed to him has ceased, when the official recall of his powers has been directly notified to him, or when his act of resignation as a delegate has been accepted and confirmed by his delegating superiors. His powers are not lost *ipso facto* with the cessation of power in the one who delegated him, except in two contingencies of which canon 61 makes express mention (canon 207, § 1). These two cases occur 1) when a departure from the more ordinary and normal course in the act of delegation becomes evident from the rescript itself, for example, by the use of such phrases as "*ad beneplacitum nostrum*", "*donec voluero*", "*donec mihi placuerit*", for these phrases or clauses in a rescript presuppose a perseverance of the grantor in his original will, which does not continue and can not exist when the person has died or his juridicial status has come to an end; 2) when a favor or privilege is so granted that it must be used for definitely designated persons and the grantor has lapsed from office before the delegate has begun the use or exercise of his committed powers or faculties.—Cfr. O'Neil, *Papal Rescripts of Favor,* The Catholic University of America, Canon Law Studies, n. 57 Washington: The Catholic University of America, 1930, p. 198 seq.

by an act of revocation by the superior, whether by way of a personal recall or an erroneous decision or judgment, or whether by way of reversal of judgment granted through an appeal to a court of higher instance.[2]

THOSE WHO MAY REMIT AND CONDITIONS NECESSARY FOR REMISSION. In those cases in which a superior has the faculty to free one from the observance of a law, he likewise enjoys the power to remit the penalty attached to the law.[3] This applies even though the faculty to free one from the observance of a law comes by way of delegation, either from common law or from the grant of a superior.[4] Thus, if a bishop communicated to the deans throughout the diocese the faculty of exempting individual clerics from compliance with the ordinance which, under threat of a reserved *latae sententiae* suspension *ab officio* operative for two months, forbids them to drive automobiles, then these deans would also have the faculty to remit the vindictive suspension incurred upon the violation of this ordinance.

The Pope by reason of his universal and unlimited jurisdiction has the power to remit vindictive suspensions anywhere in the world. The various Congregations, too, within their competence have this right. Metropolitans enjoy the faculty only during the time of their canonical visitation in a suffragan diocese of the province, and in cases of appeal from a declaratory sentence, because of the fact that such an appeal seems to be *in devolutivo tantum.*[5] In the question of an appeal from a condemnatory sentence, there is no need to remit the vindictive penalty. Since appeals are *in suspensivo,*[6] there is a stay of execution relative to the sentence of the lower court. The lack of conformity between the sentence of the higher and lower courts rather makes that stay of execution something permanent. It is not a remission of the penalty already incurred. In regard to Ordinaries, all may of course dispense from

[2] Canons 2236, § 1; 2289; 2290, § 1.

[3] Canon 2236, § 2.

[4] A Coronata, *Institutiones Iuris Canonici,* IV, n. 1736; Ayrinhac, *Penal Legislation in the New Code of Canon Law,* n. 66.

[5] Canon 274, n. 5, n. 7.

[6] Canon 2287.

those suspensions which they themselves have instituted or inflicted. They enjoy the power to dispense from *latae sententiae* suspensions flowing from the common law only in as far as the conditions mentioned in canon 2237 have been verified. The Vicar General lacks all power to remit penalties which have already been inflicted, unless he possesses a special mandate to that effect. He may however remit those *latae sententiae* suspensions which are reserved by common law or by diocesan law to the Ordinary, since by virtue of canon 198, § 1, he himself is an Ordinary.

Once an ecclesiastical judge *ex officio* applies a penalty of suspension decreed by law or by a superior, as canon 2236, § 3 directs, he is powerless to remit this suspension. However, if a judge, after consulting the Ordinary, acts in his own name,[7] he therefore can remit the penalties so inflicted or so applied. But, this power to remit these penalties is extant only as long as the process of the trial is in progress. At the completion of the trial the jurisdiction of the judge ceases for this case, and the delinquent has no other choice but to seek remission from the Holy See, or the Ordinary, or the superior who gave delegation to the judge.[8]

Relative to the remission of *latae sententiae* vindictive suspensions which have been enacted or established by the common law, the same norm is to be invoked as that which is contained in canons 2236-2237 in reference to the absolution from censures.

In public cases every Ordinary without distinction has jurisdiction by law to remit *latae sententiae* vindictive suspensions which are enacted by the common law. As exceptions to this general rule he may not remit a perpetual suspension, nor one which is reserved to the Holy See, nor one that is connected with a case brought before a civil or an ecclesiastical tribunal.[9]

[7] Canon 2220, § 1 with canons 1640 and 1743—"pollet potestate praecepta imponendi." Cfr. *AAS*, XXIII (1931), 465.

[8] A Coronata, *Institutiones Iuris Canonici*, IV, n. 1736.

[9] A Coronata, *Institutiones Iuris Canonici*, IV, n. 1737; Blat, *Commentarium*, V, n. 59. Both of these canonists assert that there is a doubt concerning the correct interpretation of the phrase *deductum ad forum contentiosum*. Because of this fact, recourse must be had to the old law for the real meaning this phrase is to convey, since the present law in the Code is based substantial-

Of course, a bishop can, so at least it would seem, grant remission from vindictive suspensions regarding cases which are not reserved to a higher authority, even after he has taken public cognizance of the case in an administrative manner. If this were not true, it would be hard to see how in some cases he could arrive at the prudent decision required for the exercise of his power to remit the penalty.

Canon 2237 § 2 limits in no way the jurisdiction of Ordinaries concerning *latae sententiae* vindictive suspensions which the common law has enacted. Hence, no matter whether these suspensions are reserved or not, the Ordinaries possess the power to remit them.

What about cases in which a *latae sententiae* vindictive suspension has been incurred because of the violation of a particular law or of a preceptive ordinance *ad instar legis?* In such circumstances, it is necessary too to have recourse to the general principles of law. Canon 2289 plainly directs that dependence on canon 2236 is to be sought regarding the remission of vindictive penalties. Consequently, when the suspension is reserved, he primarily enjoys the power to remit this penalty who enacted the particular law or decreed the particular precept. The same right is also possessed by his superior, his successor, or any one delegated for this purpose. The confessor has only that power over vindictive penalties which the Code gives him in canon 2290. In occult cases, he may only temporarily suspend the obligation of observing the penalty and urge recourse in the meantime to the one properly qualified to receive it. He may even dispense entirely from the penalty when the making of recourse to a superior is morally impossible for the penitent. As to public penalties, these can not at any time be remitted by one who has no jurisdiction in the external forum over the penitent. This is true even amid the circumstances contemplated in canon 2290.

ly on a similar legislation by the Council of Trent—Sess. XXIV, *de ref.*, c. 6. Relative to this Gasparri says that, prescinding from the opinion of other authors, he holds the view, that the phrase *deductum ad forum contentiosum* signifies that the case is brought to either an ecclesiastical or a lay tribunal of justice. Consequently, he continues, a crime is said to be *deductum ad forum contentiosum* when it is prosecuted in this tribunal of justice through a denunciation or accusation before an approved judge. Or as they commonly say, when *la justice est saisie.*—*De Sacra Ordinatione*, I, n. 225.

It must also be remembered that, in general, a dispensation granted for the remission of a vindictive penalty may be conceded either orally or in writing. It may be imparted absolutely or conditionally. It may be given in the internal or in the external forum. It may be granted to those who are absent or to those who are present. The particular manner of proceeding will be indicated by the needs and the circumstances of each separate case. But, although the law states that, in general, the dispensation may be granted orally or in writing, it also declares that if the penalty has been inflicted in writing, the act of remission should likewise be in writing.[10]

Regarding the more urgent cases which have not yet become public and concerning which publicity is not imminent, the following conditions, provided by canon 2290 must be borne in mind. First of all, in § 1 there is no question of an outright dispensation or remission. The confessor, acting in the internal sacramental forum, has only the faculty to suspend the external observance of such *latae sententiae* vindictive penalties as have been incurred through the violation of a common law, a particular law, or a mandate or precept issued *ad instar legis*. This faculty, however, is not absolute. Its use is contingent upon the verification and fulfillment of a number of conditions.

The contraction by the penitent of the vindictive penalty must still be a fact that is secret or occult, at least in the vicinity where the confessor is exercising his faculty. Again, the urgency for the use of his faculty must be occasioned by the consideration that an observance of the penalty would betray the penitent before the public and thus either certainly, or at least probably, attach infamy to his character, or give occasion for scandal. Moreover, the confessor must oblige the penitent, under penalty of reincurring the same penalty, to have recourse within a month to the competent superior and to abide by the injunctions which the superior will impose upon him. The penitent is free, when instituting his recourse, to do so either by letter or through the mediation of the confessor. The penitent's identity will of course remain veiled through the use of a fic-

[10] Canon 2239, § 1, § 2.

titious name. He is excused from instituting a recourse only when such effort would entail a serious embarrassment or perplexing difficulty.

When recourse remains possible, it may first of all be brought to the attention of the Sacred Penitentiary, whenever the nature of the case reserves the power of remission to the Holy See. But, this is not necessary in the case of a vindictive suspension except when the reservation is indicated outside of common law. For, all occult cases of *latae sententiae* vindictive penalties of suspension as established by the common law, the episcopal or religious Ordinary also enjoys a proper competence in virtue of the powers conceded him by canon 2237, § 2. Hence, in all these cases recourse is admissible to him as well as to the Sacred Penitentiary. If the bishop should enjoy privileged faculties which enable him to handle even such cases of *latae sententiae* penalties which the Holy See has established outside of the common law, then recourse could be made to him in all cases without exception. Since the matter, concerning which the recourse is to be made pertains to the sacramental forum, all care must be taken to shield the sacramental seal. Any likely danger or any precarious undertaking in this respect would excuse all obligation of recourse and thus allocate the case under the special rulings which canon 2290 § 2 provides for cases of extraordinary character.

The law of canon 2290, § 1 ordains that the mandate given by the superior must be observed. There is no mention, however, that it must be executed under threat of reincurring the suspension if the duty be deliberately neglected. The reason is evident, namely, because the suspension has not been remitted. Its observance has been stayed by the confessor in lieu of the fact that the penitent promised to make recourse. Should the latter fail to execute the promise, he must again observe the suspension.

If the urgency for which the confessor suspended the observance of the penalty has ceased, the cleric would not have to begin again to obey the prohibitions of his penalty. The law of canon 2290 § 1 merely demands a promise from the penitent to have recourse within a month. Before this month has elapsed the cleric would not have to observe the penalty, because the very promise, by which he was liberated from observing the penalty, is violated only when a month has passed without making the recourse. Nor would the cleric be bound by his suspension once he has made the recourse, because, again, he has fulfilled a condition prescribed by the canon, and hence, may continue to enjoy the benefits of the law.[11] It is in this fact precisely that the penitent reaps a distinctive gain over and above the concession granted him by canon 2232, § 1, for, whilst this latter canon excuses him from externally observing a penalty whenever its observance would bring infamy upon him, the faculty which a confessor has and uses in accordance with canon 2290, § 1 liberates the penitent once for all from any further external observance of the penalty, even though either infamy or scandal would no longer have to be feared as a result of the observance.[12]

In extraordinary circumstances when recourse is impossible, the law empowers the confessor to dispense fully from the effects of the vindictive penalty. He must, however, obtain a promise from the penitent to make suitable satisfaction and to repair the scandal and then impose a proportionate penance to be executed within a space of time determined by him. The substantial fulfillment of these conditions is so essential on the part of the penitent that in the event of their culpable neglect, the delinquent will fall back into the very same kind of penalty from which he was dispensed.[13]

The confessor may never dispense from a public suspension, no matter how urgent the case may be. To obtain remission from this type of a penalty, he must refer the matter to the Holy See, or to the Ordinary, or their delegates,[14] as the nature of the case may demand. If a case is brought to an Ordinary who has no other faculties than those accorded by common law, he can grant a dispensation only in so far as he exercises his powers within the limits set by canon 2237, § 1.

No one who has faculties to dispense from a public vindictive suspension is bound in justice to exercise that power in view of a cleric's restored moral integrity of life. When approached for the

[11] Vermeersch-Creusen, *Epitome,* III, n. 491.

[12] Cfr. A Coronata, *Institutiones Iuris Canonici,* IV, n. 1823 in fine.

[13] Canons 2290, § 2; 2254, § 3.

[14] Canon 2236, § 1.

remission of the penalty, the superior must bear in mind the decisive factors which bear upon every case, namely, the obviation of the scandal which resulted from the delictual act and the public expiation of the crime which was publicly known along with the making of satisfaction, or at least of a sincere and efficient promise to repair the subsequent harm and injury.[15] When a penalty, specifying the time for the duration of its observance, has been incurred or inflicted, nothing needs to be done by the superior to curtail its duration. The lawgiver in his law or precept has prudently predetermined the time requisite for the expiation of the crime. On the other hand, if it be inflicted without the indication of a definite time-limit, it is to be regarded as continuing in its binding force up to that time when authority, in its prudent observation of the case, will consider all harm sufficiently repaired in actuality, or, at least, in sincere desire, to invite an intervention through a remission of the penalty.

The Code draws upon the salutary instructions of the Council of Trent[16] to counsel benevolence above austerity, exhortation above threats, charity above dominant power in the infliction of the censure of excommunication. Inflexible rigor is to be tempered with a benign humanity, justice with mercy, severity with indulgence, in order that the aims of fraternal correction may bear ultimate fruit.[17]

A similar spirit of intelligent kindliness and compassionate forbearance animates the Church's law in canon 2288, when the lawgiver leaves it to the judgment of prudence to suspend the execution of inflicted penalties following upon an initial offense. Only when the recipient of this benevolent favor has rendered himself unworthy of it in the course of the ensuing three years, either by repeating the commission of the same crime, or by perpetrating some other similar offense, will there be need of punishment. The punishment will then be the expiation of both crimes.

For a case in which the danger of death is present canon 882 ordains that any priest may absolve from all sins and censures, no

[15] Canon 2286.

[16] Sess. XXV, *de ref.*, c. 3.

[17] Canon 2214, § 2.

matter in whatsoever manner they be reserved. The canon in no way indicates any special faculties for the remission of vindictive penalties. Perhaps the law is silent on this point in this canon and elsewhere, because of its liberal concessions in canon 2232, § 1 and canon 2290. Perhaps it is silent because the vindictive penalty of suspension, does not in any way interfere with the reconciliation of a soul before meeting its Maker in judgment that follows death. Perhaps the Code makes no provision for this particular situation because it does not conceive of any possibility of infamy to the character or of the likelihood of scandal arising from the prohibition to exercise rights which a cleric in danger of death could actually exercise. It might even be because no vindictive penalty accompanies any one into the next life—for they all cease at death—that the law shows no specific concern for their remission when the penitent is in danger of death. For this silence who would venture to assign an apodictical reason?

Granted, however, for the sake of a further question, that the same conditions for which canon 2290 has made provision do exist for a penitent in danger of death, must the confessor be denied the power to suspend the obligation of the observance of the penalty, or even of remitting it entirely? An affirmative answer would seem inequitable since its confirmation could only be sought in the negative argument which is derived from the silence of the law. Never is the Church more considerate of human limitation than when she attends her sick and dying children. The very least that would be expected of her in order to sustain proof of that solicitude is that she enable a confessor to suspend the obligation of observing the occult penalty and thus avail himself of the faculties outlined for him in canon 2290, § 1. Given the actual conditions which would render a case of danger of death the equivalent of the exceptional emergency contemplated in canon 2290, § 2, it appears perfectly logical to allow the confessor to remit the penalty and to impose a canonical penance along with the duty of satisfaction, whose fulfillment will be conditioned upon recovery from sickness. The penitent, after convalescense must fulfill the injunctions given him and execute them in the interval of time specified by the confessor for their discharge. It is only when it is prudently deemed impossible to institute recourse during the ensuing month or longer after convalescence, that the confessor may remit the penalty entirely, and free the penitent from the obligation of recourse.

Canon 2290 points to a *confessor* as having the special faculties outlined there. Will this exclude a non-approved priest who might be called upon to exercise his priestly powers in behalf of a penitent who is in danger of death? It seems not. Whenever the circumstance of danger of death is present for a penitent, the law constitutes all priests confessors irrespective of their jurisdictional disabilities,[18] and supplies the needed jurisdiction for the valid and fruitful administration of the sacrament of Penance. Since a stay of execution in the operation of vindictive penalties or even their total remission may constitute a fruitful, if not a necessary adjunct in the administration of the sacrament of Penance, one must presume that the non-approved priest enjoys all the necessary faculties. Thus, it seems beyond doubt that he enjoys the same faculties which the Code grants the confessor in canon 2290.

No provision is made in the Code for the remission of a public or a notorious suspension to be granted by a confessor to a penitent who is in danger of death. Only the Ordinary, his superior, his successor and his specially privileged delegate have this power, for only they are empowered to act in and for the external forum, in which domain the remission of public penalties rests. A priest or a confessor who enjoys no other faculties than those entrusted to him by canon 2290 can do no more than absolve his clerical penitent from his sins and censures. He will then, if time permits, petition the bishop, or some other competent Ordinary or superior to grant a direct dispensation or commit the necessary faculties to himself to effect the remission of the vindictive penalty. Unless the privileged delegate mentioned in canon 2236, § 1 had also the power to subdelegate his faculties,[19] he could at most grant a dispensation or remission of the penalty *in absentem.*

[18] Canons 882; 884; 2261, § 2, § 3; 2275, n. 2; 2284.

[19] Canon 199, § 3.

APPENDIX

A. *Latae Sententiae* Censures of Suspension.

I. Those Reserved to the Holy See:

1) Canon 671, n. 1: Those clerical religious with perpetual vows who have been dismissed from their institutes for crimes whose nature is in law considered less grave than the delinquencies mentioned in canons 646 and 670, *ipso facto* incur a *general* suspension, whose effects are to endure until these religious have obtained absolution from the Holy See.

2) Canon 2371: All clerics *ipso facto* incur a *general* suspension reserved to the Holy See, who through simony knowingly confer or receive orders, or receive or administer the sacraments.

3) Canon 2372: Those clerics who presume to receive orders from a notorious apostate, heretic, schismatic, or from one upon whom there has been pronounced a declaratory or condemnatory sentence of excommunication, suspension or interdict incur *ipso facto* a suspension *a divinis* reserved to the Holy See.

II. Those Reserved to the Ordinary:

Canon 2341: Clerics who without due permission of the local Ordinary sue in the civil court another cleric or religious inferior to a bishop, *ipso facto* incur the suspension *ab officio*, whose remission is reserved to the Ordinary.

III. Those Reserved to the Major Superior:

Canon 2386: A cleric in major orders who is a fugitive from his religious institute incurs *ipso facto* a *general* suspension which is reserved to his major superior.

IV. Those Reserved to No One:

1) Canon 2366: Priests who presume to hear confessions without the proper jurisdiction are *ipso facto* suspended *a divinis;* those who presume to absolve from reserved sins are *ipso facto* suspended *ab audiendis confessionibus.*

2) Canon 2374: Those who maliciously receive orders without dismissorial letters or with forged ones, or who receive orders before attaining the canonical age, or who intentionally receive orders *per saltum*, are *ipso facto* suspended *a recepto ordine.*

3) Canon 2400: A suspension *a divinis* is *ipso facto* incurred by those clerics who presume to resign an office, benefice, or ecclesiastical dignity into the hands of lay persons.

4) Canon 2402: An abbot or a prelate *nullius* who delays the prescribed blessing for three months after receiving the papal letters, *ipso facto* incurs a suspension *a iurisdictione.*

5) Canon 2409: A vicar capitular who grants dimissorial letters for ordination contrary to canon 958, § 1, n. 3, *ipso facto* incurs a suspension *a divinis.*

B. *Latae Sententiae* VINDICTIVE SUSPENSIONS.

I. THOSE RESERVED TO THE HOLY SEE:

1) Canon 2370: If without an apostolic mandate any bishop should undertake to consecrate another bishop, then he and the bishops or in the place of the bishops, the priests assisting him, as well as the recipient of the consecration *ipso facto* incur a *general* suspension, whose effects continue to bind until the Holy See dispenses therefrom.

2) Canon 2373: A suspension *ab ordinum collatione* for a year reserved to the Holy See is *ipso facto* incurred by: a) those who ordain without the proper dimissorial letters one who is not their subject; b) those who in the absence of proper testimonial letters ordain a subject in violation of the prescriptions of canons 993, n. 4 and 994; c) those who ordain one to major orders who is not provided with a proper canonical title; d) aside from any legitimate privilege and aside from the cases admitted by canon 966, those who ordain a religious belonging to a religious house situated outside of the territory of the ordaining prelate.

3) Canon 2387: A religious in major orders whose profession is null and void on account of deceit on his part is *ipso facto* under a *general* suspension until the Holy See dispenses him.

4) Canon 2394, n. 3: Chapters, communities and all other moral persons of this kind, who admit a person who has been elected, presented or nominated, without previously demanding his official letters of confirmation or appointment are *ipso facto* suspended *from the right to elect, nominate or present,* and remain thus suspended until the Holy See remits the suspension.

II. THOSE RESERVED TO NO ONE:

Canon 2410: Religious superiors who in violation of canons 965-967 send their subjects for ordination to another bishop, are *ipso facto* suspended for one month *a Missae celebratione.*

ALPHABETICAL INDEX

BIOGRAPHICAL NOTE

Eligius George Rainer was born at Baltimore, Md., January 26, 1907. After completing his elementary education in Sacred Heart's School of that city, he began his preparatory studies for the priesthood with the Congregation of the Most Holy Redeemer at St. Mary's College, North East, Pa. On May 21, 1927, he was graduated, and entered the Novitiate of the same Congregation at Ilchester, Md., where he made his religious profession on August 2, 1928. Thence, he was sent to the Redemptorist House of Studies at Esopus, N. Y., to pursue the prescribed seminary courses. On Pentecost Saturday, June 10, 1933, he was ordained to the Holy Priesthood by the Most Rev. John J. Dunn, the Auxiliary Bishop of New York. At the completion of his seminary course, his superiors sent him to the Redemptorist College at Washington, D.C., to take up graduate studies in the School of Canon Law at the Catholic University of America, where he received the degrees of Bachelor of Canon Law in 1935 and of the Licentiate in Canon Law in 1936.

CANON LAW STUDIES

1. FRERIKS, REV. CELESTINE A., C.PP.S., J.C.D., Religious Congregations in Their External Relations, 121 pp., 1916.
2. GALLIHER, REV. DANIEL M., O.P., J.C.D., Canonical Elections, 117 pp. 1917.
3. BORKOWSKI, REV. AURELIUS L., O.F.M., J.C.D., De Confraternitatibus Ecclesiasticis, 136 pp., 1918.
4. CASTILLO, REV. CAYO, J.C.D., Disertacion Historico-Canonica sobre la Potestad del Cabildo en Sede Vacante o Impedida del Vicario Capitular, 99 pp., 1919 (1918).
5. KUBELECK, REV. WILLIAM J., S.T.B., J.C.D., The Sacred Penitentiaria and Its Relation to Faculties of Ordinaries and Priests, 129 pp., 1918.
6. PETROVITS, REV. JOSEPH, J.C., S.T.D., J.C.D., The New Church Law on Matrimony, X-461 pp., 1919.
7. HICKEY, REV. JOHN J., S.T.B., J.C.D., Irregularities and Simple Impediments in the New Code of Canon Law, 100 pp., 1920.
8. KLEKOTKA, REV. PETER J., S.T.B., J.C.D., Diocesan Consultors, 179 pp., 1920.
9. WANENMACHER, REV. FRANCIS, J.C.D., The Evidence is Ecclesiastical Procedure Affecting the Marriage Bond, 1920 (Printed 1935).
10. GOLDEN, REV. HENRY FRANCIS, J.C.D., Parochial Benefices in the New Code, IV-119 pp., 1921 (Printed 1925).
11. KOUDELKA, REV. CHARLES J., J.C.D., Pastors, Their Rights and Duties According to the New Code of Canon Law, 211 pp., 1921.
12. MELO, REV. ANTONIUS, O.F.M., J.C.D., De Exemptione Regularium, X 188 pp., 1921.
13. SCHAAF, REV. VALENTINE THEODORE, O.F.M., S.T.B., J.C.D., The Cloister, X-180 pp., 1921.
14. BURKE, REV. THOMAS JOSEPH, S.T.D., J.C.D., Competence in Ecclesiastical Tribunals, IV-117 pp., 1922.
15. LEECH, REV. GEORGE LEO, J.C.D., A Comparative Study of the Constitution "Apostolicae Sedis" and the "Codex Juris Canonici," 179 pp., 1922.
16. MOTRY, REV. HUBERT LOUIS, S.T.D., J.C.D., Diocesan Faculties According to the Code of Canon Law, II-167 pp., 1922.
17. MURPHY, REV. GEORGE LAWRENCE, J.C.D., Delinquencies and Penalties in the Administration and the Reception of the Sacraments, IV-121 pp., 1923.
18. O'REILLY, REV. JOHN ANTHONY, S.T.B., J.C.D., Ecclesiastical Sepulture in the New Code of Canon Law, II-129 pp., 1923.
19. MICHALICKA, REV. WENCESLAS CYRILL, O.S.B., J.C.D., Judicial Procedure in Dismissal of Clerical Exempt Religious, 107 pp., 1923.
20. DARGIN, REV. EDWARD VINCENT, S.T.B., J.C.D., Reserved Cases According to the Code of Canon Law, IV-103 pp., 1924.

21. GODFREY, REV. JOHN A., S.T.B., J.C.D., The Right of Patronage According to the Code of Canon Law, 153 pp., 1924.
22. HAGEDORN, REV. FRANCIS EDWARD, J.C.D., General Legislation on Indulgences, II-154 pp., 1924.
23. KING, REV. JAMES IGNATIUS, J.C.D., The Administration of the Sacraments to Dying Non-Catholics, V-141 pp., 1924.
24. WINSLOW, REV. FRANCIS JOSEPH, O.F.M., J.C.D., Vicars and Prefects Apostolic, IV-149 pp., 1924.
25. CORREA, REV. JOSE SERVELION, S.T.L., J.C.D., La Potestad Legislativa de la Iglesia Catholica, IV-127 pp., 1925.
26. DUGAN, REV. HENRY FRANCIS, A.M., J.C.D., The Judiciary Department of the Diocesan Curia, 87 pp., 1925.
27. KELLER, REV. CHARLES FREDERICK, S.T.B., J.C.D., Mass Stipends, 167 pp., 1925.
28. PASCHANG, REV. JOHN LINUS, J.C.D., The Sacramentals According to the Code of Canon Law, 129 pp., 1925.
29. POINTEK, REV. CYRILLUS, O.F.M., S.T.B., J.C.D., De Indulto Exclaustrationis necnon Saecularizationis, XIII-289 pp., 1925.
30. KEARNEY, REV. RICHARD JOSEPH, S.T.B., J.C.D., Sponsors at Baptism According to the Code of Canon Law, IV-127 pp., 1925.
31. BARTLETT, REV. CHESTER JOSEPH, A.M., LL.B., J.C.D., The Tenure of Parochial Property in the United States of America, V-108 pp., 1926.
32. KILKER, REV. ADRIAN JEROME, J.C.D., Extreme Unction, V-425 pp., 1926.
33. MCCORMICK, REV. ROBERT EMMETT, J.C.D., Confessors of Religious, VIII-266 pp., 1926.
34. MILLER, REV. NEWTON THOMAS, J.C.D., Founded Masses According to the Code of Canon Law, VII-93 pp., 1926.
35. ROELKER, REV. EDWARD G., S.T.D., J.C.D., Principles of Privilege According to the Code of Canon Law, XI-166 pp., 1926.
36. BAKALARCZYK, REV. RICHARDUS, M.I.C., J.U.D., De Novitiatu, VIII-208 pp., 1927.
37. PIZZUTI, REV. LAWRENCE, O.F.M., J.U.L., De Parochis Religiosis, 1927. (Not Printed.)
38. BLILEY, REV. NICHOLAS MARTIN, O.S.B., J.C.D., Altars According to the Code of Canon Law, XIX-132 pp., 1927.
39. BROWN, MR. BRENDAN FRANCIS, A.B., LL.M., J.U.D., The Canonical Juristic Personality with Special Reference to its Status in the United States of America, V-212 pp., 1927.
40. CAVANAUGH, REV. WILLIAM THOMAS, C.P., J.U.D., The Reservation of the Blessed Sacrament, VIII-101 pp., 1927.
41. DOHENY, REV. WILLIAM J., C.S.C., A.B., J.U.D., Church Property: Modes of Acquisition, X-118 pp., 1927.
42. FELDHAUS, REV. ALOYSIUS H., C.PP.S., J.C.D., Oratories, IX-141 pp., 1927.

43. Kelly, Rev. James Patrick, A.B., J.C.D., The Jurisdiction of the Simple Confessor, X-208 pp., 1927.
44. Neuberger, Rev. Nicholas J., J.C.D., Canon 6 or the Relation of the Codex Juris Canonici to the Preceding Legislation, V-95 pp., 1927.
45. O'Keefe, Rev. Gerald Michael, J.C.D., Matrimonial Dispensations, Powers of Bishops, Priests, and Confessors, VIII-232 pp., 1927.
46. Quigley, Rev. Joseph A.M., A.B., J.C.D., Condemned Societies, 139 pp., 1927.
47. Zaplotnik, Rev. Johannes Leo, J.C.D., De Vicariis Foraneis, X-142 pp., 1927.
48. Duskie, Rev. John Aloysius, A.B., J.C.D., The Canonical Status of the Orientals in the United States, VIII-196 pp., 1928.
49. Hyland, Rev. Francis Edward, J.C.D., Excommunication, Its Nature, Historical Development and Effects, VIII-181 pp., 1928.
50. Reinmann, Rev. Gerald Joseph, O.M.C., J.C.D., The Third Order Secular of Saint Francis, 201 pp., 1928.
51. Schenk, Rev. Francis J., J.C.D., The Matrimonial Impediments of Mixed Religion and Disparity of Cult, XVI-318 pp., 1929.
52. Coady, Rev. John Joseph, S.T.D., J.U.D., A.M., The appointment of Pastors, VIII-150 pp., 1929.
53. Kay, Rev. Thomas Henry, J.C.D., Competence in Matrimonial Procedure, VIII-164 pp., 1929.
54. Turner, Rev. Sidney Joseph, C.P., J.U.D., The Vow of Poverty, XLIX-217 pp., 1929.
55. Kearney, Rev Raymond A., A.B., S.T.D., J.C.D., The Principles of Delegation, VII-149 pp., 1929.
56. Conran, Rev. Edward James, A.B., J.C.D., The Interdict, V-163 pp., 1930.
57. O'Neil, Rev. William H., J.C.D., Papal Rescripts of Favor, VII-218 pp., 1930.
58. Bastnagel, Rev. Clement Vincent, J.U.D., The Appointment of Parochial Adjutants and Assistants, XV-257 pp., 1930.
59. Ferry, Rev. William A., A.B., J.C.D., Stole Fees, V-136 pp., 1930.
60. Costello, Rev. John Michael, A.B., J.C.D., Domicile and Quasi-Domicile, VII-201 pp., 1930.
61. Kremer, Rev. Michael Nicholas, A.B., S.T.B., J.C.D., Church Support in the United States, VI-136 pp., 1930.
62. Angulo, Rev. Luis, C.M., J.C.D., Legislation de la Iglesia sobre la intencion en la application de la Santa Misa, VII-104 pp., 1931.
63. Frey, Rev. Wolfgang Norbert, O.S.B., A.B., J.C.D., The Act of Religious Profession, VIII-174 pp., 1931.
64. Roberts, Rev. James Brendan, A.B., J.C.D., The Banns of Marriage, XIV-140 pp., 1931.
65. Ryder, Rev. Raymond Aloysius, A.B., J.C.D., Simony, IX-151 pp., 1931.

66. CAMPAGNA, REV. ANGELO, PH.D., J.U.D., Il Vicario Generale del Vescovo, VII-205 pp., 1931.
67. COX, REV. JOSEPH GODFREY, A.B., J.C.D., The Administration of Seminaries, VI-124 pp., 1931.
68. GREGORY, REV. DONALD J., J.U.D., The Pauline Privilege, XV-165 pp., 1931.
69. DONOHUE, REV. JOHN F., J.C.D., The Impediment of Crime, VII-110 pp., 1931.
70. DOOLEY, REV. EUGENE A., O.M.I., J.C.D., Church Law on Sacred Relics, IX-143 pp., 1931.
71. ORTH, REV. CLEMENT RAYMOND, O.M.C., J.C.D., The Approbation of Religious Institutes, 171 pp., 1931.
72. PERNICONE, REV. JOSEPH M., A.B., J.C.D., The Ecclesiastical Prohibition of Books, XII-267 pp., 1932.
73. CLINTON, REV. CONNELL, A.B., J.C.D., The Paschal Precept, IX-108 pp., 1932.
74. DONNELLY, REV. FRANCIS B., A.M., S.T.L., J.C.D., The Diocesan Synod, VIII-125 pp., 1932.
75. TORRENTE, REV. CAMILO, C.M.F., J.C.D., Las Processiones Sagradas, V-145 pp., 1932.
76. MURPHY, REV. EDWIN J., C.PP.S., J.C.D., Suspension Ex Informata Conscientia, XI-122 pp., 1932.
77. MACKENZIE, REV. ERIC F., A.M., S.T.L., J.C.D., The Delict of Heresy in its Commission, Penalization, Absolution, VII-124 pp., 1932.
78. LYONS, REV. AVITUS E., S.T.B., J.C.D., The Collegiate Tribunal of First Instance, XI-147 pp., 1932.
79. CONNOLLY, REV. THOMAS A., J.C.D., Appeals, XI-195 pp., 1932.
80. SANGMEISTER, REV. JOSEPH V., A.B., J.C.D., Force and Fear as Precluding Matrimonial Consent, V-211 pp., 1932.
81. JAEGER, REV. LEO A., A.B., J.C.D., The Administration of Vacant and Quasi-Vacant Episcopal Sees in the United States, IX-229 pp., 1932.
82. RIMLINGER, REV. HERBERT T., J.C.D., Error Invalidating Matrimonial Consent, VII-79 pp., 1932.
83. BARRETT, REV. JOHN D. M., SS., J.C.D., A Comparative Study of the Third Plenary Council of Baltimore and the Code, IX-221 pp., 1932.
84. CARBERRY, REV. JOHN J., PH.D., S.T.D., J.C.D., The Juridical Form of Marriage, X-177 pp., 1934.
85. DOLAN, REV. JOHN L., A.B., J.C.D., The Defensor Vinculi, XII-157 pp., 1934.
86. HANNAN, REV. JEROME D., A.M., S.T.D., LL.B., J.C.D., The Canon Law of Wills, IX-517 pp., 1934.
87. LEMIEUX, REV. DELISLE A., A.M., J.C.D., The Sentence in Ecclesiastical Procedure, IX-131 pp., 1934.

88. O'Rourke, Rev. James J., A.B., J.C.D., Parish Registers, VII-109 pp., 1934.
89. Timlin, Rev. Bartholomew, O.F.M., A.M., J.C.D., Conditional Matrimonial Consent, X-381 pp., 1934.
90. Wahl, Rev. Francis X., A.B., J.C.D., The Matrimonial Impediments of Consanguinity and Affinity, VI-125 pp., 1934.
91. White, Rev. Robert J., A.B., LL.B., S.T.B., J.C.D., Canonical Ante-Nuptial Promises and the Civil Law, VI-152 pp., 1934.
92. Herrera, Rev. Antonio Parra, O.C.D., J.C.D., Legislacion Ecclesiastica sobra el Ayuno y la Abstinencia, XI-191 pp., 1935.
93. Kennedy, Rev. Edwin J., J.C.D., The Special Matrimonial Process in Cases of Evident Nullity, X-165 pp., 1935.
94. Manning, Rev. John J., A.B., J.C.D., Presumption of Law in Matrimonial Procedure, XI-111 pp., 1935.
95. Moeder, Rev. John M., J.C.D., The Proper Bishop for Ordination and Dimissorial Letters, VII-135 pp., 1935.
96. O'Mara, Rev. William A., A.B., J.C.D., Canonical Causes for Matrimonial Dispensations, IX-155 pp., 1935.
97. Reilly, Rev. Peter, J.C.D., Residence of Pastors, IX-81 pp., 1935.
98. Smith, Rev. Mariner T., O.P., S.T.Lr., J.C.D., The Penal Law for Religious, VII-169 pp., 1935.
99. Whalen, Rev. Donald W., A.M., J.C.D., The Value of Testimonial Evidence in Matrimonial Procedure, XIII-297 pp., 1935.
100. Cleary, Rev. Joseph F., J.C.D., Canonical Limitations on the Alienation of Church Property, VIII-141 pp., 1936.
101. Glynn, Rev. John C., J.C.D., The Promoter, of Justice, XX-337 pp. 1936.
102. Brennan, Rev. James, S.S., J.C.L., The Simple Convalidation of Marriage, 1937.
103. Bruini, Rev. Joseph Bernard, A.B., S.T.B., J.C.L., Clerical Obligations of Canons 139 and 142, 1937.
104. Connor, Rev. Maurice, J.C.L., The Administrative Removal of Pastors, 1937.
105. Guilfoyle, Rev. Merlin Joseph, J.C.L., Custom, 1937.
106. Hughes, Rev. James A., A.B., A.M., J.C.L., Witnesses in Criminal Trials of Clerics, 1937.
107. Jansen, Rev. Raymond J., A.B., S.T.L., J.C.L., Canonical Provisions for Catechetical Instruction, 1937.
108. Kealy, Rev. John J., A.B., J.C.L., The Introductory Libellus in the Church Court, 1937.
109. McManus, Rev. James Edward, C.SS.R., J.C.L., The Administration of Temporal Goods in Religious Institutes, 1937.
110. Moriarty, Rev. Eugene James, J.C.L., Oaths in Ecclesiastical Courts, 1937.

111. Rainer, Rev. Eligius George, C.SS.R., J.C.L., Suspension of Clerics, 1937.
112. Reilly, Rev. Thomas F., C.SS.R., J.C.L., Visitation of Religious, 1937.

www.ingramcontent.com/pod-product-compliance
Lightning Source LLC
LaVergne TN
LVHW050252080826
844660LV00012B/627
* 9 7 8 0 8 1 3 2 2 3 0 0 1 *